W9-AKU-650

Inventing Iraq

The governing districts and major towns in Iraq during the Mandate

Inventing Iraq

The Failure of Nation Building and a History Denied

Toby Dodge

COLUMBIA UNIVERSITY PRESS   NEW YORK

COLUMBIA UNIVERSITY PRESS
Publishers Since 1893
New York   Chichester, West Sussex

Copyright © 2003 Columbia University Press
All rights reserved

Library of Congress Cataloging-in-Publication Data
Dodge, Toby.
Inventing Iraq : the failure of nation-building and
a history denied / by Toby Dodge.
p. cm.
Includes bibliographical references (p.) and index.
ISBN 0–231–13166–6 (cloth : alk. paper)
1. Iraq—Relations—Great Britain.
2. Great Britain—Relations—Iraq.
3. National state. 4. Sovereignty.
5. United States—Politics and government—2001–
6. Iraq War, 2003. I. Title
DS70.96.G7D633   2003
956.704'1—dc21   2003051453

∞

Columbia University Press books are printed on
permanent and durable acid-free paper.

Printed in the United States of America
c 10 9 8 7 6 5 4 3 2 1

For Clare

CONTENTS

Preface: Iraq and the Ordering of the Postcolonial World

FROM WOODROW WILSON TO GEORGE W. BUSH

In Iraq today, the United States is presiding over a country about which it has a limited understanding. The United States is attempting to rebuild Iraqi state institutions and reform their interaction with society. Post–Cold War military interventions into failed or rogue states with the overt aim of reforming their political systems are becoming increasingly common but, to date, these interventions have been uniformly unsuccessful. It is not surprising therefore, that attention is increasingly being focused on Britain's own inadequate attempts to build a modern democratic state in Iraq during the eighteen-year period between 1914 and 1932.

At the beginning of a very hot Iraqi summer I interviewed a senior British diplomat in the garden of what had been the British High Commission on the banks of the Tigris River in Baghdad. He was optimistic, even bullish. The lawlessness that had been the focus of much media coverage over the previous month was, he said, overstated. Order would soon return to the capital's streets and the country beyond. Criticism, both Iraqi and international, of the nascent representative structures being fostered by the occupying powers was inaccurate. They were not, as detractors argued, dominated by an irrelevant minority of carpetbaggers, but were instead the foundations of a democratic process that would slowly evolve into a vibrant and sustainable polyarchy—a stable coordinated rule of multiple institutions representing diverse social forces and interests.

The interview took place at the end of May 2003 as British and American forces, having unseated Saddam Hussein, struggled to impose order on Iraq and wondered how to reform its political structures. However, the conversation could well have taken place at the end of May 1920. Instead of Christopher Segar, Head of the British Office in Baghdad, answering the questions, it would, in 1920, have been Arnold Wilson, the acting Civil Commissioner, responsible for building a state in Iraq in the aftermath of the First World War. Wilson was a confident and bullish colonial official who was wrestling with a serious dilemma. How, under intense international scrutiny, could he control a well-armed society that had become increasingly resentful about the occupation of their country? Wilson himself never found satisfactory answers to this question. On July 2, 1920, a revolt, or *thawra*, broke out along the lower Euphrates. Fueled by a population resentful at the heavy-handed approach of the occupying forces, the rebellion quickly spread across the south and center of the country. Faced with as many as 131,000 armed opponents, the British army did not regain full control until six months later in February 1921. The cost in lives and money of the revolt made the continued occupation of Iraq very unpopular with British public opinion. It also cost Wilson his job. From 1921 onward the British continually strove to cut the costs of their presence in Iraq. Ultimately the decision was made to extricate themselves from the country as quickly as possible. The result was a failure to build a liberal or even a stable state in Iraq.

The similarity between the British occupation of the 1920s and the role of the United States's Coalition Provisional Authority (CPA) in 2003 becomes more striking at the CPA's headquarters in downtown Baghdad. In the 1920s, deep divisions amongst British civil servants undermined their attempt to build a functioning state. Arguments concerned not only the type of state to be built, but which Iraqis should staff the government and how state institutions should interact with the wider population. The CPA, resident in what used to be Saddam's most important palace, is not a well-organized or harmonious organization. The ideological disputes wracking the Republican administration in Washington have been transplanted, even exacerbated, in Baghdad. A senior American official I interviewed in Iraq marveled at the speed with which decisions, collectively agreed to at the CPA, were then undermined once the representatives of the different factions had called Washington to find out what their masters wanted them to do. For the squabbling factions in Washington, the heart of the dispute about Iraq is the depth of U.S. commitment to reforming the country's political structures. Paul Wolfowitz, the neoconservative Deputy Secretary of Defense, personifies one group. His approach is macrotransformationalist. Under U.S. supervision Iraq can be totally transformed, becoming a beacon of liberal democracy for the

Middle East and wider developing world. The other approach, associated with Secretary of State Colin Powell and the CIA, is minimalist. Worried about the costs—political and economic—of a long term U.S. commitment to Iraq, this approach is concerned with establishing order and stability by changing the highest echelons of the governing elite but conserving the existing governing structures.

Another pertinent similarity between the U.S. occupation of Iraq in 2003 and that of the British in the 1920s is how both interact with society. British colonial rule had traditionally been heavily dependent of scientific quantification to understand the societies they sought to dominate. Colonial officials were used to taking a great deal of time compiling censuses and cadastral surveys, or records of property boundaries, subdivisions, buildings, and related details. The British in Iraq, because of restrictions on money and troops, could not do this. Instead they interacted with Iraqi society on the basis of what they thought it *should* look like. In lieu of detailed investigations and engagement with actual conditions and practices, Iraq was understood through the distorted shorthand supplied by the dominant cultural stereotypes of the day.

The sense of incoherence and political division at the heart of American attempts to rebuild Iraq has been seriously exacerbated by the CPA's inability to establish meaningful communications with Iraqi society. Short of Arabic speakers and devoid of any Iraqi expertise themselves, the coalition has been forced to rely on the Iraqi political parties formed in exile to act as their intermediaries. In fact, the nature of these organizations has increased the divide between U.S. forces and Iraqis. Despite setting up numerous offices around Baghdad, publishing party newspapers, and spending large sums of money, the two main exiled groups, the Iraqi National Congress and Iraqi National Accord, have failed to mobilize significant support. All the Iraqis I met—rich or poor, religious or secular—showed at best indifference and more often outright hostility to the returned exiles. This was especially the case with the INC and INA, whose avowed secular outlook identifies them with external manipulation.

If one were able to pick up Iraq like a good piece of china and turn it over, it would bear the legend: "Made in Whitehall, 1920." Britain's failed attempt, during the 1920s and 1930s, to build a liberal state in Iraq forms the historical backdrop against which the removal of Saddam Hussein in

2003 and its aftermath should be understood. This book does not focus on Iraqis in Iraq in the 1920s. It is an examination of British colonialism's dying days. This is not to detract from the decisive role played by Iraqis, whether as members of political elites or as ordinary people. Rather, my book emphasizes the critical impact upon events exercised by how key colonial civil servants, caught up in a rapidly changing international system, understood the society they were interacting with. How the British understood Iraq made it impossible for them to accomplish what they had initially set out to do: build a liberal, modern, sustainable state capable of reshaping the lives of the Iraqi people. The British did not mean to undermine the nascent Iraqi state. But, hobbled by an ideologically distorted view of Iraqi society and facing financial and political limits, they did. The United States in Iraq today must understand that it is both living with the consequences of that failure and is in danger of repeating it.

Ordering the Postcolonial World

Woodrow Wilson, in the aftermath of the First World War, and George W. Bush, in the aftermath of the Cold War, were faced with a similar conundrum: how to protect the United States by imposing order on an international system they perceived to be both fractured and dangerously unstable. For both, the dangers of instability came from the periphery of the system. The dilemma that both presidents faced was the extent to which radical reform was needed in order to secure long-term stability. Radical reform, by its very nature, would threaten the interests of the United States and her allies. Both presidents sought instead to reimpose stability by reworking the Westphalian notion of state sovereignty and then reapplying it to the states of the developing world. This was done to guarantee international order whilst forwarding what Wilson believed—and Bush now believes—to be the interests of the United States. In 1920, and once again in 2003, this quest for international order has had a profound impact on the domestic politics of Iraq. In 1920, it forced the British to build a self-determining state; in 2003 it has led the United States to undertake regime change and George W. Bush to publicly commit the United States to building a liberal government in its aftermath.

During the twentieth century and now in the twenty-first century, order is predicated on the universal unit of the state. The system operates by granting rights exclusively to states. The shared goal of the majority of states in the system is the defense of individual state sovereignty but also the safeguarding of systemic stability by limiting the extent and nature of violence.[1]

The crucial defining aspect of all rights bearing actors in the system is sovereignty. The Westphalian system of states was founded on the principle of sovereign nonintervention. But until the end of the First World War, sovereignty had to be earned. To gain legal personality a state had to prove positive sovereignty, an ability to control a delineated and stable geographic territory, provide political goods for its citizens, and interact internationally on the basis of equality and reciprocity with other states.[2]

At the end of the First World War, Wilson and the briefly assertive United States strove to rework the Westphalian system on a global, extra-European basis. At the heart of this project was the mandate ideal, based on the universal application of the sovereign state even to those regions and peoples whose histories had been lived outside its framework. Open markets and politically independent governments would bring about a world without empire and would prevent another cataclysm like the one just endured.

The universalizing ideology of Wilson, combined with America's propagation of unrestricted markets, meant that European powers found it impossible to justify the annexation of territory they had acquired by the end of the war. Sovereign territorial states now became the central means of understanding and organizing the international sphere. Although Wilson's international presence was short-lived, his vision could not be ignored. It articulated a framework for understanding and establishing a workable international political order in the midst of the moral and ideological wreckage of empire.

Iraq, by highlighting the tortured birth of the postcolonial state in international relations, played a groundbreaking role in world politics. Its three provinces were one of the first areas of the Ottoman Empire to be invaded by British troops at the outset of the First World War. In 1932, Iraq became the first mandated state to gain its independence, entering the League of Nations as a full, self-determining member. It had escaped both the clutches of the Ottoman and total absorption within the British imperial system.

The implications and reorientation represented by Wilson's vision of self-determination and the mandate system fully came into their own with the "revolt against the west" in the aftermath of the Second World War.[3] It was officially codified in the 1960 United Nations General Assembly Declaration on the Granting of Independence to Colonial Countries and Peoples, which stated that "all peoples have the right to self-determination" and the "inadequacy of political, economic, social and educational preparedness should never serve as a pretext for delaying independence."[4] All newly independent states now legally entered the international system officially organized by the norm of sovereign non-interference. Article 2, paragraph 7 of the United Nations Charter ruled out intervention in the internal affairs of any member state.[5]

Iraq, one of the first postcolonial states, exhibited from the beginning the instability that would come to haunt international relations in the aftermath of decolonization. After entry into the League of Nations in 1932, formal state commitments to liberal democracy were quickly dispensed with and the polity was rocked by a series of bloody coups, culminating in the Baath Party's seizure of power in 1968. In the 1970s, oil wealth and the growth of a rentier economy allowed the government of Saddam Hussein to gain unprecedented autonomy from, and power to rule over, Iraqi society.

The internal instability of some postcolonial states similar to that evidenced by Iraq, with its potential to destabilize the international system, has led to the questioning of sovereignty as an unalienable right. Ultimately it has led to the rise of the Bush doctrine of preemptive war. The undermining of postcolonial sovereignty began in the economic sphere with the rise of the "Washington consensus" in the 1980s. The International Monetary Fund and the World Bank set about applying the "wisdom of market reliance" to developing countries in economic difficulty. In return for loans, these organizations demanded not only free trade but also the liberalization of capital and financial markets.[6] By the middle of the 1980s, structural adjustment loans accounted for more than 25 percent of World Bank lending and came to be seen by both the World Bank and the IMF as a precondition for further lending.[7] These loans had a large number of policy conditions attached that were designed to reduce drastically the state's role in the economy. The removal of import quotas, the cutting of tariffs and interest rate controls, the devaluation of currencies, and the privatization of state industries were all imposed on the governments of postcolonial developing countries.

The end of the Cold War, the breaking up of the bipolar division and the increasing complexity of international relations led to an unprecedented scrutiny of postcolonial sovereignty. As early as 1990, international-relations scholars were arguing that decolonization had eclipsed "empirical statehood." That is, they noted that legal state sovereignty need no longer be correlated with measurable political capacity or national unity. The right to sovereignty, they pointed out, could now be based solely on the demands of former colonial territories independent of their governments' ability to adequately embody and exercise any clear national autonomy.[8] The conclusions U.S. policy advisers drew from such observations were that a state's right to sovereignty "is not unconditional or normatively superior to the right to security of the polity."[9] Such conclusions clearly implied that governing elites of errant states could be conceptually separated from the mass of the population. International intervention in formally sovereign states could now be justified in the name of their suffering populations.

Given these developments, the end of the Cold War gave rise to coercive diplomacy by the international community in the name of global governance. Military intervention and economic sanctions were used to promote a liberal global order in the name of protecting human rights and furthering democracy. In 1990, in the aftermath of the invasion of Kuwait, Iraq appeared to offer a suitable target for such action. Not only had it transgressed the rules of the old Westphalian system by invading Kuwait, but it had offended the emerging rules of liberal governance by oppressing the human and democratic rights of its own population. Heavily dependent on oil exports, the Iraqi regime appeared extremely vulnerable to the economic blockade placed on it. But even after ten years of the most comprehensive economic blockade in modern history with its incalculable toll in human suffering, the Iraqi state could not be coerced into reform or internal collapse.

The rise of the Bush doctrine in the aftermath of September 11, 2001, and the invasion of Iraq in 2003 represent the heaviest blow to date against state sovereignty in the developing world. The influence of this international norm, born of Woodrow Wilson's attempts to universalize the Westphalian system in the aftermath of the First World War, has reached a nadir from which it is now difficult to imagine it recovering. In many respects the Bush doctrine represents a conscious attempt to codify changes to international relations in the post–Cold War era. It recognizes and institutionalizes the political effects of attacks on economic sovereignty under the "Washington Consensus" of the 1980s. Likewise it asserts a basis for the military enforcement of demands for liberal good governance developed in the 1990s. Ultimately the Bush doctrine is an attempt to return to the pre–Woodrow Wilson international system, where the right to sovereignty has to be earned. The question haunting the Bush doctrine is what to do with those states that will not—or more problematically cannot—earn their sovereignty in the ways demanded by the United States.

For the Bush administration, as it set about applying its new doctrine in the aftermath of 9/11, the Baathist regime in Baghdad was a potent symbol of a defiant Third World state. Over the course of the 1990s, despite invasion, continuous bombing, and a decade of the harshest sanctions ever imposed, Iraq continued to reject the demands of the United States and the international community. It was proof, for those states of a rebellious disposition, that autonomy could be indigenously defended in a world dominated by a single hegemon. By engineering regime change in Baghdad, Washington has clearly signaled its commitment to the Bush doctrine as well as the lengths it will go to achieve its core foreign policy goals. To quote Under Secretary of State for Defense Planning Douglas Feith, "one of the principal reasons that we are focused on Iraq as a threat to us and to our interests is because we are focused on this connection between three things: terrorist organizations, state sponsors, and weapons of mass destruction."[10]

It is important to recognize that the strategic goals of the Bush doctrine were not born from the ash and rubble of the twin towers. The geopolitical thinking behind them became apparent as early as 1992. In the dying days of Bush senior's presidency, the then Secretary of Defense, Dick Cheney, assembled a team to plan U.S. foreign policy in the aftermath of the Cold War. The result, the forty-six page *Defense Planning Guidance*, was drafted under the supervision of Paul Wolfowitz. It recommended that the United States should strive to lock in its unilateral dominance of the international system. To do so, it should distance itself from the standing mulilateralism of the UN and rely instead on ad hoc coalitions of the willing. To counter asymmetrical threats from weaker states, it aggressively had to stop the proliferation of weapons of mass destruction. Over the long-term, the United States was to use its military power to enlarge a zone of democratic peace.[11]

These recommendations, originally considered too harsh and burdensome in the midst of the optimism that greeted the end of the Cold War, have now come to dominate U.S. foreign policy in the aftermath of 9/11. In the perspective of George Bush's foreign policy team, 9/11 "ended the decade of complacency."[12] It allowed them, in their own view, to successfully overcome public hostility to U.S. military action overseas and develop the forward-leaning approach to reordering world politics that key members of the administration had been advocating for more than a decade.[13] The Bush doctrine is the attempt to collapse three distinctly separate problems—terrorism, weapons of mass destruction, and the weakness of postcolonial states—into one policy. It was Saddam Hussein's regime that provided the vehicle for this aspiration.

An attack at the center of U.S. public life on September 11, 2001, gave the American public a heightened sense of their own collective vulnerability.[14] The Bush administration strove to convince the electorate that the unilateral deployment of America's military dominance was the key to making sure that this new asymmetrical warfare did not come to haunt the world's remaining superpower. In the immediate aftermath of the September 11 attacks, the administration was divided about how to approach the war against terrorism. Leading hawks, most notably Dick Cheney and Donald Rumsfeld, made a strong case for the broadest possible definition of terrorism, going well beyond the immediate hunt for al Qaeda.[15] Although Bush was initially reluctant to do this, by the time of the State of the Union Address on January 29, 2002, terrorism had now been defined in the broadest way. The "axis of evil" facing America had now become Iraq, Iran, and North Korea, "and their terrorist allies." These three rogue states were a grave and growing danger not only because they were "seeking weapons of mass destruction," but also because they "could provide these arms to terrorists, giving them the means to match their hatred."[16]

In the State of the Union Address and then more clearly in *The National Security Strategy of the United States*, published that September, the issues of rogue states, WMD, and terrorism had been forged into one homogenous threat to the continued security of the American people.[17] This new "grand strategy" mapped out a solution to the threat posed from the weaker creations of decolonization. The "right" to sovereignty was now only to be granted when a state had met its "responsibilities" to the international community.[18] These responsibilities concern the suppression of all terrorist activity on their territory, the transparency of banking and trade arrangements, and the disavowal of weapons of mass destruction.

All means necessary—diplomatic, financial, and military—were to be deployed to convince the ruling elites of errant states that it was in their interests to conform to these new demands. But the doctrine faced two problems: failed or rogue states too weak to impose these new responsibilities on their populations and states that simply refused to be coerced. Even amongst the neoconservatives that dominate the present administration, there appears to be differences concerning the role U.S. troops and American civil servants will play in coercing or reforming the rogue, the weak, and the recalcitrant.

Vice President Richard Cheney and the Secretary of Defense Donald Rumsfeld's political inclinations can best be described as both realist and unilateralist. In the post–Cold War era, the United States is clearly the unchallenged hegemon whose power cannot and should not be rivaled. However, such unmatched influence brings with it temptations that should be resisted.[19] In clear realist terms, the foreign policy interests of the United States should be precisely and very narrowly defined. There should be no "foreign policy as social work," no extended forays into state building like those that bogged the Clinton administration down in far flung countries that were of little direct interest to the United States. It is this approach that has limited the numbers and role of U.S. troops in post-Taliban Afghanistan.[20]

Deputy Secretary of Defense Paul Wolfowitz, on the other hand, personifies the other wing of neoconservative thought. In Wolfowitz's philosophical approach, we find strong echoes of nineteenth-century Utilitarian thought. It is both liberal and universal. It is the governing systems of countries that distinguish them as different and problematic. Remove state tyranny from the Middle East and the wider developing world, and

rational individual democrats will spring forth, free to chose liberal political and economic systems within which to order their lives. But "draining
the swamp" of Middle East terrorism, even if only in Iraq, would be a long-
term and costly business. Ideally the Wolfowitzian model would involve
U.S. personnel in root and branch reform of Iraq's governing structures and
state-society relations. This could take anything up to a generation.

President Bush's position on this, the defining issue of his foreign policy, appears ambiguous. His views on the use of U.S. troops has in the
past appeared to mirror the military's own distaste for state building. In
the presidential campaign and again in the run-up to the war against the
Taliban in Afghanistan, he made it clear on numerous occasions that he
did not want U.S. troops to be deeply involved in rebuilding the country.[21] However, in more recent speeches, Bush appears to have shifted to
a more liberal approach, committing American military power, by implication at least, to reforming the internal political structures of postcolonial states and thence building a new liberal world order.[22]

The evolution and resolution of this most difficult but most important aspect of the Bush doctrine will take place in Iraq. If successful it
could result in the imposition of a coherent model for post–Cold War
international relations across the world.[23] If it fails, the result could be a
rapid curtailment of America's international ambitions and a drastic scal-
ing back of its commitments. The removal of Saddam Hussein's regime
and the growth of a stable and hopefully democratic government in its
place would send a message to the rest of the developing world, not only
about the lengths Washington would go to achieve its core foreign policy
goals, but also the type of international system those goals were aimed at
creating. To quote the President himself, "a new regime in Iraq would
serve as a dramatic and inspiring example of freedom for other nations in
the region."[24]

But the removal of Saddam Hussein was the beginning, not the culmination, of a long and very uncertain process of reform. It was also the
continuation of a failed effort to create a modern liberal state on the part
of the world's leading hegemon as part of a new world order. The nature
of and reaction to an American presence in Iraq over the next decade will,
to a large degree, determine the type of state that emerges in the aftermath of any future war and the role of the United States in the international system for the next generation.

Inventing Iraq

Chapter One

Understanding the Mandate in Iraq

I spent several hours by his bedside while the old man lamented the passing of the good old days. It was impossible to listen to the words of this old aristocrat without an overwhelming sense of the smallness of the world and the sameness of human nature. With a few changes in names and localities, his words might have been used by any old English landowner of a generation ago. . . . Government was undercutting the roots of the old society, by strengthening the lower classes and by sacrificing the noble. —*John Glubb, reporting a conversation with the dying Fahad ibn Hadhdhal, Shaikh of the Amart division of the Anaizd in June 1923.*[1]

Between 1914 and 1932, the British government created the modern state of Iraq. In the aftermath of the World War I British foreign policy was dominated by financial and military weakness, as President Woodrow Wilson and the United States were driving attempts to re-establish international order. Wilson strove to rework the Westphalian system, dating back to 1648, on a global, extra-European basis. At the heart of this project was the Mandate system, designed to establish the universal ideal of the sovereign state, with comparatively open markets and politically independent government. The creation of the Iraqi state represented a break with traditional territorial imperialism and signaled the beginning of the end of British international dominance. Under the Mandate system real political power had to be devolved to the institutions of the nascent Iraqi state and the Iraqi politicians running them.

Once British tutelage and supervision over the creation of Iraq gained international recognition through the League of Nations in 1920, it was perceptions of Iraqi society by its British rulers that had the major influence on how the state was built. Inserted into an unfamiliar society and charged with building the institutions of a modern state, British colonial officials had little choice but to strive to understand Iraq in terms that were familiar to them. The conception of society that colonial officials deployed to order an alien population, sprang in large part from their own understandings of the evolution of British society.[2] At the heart of British thinking was a dichotomy between the explanatory weight to assign to individuals as independent agents and that to assign to social structure and 'traditional' institutions and practices.[3] Rational individualism was dominant, but a romantic collectivism also played an important role.[4] British attempts at state-formation in Iraq revolved around arguments between these two positions. Should the state form direct institutional links with individuals, or should it rule through tribal organizations and their shaikhs? The conflict between these two competing conceptions of social order ultimately determined——and doomed——British attempts to successfully create state institutions through which the Iraqi people could exercise national sovereignty and self-determination within a reestablished system of international order.

The goal of creating a self-consciously 'modern' state made British colonial presence in Iraq different from previous versions of British rule throughout its Empire. After 1920, as new governmental institutions were built, it slowly became apparent to British officials that the Iraqi state was to be run by and for Iraqis. By the mid-1920s it was realized (if not accepted) by the British administration that, with Iraq's entry into the League of Nations, the Iraqis running the state would, within a very short period of time, be given autonomy. Far from consciously creating an 'informal empire' in the Middle East, as some scholars have argued, the British in Iraq were very aware of the temporary nature of their tutelage.

The period during which modern Iraq was created, 1914–1932, is situated in the interregnum between two epochs —— that of free-trade imperialism dominated by the British and U.S.–promoted international liberalism. The First World War delivered a systemic shock and represented the culmination of several trends within the international system. The three pillars of nineteenth-century international relations —— British hegemony, free trade imperialism and international stability —— all came under siege from forces whose origins dated from early in the previous century. The obvious failure of the system to prevent war, the economic and military strain that the conflict placed on the British treasury and army, and the social turmoil that erupted in the aftermath of the cease-fire highlighted a long-term international crisis.

Britain as the first industrialized power, was clearly going to find it difficult to defend its head start, as industrialization spread throughout Europe and beyond. From the 1870s onwards, although Britain's output of coal, textiles and iron increased in absolute terms, it began to decrease in relation to other producers.[5] The First World War exacerbated this decline in economic dominance as Britain's trade deficit with the United States greatly expanded. The combined effects of these developments caused the center of gravity of the international economy to shift to the United States. Britain exercised decreasing control over the European balance of power.[6]

After the economic chaos of war, the United States reverted to the Gold Standard in 1919, followed by the rest of Europe in the 1920s. The rise of protectionism was matched by a decline in the economic dominance of the City of London. Despite British government attempts, the City could not regain its authoritative position at the heart of a free trading world economy. Global economic consensus was not regained until 1945.[7] This breakdown in the system of international economics, due in part to a decline in British hegemony, was matched by the end of the balance of power system in the run up to the First World War. No alternative system of international power appeared to take its place in the Great War's aftermath.

The rise in American economic power led, initially at least, to a more assertive U.S. post-war foreign policy. An ascendant America, in conjunction with the old hegemon Britain, attempted to provide solutions to international economic instability and the revolutionary political movements sweeping across Eastern Europe. Like Britain in 1815, the U.S. attempted to reestablish, along reformed lines, the Westphalian system. It was hoped that reformed Westphalian principles would create a coalition of states who would act collectively in ways that favored the United States. Unlike Britain and in reaction to the overtly internationalist stance of the Bolsheviks in Moscow, President Woodrow Wilson proposed remaking the Westphalian system into a global order that would extend the principle of state sovereignty beyond Europe and use it to meet the world-wide challenges of revolution and instability.[8]

It is within the international system of the twenty-year crisis, during which no hegemonic state dominated, that Iraq was constructed.[9] The slow international decline of Britain combined with the tentative assertion of U.S. power, created an international system organized around two poles. Materially British economic and military power was in disarray. The United States' economy, expanding since the end of the Civil War behind an array of tariff barriers, was now of a size and dynamism to cast its influence across the world. Conceptually Woodrow Wilson's dominance of the Paris Peace Conference along with his demands for open seas, open markets and self-determination, gave rise to the possibility of a new organizing principle for the international system. Order would be based on the universal unit of the sovereign state, fostering comparatively open world markets and politically independent governments. Even with Wilson's death U.S. isolationism was confined to the political sphere. Economically the U.S. continued to push for open markets for its exports. Politically Britain's comparative post-war weakness led to the interregnum, with a dying hegemon unable to assert its dominance, but with the nascent hegemon unprepared and unwilling to assume the burdens of world leadership.

The structural and material changes, on both the domestic and international levels, had far-reaching ramifications for British politics and foreign policy. The historic bloc that structured the British state had to be reconfigured to meet destabilizing economic and political challenges. Lloyd George's wartime coalition government had already increased the power of the state to intervene in and direct the economy.[10] Post-war domestic instability and the global decline of the City of London, gave further impetus to this process. Gentlemanly capitalists and industrialists were forced to cede power to civil servants and politicians.

British politicians, diplomats and colonial civil servants were experiencing the change in the international system from 1920–1932 first hand. Their understanding of this change was the immediate response of people reacting to day-to-day events, with little time to devote to gauging the larger mechanisms at work.[11] The majority of them nonetheless perceived that far-reaching changes were taking place. The degree to which these changes heralded an absolute break with the past and were initiating a new system of international politics was a matter of debate amongst those involved in policy formation and implementation. Few had the time or inclination to speculate on the meaning of the larger process in which they were caught up.

Chapter Two

The Mandate System, the End of Imperialism, and the Birth of the Iraqi State

The award from the League of Nations of the Mandate for Iraq to Great Britain in 1920 was the result of far-reaching changes to the international system. One of the most public expressions of the end of Britain's predominant role in the world was the creation of the Mandate system placed at the heart of the League of Nations. The Mandates marked the beginning of the end of a world order organized by European imperialism—by territorial annexation and domination based on notions of cultural and racial superiority.

The decline of British hegemony and free trade imperialism had transformative global effects. The United States under Woodrow Wilson, drawn into the war against its better judgement, set about planning to impose economic and political stability on the post-war world. But U.S. international liberalism had distinct and potentially far-reaching differences from the ideology which had organized the pre-war world. An indication of future policy was the U.S. Secretary of State's 1899 declaration of policy towards China. In place of spheres of interest and colonial annexation there was now to be the "open door."[1] America's growing economic superiority was to be championed by open export markets across the globe. The logical corollary of such a position was the delegitimation of the colonial state. If markets were to be open, if consumers across the world were to be allowed freedom of choice, then there was little room for colonial notions of tutelage and protected markets. This argument gained ideological coherence when Wilson began to counter Lenin's internationalist appeals to the working class with propaganda aimed at extolling the freedoms and prosperity to be achieved by self-determining nations.[2]

The retreat of America into isolationism after Wilson's death and the incapacity of the Soviet Union due to civil war and famine meant that the international system of the period appears chaotic and structureless. This appearance, while partially accurate, masks longer term trends that became manifest only in 1945.[3]

The universalizing ideologies of both Wilson and Lenin, combined with America's propagation of unrestricted markets, meant that European powers found it impossible to justify the annexation of territory they had acquired by the end of the war. The new ideological centrality of specifically collective structures (nationally, culturally, or economically defined) for delivering order meant that territorial states in the non-European world now became central to organizing the international sphere. Wilson's attempts to institutionalize a U.S.-led post-war world extended to replacing colonial annexation with the self-determination of nations. Although Wilson's international presence was short-lived, his philosophy represented the alignment of powerful forces which could not be ignored as a result of his death or America's retreat into political isolationism.

Woodrow Wilson's philosophy can sometimes appear as an unstable combination of personal arrogance and general ignorance of European and international history.[4] His philosophy was still very much in flux as the First World War began. Nevertheless he was able to capitalize on the shock produced across Europe by the devastation of the war. He combined moral assurance with a liberal idealism influential amongst U.S. intellectuals and industrialists at the beginning of the twentieth century. The result was a political platform that temporarily managed to harness the two dominant impulses of U.S. foreign policy, a desire for both political isolationism and economic expansionism.[5] Wilson capitalized on the historical aversion of the United States to territorial imperialism and suspicion of European politics by playing to a sense of the superiority of the American system of government and its suitability for the rest of the world.[6]

This anti-imperialism manifested itself in Wilson's backing for the "open door" policy of free and equal access to markets around the world. This policy had been pursued by Wilson himself in Latin America before the outbreak of war. States were intimidated by the US's superior military force into reshaping their economic systems. Primarily they had to guarantee private property rights and underwrite business contracts.[7] The free trade and open seas at the heart of Wilson's fourteen-point manifesto appealed to aspiring nations while securing America's position as the dominant world economic power.

Wilson's approach to open markets and self-determination was to be married with the projection of the then current belief in institutional management onto the international sphere. The rise of the philosophy of state interventionism in Europe was matched by Wilson's demand for collective management at the international level. Strong global governance driven by disinterested technical knowledge could be deployed to solve international as well as national instabilities.[8] Wilson's managerial approach caught the popular zeitgeist in Europe. With the old ideological approaches so thoroughly discredited, the apparent fresh idealism and confident interventionism of the U.S. president mobilized British public opinion.[9]

The universal unit of the state became the definitive way the international system was to be grasped and ordered. Imperialism, with its empire-building and policy of annexation, gradually became unacceptable. The idea of the self-determining state in the developing world, a novelty at the beginning of this period, became dominant by the mid-1930s. In London the reduction in Britain's material power had effects on the institutional structures of the state. The foreign policy-making power of the Government of India decreased as the Middle East department in the Colonial Office was set up in London to centralize decision-making.[10] Internationally, the League of Nations was left to function without U.S. support and faced increasing uncertainty in the international system without a hegemonic state to oversee good order. But the League and the notion of international arbitration, even without U.S. backing, still exerted a powerful influence on British foreign policy.[11]

Both international and domestic change during the period 1914 to 1932 was rapid. As it became apparent that a radical shift in policy was required, British officialdom became divided. During the war three distinct centers of Middle East policy-making emerged: Cairo, Delhi, and London. Each exercised competing influence on policy in Iraq.[12] It was Delhi that proved unable to adjust to managing the Middle East. For those in Delhi, cut off from the post-war European turmoil and insulated from the effects of Wilson's liberal rhetoric, the adjustment needed for this nascent new world order came much more slowly than elsewhere.[13] This inability to escape the constraints of the old imperialist model was heavily present in the Indian Political Service which "tended to approach administrative problems along the lines which they had been taught in India".[14]

Pitted against this static view were those in the cabinet and civil service who saw the need for quick and decisive changes. Sir Arthur Hirtzel, head of the Political Office at the India Office in London, continuously wrote to Baghdad between 1919 and 1920 urging that real and tangible power be given to Arab politicians. This view was strengthened publicly by T.E. Lawrence writing to *The Times* during the summer and autumn of 1920. He pointed out that British civil authorities in Iraq were abusing the autonomy they had built up during the war and were now blocking any change in policy. Those in Baghdad contested every suggestion of real self-government sent them from home. A proclamation about autonomy was hastily drafted and published in Baghdad in an attempt to forestall a more liberal statement in preparation in London.[15]

It was the acting Civil Commissioner, A. T. Wilson, who came to personify the "Indian" view. Wilson, who joined the Indian Political Service as soon as he graduated from Sandhurst, refused to acknowledge that the rise of colonial nationalisms and American liberalism was forcing the British to change their foreign policy. With the tribal uprising in Iraq that began in the summer of 1920, Wilson presented London with two stark alternatives: to hold Mesopotamia by force or leave. Hubert Young, the Secretary of Curzon's Middle East Committee, highlights the extent of Wilson's misjudgment.

> He makes no mention of the third alternative, which is, and has been, the policy of His Majesty's Government, namely to remain in Mesopotamia with the good will of the people. The reason for this is not far to seek. It is because he knows that we cannot obtain the good will of the people without instituting a predominantly Arab government, and this I am perfectly certain Colonel Wilson will use every effort to prevent.[16]

The removal of A.T. Wilson reasserted London's control over the situation. The revolt, or *thawra*, along the lower Euphrates started in Rumaithah on July 2, 1920. Now grown in Iraqi political mythology to become the founding act of the nation, its origins probably lay in anger at the military imposition of efficient tax gathering. At its height at the end of August it had spread to the upper Euphrates and the area surrounding Baghdad.[17] British forces, faced with as many as 131,000 men, took until February 1921 to regain full control of the country at a cost of £40 million and many British casualties. The extent and ferocity of the revolt combined with the realization of the long-term effects of the post-war settlement, marked a decisive shift in the attitudes and perceptions structuring British government discussions and colonial officials' actions.[18]

The evolution of British policy, under the pressure of both international and domestic developments can be divided into four interconnected stages. From the beginning of the war until 1918, the consensus of British official opinion held that Basra, the most strategic and economically important area of Iraq, would be annexed after the war. By 1919, with the rise of American power and President Wilson's liberalism, it became increasingly obvious that annexation was not an option. This understanding evolved in conjunction with the construction of the League of Nations and negotiations on the terms of the Mandates. Officials based in London were the first to recognize the impossibility of annexation while those in India only grudgingly came to accept the new reality. Those in Baghdad, foremost among them A.T. Wilson, cut off by geography and experience, did not gauge the nature and extent of international change and were loath to accept new policy constraints.[19] It was not until the revolt of 1920 that the extent of the shift in international affairs became apparent to all.

Growing nationalism amongst the urban populations of Iraq became the major influence driving British policy after 1920. The organization of mass protest against the Mandate in Iraq, and the resentment of the term itself by the urban educated classes, meant that from 1923 onwards the British had to further redefine their policy. This involved a move away from Mandated control, since that was associated with direct long-term rule, however constrained. For 1923–1927 the approach of the authorities in Baghdad and their masters in London can best be described as advisory. Iraq was to become independent sooner than anyone had predicted. The British role was to ensure that the state be constructed as efficiently as possible. The contradictions inherent in this policy — driven by conflicting pressures internationally within Britain and in Iraq — meant that by 1927 there was one more final shift. The idea of creating a legitimate, stable state with the ability to rule efficiently over its population was dropped altogether. Britain's primary policy goal from 1927 onward was to unburden itself of its international responsibilities towards Iraq as quickly as possible. Reports to the League of Nations Mandate Committee were intentionally falsified. Those in Iraq complaining about the sham of central government rule were silenced or ignored. Britain decided to construct a "quasi-state," one which bore the appearance of a *de jure* national polity but whose institutions were in fact a facade built in order to allow Britain to disengage.[20]

From Annexation to Mandate, 1914 to 1923

The occupation of Basra in November 1914, indicated its strategic and economic value to the British Empire. In the political climate of the war's early years, the idea that, once taken, Basra would be handed back to the Turks or to its indigenous inhabitants seemed ludicrous to those involved in the execution of the military operation. "In those early days I naturally assumed, with everyone else out there, that Mesopotamia would be annexed to the British Empire, the only doubt being whether it would come under India or not."[21] Although at this stage there was no explicit confirmation of this policy from the Government of India, the size and nature of the civil administration being set up behind the advancing British troops gave the impression of the permanence of the British presence.[22] The country was organized along Indian lines with political districts run by British officers who reported back to the central administration.[23]

The capture of Baghdad in March 1917 after a long and costly campaign led to a formally codified policy on Iraq. The ambitious nature of this policy, the certainty with which it was stated and the ideology which justified it all sprang from the discourse of imperialism that had structured British foreign policy for the major part of the nineteenth century. Such coherence and confidence in policy towards Iraq would not be evident again until 1929.

In March 1917 the British government decided that Basra *Vilayet* was to be permanently retained under British rule and Baghdad should be run as an Arab state with British support.[24] This policy was further defined in May 1917 when a committee of the imperial war cabinet reported on British war aims. The report drawn up by George Curzon and accepted by the cabinet argued for the retention of both Palestine and Mesopotamia after the war.[25] A.T. Wilson noted a similar approach being expressed by British administrators while on sick leave in India in

October 1915. The idea in "official circles" was to "Indianize" Iraq by "planting military colonies such as exist in Punjab" with Basra at least becoming a dependency of India. "My imagination envisaged some form of protectorate, which might develop further along into a fully-fledged Arab State with 'Dominion status' under the British Crown."[26]

Imperial ideology justified this annexation in both strategic and civilisational terms. Imperial ideology considered "the peoples of the East" to be in no way ready for self-government. Curzon, in discussing moves towards Indian democracy in 1917, thought it would lead to "a narrow oligarchy of clever lawyers." The process should be evolutionary and slow enough to last "for hundreds of years."[27] This view was echoed by A.T. Wilson, who argued that Iraq had "no competent" authority to which to hand over power. To allow self-determination would be to sow the "seeds of decay and dissolution," an "anarchic" step.[28] These views are replicated in the correspondence of Gertrude Bell. Bell was one of the most remarkable figures of her age. In 1888 she became the first women to gain a first in Modern History from Oxford. Before the war she was an accomplished mountaineer and explorer prior to joining the Colonial Office. As the Oriental Secretary to the High Commissioner, she rose to become a key figure in the creation of the Iraqi state. In her voluminous writings she reproduces the views of her society, portraying the Iraqi population as mute and passive, favoring, when articulate at all, benign British rule. If the "vociferous minority" who called for independence were heeded then it would all end in "universal anarchy and bloodshed."[29]

The Birth of the Mandate in Europe

By the beginning of 1918 the shift in the structures constraining the British state had become apparent to those guiding policy from London. In reacting to and attempting to shape these new realities diplomats and politicians added momentum to the dynamics already at work. On January 5, 1918 Lloyd George gave a speech calling for Mesopotamia, along with other non-Turkish areas of the Ottoman Empire, to be recognized as having "their separate national conditions."[30] Lloyd George, in announcing British war aims and encouraging Arab nationalist hopes, was careful to avoid using the potentially costly and destabilizing words "self-determination."[31] The main object of Lloyd George's concern, and the "evil star" overshadowing British discussions on the Middle East, was US president Woodrow Wilson, and his aims for restructuring post-war international relations.[32]

In January 1917 Wilson began rallying support in the Senate for a more active role for the U.S. in world politics at the end of the war. In speaking out against the balance of power system he argued that a just and secure peace could be built only when all nations were equal. "No peace can, or ought to, last which does not recognize and accept the principle that governments derive all their just powers from the consent of the governed, and no right anywhere exists to hand peoples about from sovereignty to sovereignty as if they were property."[33] It was clear that the new economic and military power of America combined with Wilson's determined liberalism could revolutionize the way Europe treated the non-European world. George Lewis Beer, a member of an inquiry team assigned by the President to advise him on post-war problems, attempted to codify Wilson's rhetoric and apply it to the pressing problem of the non-Turkish parts of the Ottoman Empire.[34] Beer, by employing the term "Mandate," attempted to strike a balance between the interest-driven role of European colonialism and the needs of "backward peoples."[35] "Backward peoples," he argued, should be subject to "outside political control" and "foreign capital to reorganize their stagnant economic systems." It made sense to Beer that the power and capital should be supplied by the state with the largest direct interest in a given area. But, crucially, this relationship must be administered through an "international mandate embodied in a deed of trust" to protect both the native population and the interests of other foreign powers.[36]

It was the firmly asserted necessity for compromise between the interests of the great powers and the rights and needs of non-European peoples that dominated Wilson's fourteen-point speech delivered to Congress on January 8, 1918.[37] Wilson's balancing act between liberal idealism and great-power politics did nothing to lessen the impact of the speech on the foreign-policy-making élite in London. The combined effects of Lloyd George's and Wilson's pronouncements on those in the India Office as they scrambled to accommodate and limit the impact of this apparently new approach is best summed up by Mark Sykes:

If America had not come into the war, if the Russian revolution had not taken place, if the idea of no annexation had not taken root, if the world spirit of this time was the world spirit of 1887, there would be no reason why we should take any steps to consolidate our position against a peace conference, it would be good enough. . . . [But now] . . . imperialism, annexation, military triumph, prestige, White man's burdens, have been expunged from the popular political vocabulary, consequently Protectorates, spheres of interest or influence, annexations, bases etc., have to be consigned to the Diplomatic lumber-room.[38]

The effects of Wilson's rhetoric on policy towards Iraq first become visible in March 1918. In the spring of 1918, Sir Percy Cox, the Civil Commissioner in Baghdad, was brought to London to help revise policy in the light of changing circumstances. Cox was one of the most experienced colonial civil servants of his generation and came to be the chief troubleshooter for the British government in the Middle East during these turbulent years. The Political Department of the India Office framed the discussions in terms of "the great change that has taken place in the general political situation during the past year." Any claim to control Iraq would be judged by a skeptical world community and hence would have to be justified on stronger grounds than the "rights of conquest." Suddenly the nature of Iraqi society became central to the discussion. Who were these people who would now be given the right to self-determination?[39]

Cox's response to the India Office deliberations reveals the difference in perception on the part of those whose access to world opinion was filtered through the concerns of Delhi and not London. Although acknowledging the "potent influence" of President Wilson, Cox's thoughts were still structured by the twin goals of the annexation of Basra and the construction of a "veiled protectorate over the Baghdad *Vilayet.*"[40] But Cox, recognizing the new spirit of the age, was also concerned with whom in Iraq could be encouraged to take a pro-British line and so help justify British intentions.

The debates in London from 1918 until the convening of the peace conference in Paris in January 1919 remained contradictory and inconclusive. Britain's future role in Iraq shifts from the annexation of Basra to the question of how to retain a guiding influence over the country and

justify this tutelary oversight to the world. The question of British presence in Iraq was finally resolved in Paris.

The debates in Paris highlighted the clash between Wilson's liberal
conception of how international relations should be conducted and more
blatant imperialistic views. They also revealed a schism in the British
Empire's delegation. This division has been characterized as an argument
between London and the white dominions. London-based politicians led
by Lloyd George realized that the increase in economic and military
power of the United States and a change in the ideological atmosphere
brought on by the rise of colonial nationalisms meant that imperialism
now had to be justified in humanitarian terms.[41] South African and Aus-
tralian delegations wanted to create their own sub-imperial systems by
annexation. Cut off from direct contact with events in Europe these delegations did not grasp the extent to which international relations had
changed.

Jan Smuts, a prominent member of the British Empire delegation,
was able to produce a compromise between these two positions. Smuts,
unlike his fellow delegates from the British white dominions, was aware
that annexation was ideologically out of the question. It was his refor-
mulation of G. L. Beer's Mandate ideal that allowed the British dominions and Wilson each to gain what they wanted. Smuts like Beer saw
the Mandate system as the successor to Empire, but one that had to be
more explicitly codified and administered according to internationally
accepted principles. Mandates in the Middle East would help states
emerge from the wreckage of Ottoman control and prepare them for
independence. Smuts however drew a stark distinction between those
states and the colonies "inhabited by barbarians".[42] This conceptual
division formed the basis of compromise. States were to be placed in
one of three categories (A, B or C) depending on their level of development.[43]

Smuts's compromise bought off arch-imperialist sentiment with the
"C" Mandates of Africa. But his compromise also changed the basis on
which the new territories gained during the First World War could be
governed. The placing of Edmund Burke's notion of sacred trust at the
core of the compromise shifted the rationale of global power. The pre-
rogatives of the state holding the Mandate were now clearly and institutionally delimited. The Permanent Mandates Commission oversaw the

execution of the Mandate and exercised an independent authority that those running the nascent Iraqi state took very seriously.[44] For Wilson this shift was of paramount importance. He argued that world opinion had changed and that if the Paris Peace Conference accepted annexation, "the League of Nations would be discredited from the beginning."[45]

For colonial administrators running the Mandated territories of the Middle East the decision in Paris caused great concern. They were faced with an international regime that forced them to publicly devolve real power to the population. A vocal group of urban-based political activists demanded that they do just that and quickly. The officials charged with carrying out this policy, schooled primarily within an imperialist universe, found it very difficult to do so. Some managed with varying degrees of success. Others failed.

"Long-established and hitherto almost unchallenged assumptions of British imperial policy had (post Wilson's fourteen points) to be reconciled completely with a new set of requirements. In Iraq, it was necessary to adapt the existing administrative machinery, derived from Indian models, to a new and less direct form of control, which was at first unfamiliar and unpalatable to those called upon to operate it."[46]

Once those at the head of the British state realized that the Mandate had replaced annexation as the means to maintain British influence in Iraq, they faced the problem of working out the practical ramifications on the ground. The pursuit of British interests was now constrained by the League's Permanent Mandates Commission. In Britain itself the government had to contend with the deep unpopularity of continued involvement in Iraq. Both these constraints on British policy were compounded by the growth of unfavorable Iraqi public opinion. The notion of self-determination and the ideological power of nationalism meant that a segment of Iraqi society was demanding the right to represent the nation. The state institutions that emerged and evolved under the Mandate reflected all these pressures.

All came to bear on one man, A. T. Wilson. Acting Civil Commissioner in Iraq between September 1918 and June 1920, Wilson and the administration he ran were tasked with the responsibility of carrying out the decisive shift in the British government's administration of conquered territories in the Middle East. Wilson, ideologically unable to accept the new situation, set about the task of governing Iraq as if nationalism,

Woodrow Wilson and the League did not exist. Britain, he argued, could not maintain its position in Iraq "by conciliating extremists" and that, "regardless of the League of Nations," Britain should "go very slowly with constitutional and democratic institutions, the application of which to Eastern countries had been attempted of late years with so small a degree of success."[47]

Wilson's policy largely ignored urban and nationalist feeling. He believed it was unrepresentative. Britain must not be "diverted by a handful of amateur politicians in Baghdad," he declared. A conscious decision was taken not to acknowledge demonstrations of public opinion that clashed with his views.[48] When asked by the British government to ascertain popular political sentiment, he made sure that only views echoing his own on the best way forward were heard in London. [49]

Wilson could accurately claim during 1918 that his repeated requests for guidance from Delhi and London had gone unanswered. But as policy towards Iraq became more coherent, Wilson was drawn into increasing conflict with his masters in London. [50] Although there was some sympathy for Wilson's assertion that good governance, efficiency and law and order would directly suffer with the establishment of an Arab-staffed administration, the fact that he could not understand the new realities led Curzon to comment that "The whole bent of Colonel Wilson's mind was wrong, and the presence at the head of the Administration of a man whose ideas were wrong was not in my opinion practicable." [51]

By the summer of 1920 Wilson had become a useful scapegoat for the uprising that swept the country, and he was unceremoniously removed when Percy Cox finally returned from Iran. [52]

After detailed discussions with members of the British cabinet in London, Cox arrived in Iraq to take up the role of High Commissioner in October of 1920. [53] His task was to tailor Britain's role in Iraq to adhere to new international norms and conform with the pressing need to bring expenditure in line with Britain's weakened strategic and economic position. [54] In the wake of a destructive and costly tribal uprising, Cox had to find a way of forming a governing structure that would publicly devolve power to the population while codifying Britain's position under the Mandate regime. Britain's actions and policy in Iraq now had to be open to international scrutiny.

British policy planners divided Britain's medium- to long-term aims in Iraq between realizing national interests and "fulfilling international obligations." The tension between meeting these two aims controlled the evolution of state building in Iraq and shaped it in distinct ways. Economic and strategic interests ranged from preventing hostile powers from dominating the head of the Persian Gulf and maintaining Baghdad as a key link in the imperial air route to India to the protection of the Persian oil fields. But because policy makers recognized the novelty of the international situation, they were also intent upon being "regarded as the closest friend of the Arab people." "International obligations" meant that interests had to be furthered in new and varied ways. A note prepared for the Cabinet by the Middle East Department of the Colonial Office stated that Britain's

> whole course of action has deeply committed us to the creation and support of an independent Arab State in the whole area [of Iraq], and to the rendering of such advice and assistance as may be required to enable such a state to pass through the initial difficulties of its existence . . . We have committed ourselves to the support of a particular form of government, viz., that of a constitutional monarchy under King Faisal. . . . We have undertaken, under the auspices of the League of Nations and in the eyes of the world, to do our best to make this regime a success.[55]

As High Commissioner Cox was charged with executing policy designed to realize this bundle of conflicting objectives. He quickly set about speedily implementing the measures that had been despised by A.T. Wilson.[56] Within eighteen days of reaching Baghdad Cox had formed a cabinet of urban notables. Ten months later Iraq had a king, approved by what was represented as a popular referendum.

The institutional and legal basis of the new state was constructed around the twin pillars of cabinet and king. The conflicting pressures placed upon Cox were revealed in the fluctuating freedom he, as British representative, had at any given moment, in relation to the joint actions of ministers and the king. The power that the ministers wielded after 1920 was likewise tempered by their British advisers. For the Mandate to be seen to be working, the relationship between advisers and ministers had to be consensual. The adviser could not overrule the minister, the individual in whom the power of self-determination finally rested. Under this arrangement the High Commissioner, through his day-to-day inter-actions with the king and cabinet, became the only point of official British control over the new Iraqi government. [57] As it turned out, this relationship was not legally codified under the Mandate itself because of the latter's unpopularity amongst Baghdadis, but it was spelled out by formal treaty between the Iraqi and British governments.

The Council of Ministers, as the first Iraqi institution set up under the Mandate, reflected the tensions in Britain's approach between the need to give autonomy to the population of Iraq and the desire to retain control. On November 30, 1920, Cox issued the edict that all officers and depart-ments that had made up the British Civil Administration "will now come directly under the orders of the Council of State."[58] The Council had real if mediated executive power and in one of its first decisions re-divided the country's administrative districts along Ottoman lines. This "was the most obvious indication to the public that an Iraq Government was now a reality."[59]

Constraints placed on the decision-making powers of the Council of Ministers were vested in the High Commissioner. When the Council of Ministers was formed, Cox declared himself to have the "supreme authority" as the representative of the British Government over any exec-utive decisions made.[60] But as the ministers set about taking control of their ministries and running the country, the High Commissioner's power was in turn constrained by the growth and actions of state institu-tions. [61] This meant that, as the relationship between the new Iraqi gov-ernment and the High Commissioner was codified, the final sanction left to the High Commissioner was the right to "insist upon the king send-ing the bill or resolution back to the cabinet for reconsideration." [62] The High Commissioner more generally relied on sending letters to the Council's meetings recommending that certain issues be discussed or rethought.[63]

Informally, the growth of the Iraqi state and its exercise of power relied heavily on the role of the British advisers during the first few years of the Mandate. At first "Advisor" was the term applied to every British officer whose job was transferred from the British Civil Administration to the new Iraqi state. At every level from the Council of Ministers down to the Political and Assistant Political Officers spread out across Iraq, advisers went from exercising executive control to assisting Iraqi office holders: *Mutasarrifs* and *Qá'immaqams*. As time went on, budget cuts and troop demobilisations meant that the numbers of British officers attached to the Iraqi state declined sharply.[64]

As the Iraqi state grew, a limited number of key British personnel became the advisers to the ministers. The intention was to place British executive direction at the very heart of each ministry. Nevertheless, as with the formal status of the High Commissioner himself, advisors' official roles were codified in surprisingly limited ways. Legally the ministers were "requested" by the High Commissioner to take the views of their adviser "into careful consideration." If a difference of opinion arose between the two men, the minister was again asked to "call the Adviser into consultation." If this failed to produce consensus, the matter was referred to a full meeting of the Council of Ministers for discussion. But the unofficial role of the adviser was in 1920 to be the eyes and ears of the High Commissioner's staff in the institutions of the new state.[65] All information concerning the Iraqi government emanating from the High Commissioner's staff, the British Government and Army would be funneled to the ministries through the relevant adviser. Ministers were directed to discuss all courses of action with the advisers before they made decisions. Advisers were required to attend and take part in Council meetings although they could not vote.[66]

The second pillar of the Iraqi state and a further means of establishing Iraqi autonomy was the king, both as institution and central political actor. With finances under scrutiny and the rapid reduction of British personnel, the king was seen as the pivotal point of control for the High Commissioner.[67] The king was also supposed to rally the population behind the new state.[68] For the League of Nations, Faisal was a charismatic Arab head of state who had been at the Paris Peace Conference and could credibly present himself to the Iraqi people and the world as a nationalist hero.

Cox and the High Commission staff in Baghdad clearly regarded the king as an instrument. [69] The two local candidates before Faisal arrived in Iraq were discounted on the grounds that they would not appeal to the population as a whole.[70] Faisal, with no constituency of his own, appeared open to British manipulation.[71] It was hoped that he would appeal to

moderate nationalist opinion and build a coalition against radicals calling for complete British withdrawal.

The conflict between the British government's attempt to retain as
much power as possible and counter pressures from both Iraqi society
and the international community to establish Iraq as an autonomous,
sovereign state erupted almost immediately. During August 1921, in the
run up to the vote in favor of his kingship and his inauguration, Faisal
held a series of discussions with Cox to finalize the former's role. Faisal
readily agreed to British supervision of finance and foreign relations but
refused to accept that Cox would be the "ultimate power" in Iraq.[72] As
with the provisions spelling out the authority of the Council of Ministers, Cox had to compromise and hope that the "cordiality of cooperation between the Amir and the High Commissioner" would suf-
fice to keep relations working in the way Britain wanted. Cox realized
that the king would be perceived as a puppet if this measure was insisted
on. It was a sign of the constrained nature of British power that, because
"[we] have no intention of re-conquering Iraq," the final sanction could
only be the threat that Cox would resign and British troops would withdraw to Basra.[73] Churchill agreed with Cox that everything should be
done to "strengthen him [the king] in the eyes of the people." Churchill
had to go to the League of Nations and ask for its approval for the measure withdrawing "ultimate power" from the High Commissioner. He
did so on the basis that Iraq had "advanced so far towards being able to
stand alone."[74]

The hope that Faisal would reign and not rule and that ties of cordiality would be enough to ensure cooperation soon proved naive. Faisal,
aware of his dependence upon British arms and resources, set about trying to maximize his autonomy in a manner that was bound to bring him
into direct conflict with the High Commissioner and the British government. After less than eight months Faisal was threatened by Cox with
what had been seen as the final sanction, the threat of British evacuation.[75] This had little effect. Churchill and the staff of the High Commission reacted with anger and bewilderment as the limits of their power
to dictate terms became apparent.[76]

Faisal's campaign for greater power was fought on three fronts. He
attempted to influence the Council of Ministers to pass anti-Mandate legislation; he then established a power base in Hillah and Nassiriyah by

appointing loyalists to government posts and attempting to undermine tribal shaikhs he believed to be pro-British; finally, it appears he let his name be used on Pan-Arab anti-British letters emanating from his palace.[77] The campaign brought the tribes of Baghdad *Vilayet* and the Euphrates to "the verge of rebellion" and drove the *naqib*'s cabinet to resign.[78] When confronted by Cox and asked to explain both the unrest and his role in it, he answered that a tribal uprising was likely but it was to be blamed on "the uncertainty of policy and the lack of definition of responsibility as between himself and His Excellency in matters of internal administration."[79]

With relations between the High Commissioner and Faisal resting on a supposed commonality of interests, Cox had very little formal power to bring to bear on the king. The abandonment of Iraq was frequently discussed by the High Commissioner, the Colonial Secretary and the cabinet, but it was apparent to Churchill, Cox and indeed Faisal that the success or failure of British policy in the Middle East rested on the ability to deliver a quiescent Iraq. [80] When Cox confronted Faisal and demanded that he authorize the arrest of nationalist agitators, Faisal refused.[81] Cox, capitalizing on Faisal's incapacity due to sudden illness and the absence of the Council of Ministers, suspended the fledgling institutions he had spent two years nurturing. He arrested the agitators, closed down two newspapers and banned two political parties.

In the wake of these events Cox attempted to redefine Faisal's power by placing the exercise of royal power within the confines of the constitution and reinforcing the role of the High Commissioner as the chief adviser to the king.[82] Succeeding High Commissioners found that their relationship with the Palace was never stable or satisfactory. Britain's postwar strategic and economic weakness, the rise of nationalism and the ideology of self-determination meant that power had to be devolved to Iraqi-staffed institutions. The commitment to the League of Nations and the scrutiny of the Mandates Commission meant that the High Commissioner's role was exercised within international constraints and open to public interrogation. The well-organized nationalist movement inside Iraq escalated demands for greater autonomy from Britain. Faisal realized both the power and the weakness of his position. From 1921 until 1932 he continually sought to build a power base within the state and society that would give him autonomy from the nascent political élite as well as the British who had been responsible for his accession.

The speed with which Britain's role in Iraq changed from 1920 to 1922 is highlighted by the rapid shift in its legal basis. The Mandate system itself was agreed in Paris on 30 January 1919. Britain publicly accepted the Mandate for Iraq at the San Remo Conference in April 1920 announced in Baghdad on May 5. By June 1921 Cox had informed Churchill that the Mandate was "out of date" and could not be applied to Iraq.[83] The Mandate was formally replaced by a treaty of alliance and signed on October 10, 1922.

The reason for the swift transformation from Mandate to treaty was two-fold. First, the very term "Mandate" was a target for widespread resentment in Baghdad from May 1920 onwards. For the British the term was linked to the disinterested, sacred trust at the heart of Woodrow Wilson's vision of the League.[84] But the Iraqis translated the term into Arabic to suggest the sovereign rule of Britain over Iraq.[85] The abrogation of the Mandate became a key demand of the growing nationalist movement but also of the *naqib* and the king. The power of the nationalists in Baghdad drove Britain to sign a treaty with Iraq instead of attempting to administer the country under the terms of the Mandate. During the war and its immediate aftermath the British saw the nationalist movement as a positive tool to deploy against the Ottoman Empire and then as a way of unifying Iraq's disparate population.[86] But as the movement grew in power and its demands increasingly constrained the ability of the British to act, they increasingly perceived it as irrational and dangerous.

The second reason for sudden legal transformation of the relations between Iraq and Britain was the speed at which the state and its polity developed in the first two years of the Mandate. Both in London and Baghdad there seems to have been surprise at the short time it took to create the new state and the alacrity with which the urban population adapted to it:

Having set up our independent or quasi-independent state, we were bound to deal with it on terms of greater equality, and less from the point of view of a guardian towards its ward, than was originally contemplated. This being the case, the conclusion of a treaty seemed from every standpoint to be the most satisfactory way of regulating relations on the spot.[87]

The conflict between the High Commissioner and the king, which reached its peak in August 1922, was partly driven by the king and the *naqib*'s discontent with the treaty. For them the treaty did not remove the Mandate. It simply replaced it.[88] The tensions between control and devolution at the core of the British approach to Iraq were highlighted by the August crisis. Cox's response to anti-treaty feeling was to suspend government, ban nationalist newspapers and deport the leaders of the agitation against the treaty. It was only with the more active and vocal nationalist opinion cowed that conditions existed in which the king, the *naqib* and the Council of Ministers could be persuaded to accept the treaty. By his actions, however, the High Commissioner threatened to alienate the very people to whom power was to be devolved and to undermine the institutions that were supposed to assure the viability of Iraqi sovereignty.

A. (*over his narghileh*): Men say that a certain Mullah has prophesied the immediate coming of the Mahdi.
B. (*grumpily*): What good would will that be? Christ will come too and he'll be the Adviser.[89]

The twenty-year treaty that Cox had risked so much to impose was transformed in March 1923 by a protocol which limited Britain's formal involvement in Iraq to just four years. The catalyst for this abrupt change had to do with events in the wider Middle East and with developments in domestic British politics.

In September 1922, just as the Council of Ministers and the king in Iraq had been browbeaten into accepting the treaty, the coalition government led by Lloyd George faced the reality of Britain's weakening post-war power. Lloyd George's policy of supporting Greece against Turkey was being undermined by a resurgence in Turkish military power. In September British forces were surrounded by the Turkish army in the neutral zone of Chanak on the eastern side of the Dardanelles. The Prime Minister's and the Colonial Secretary's "impulsive and bellicose" handling of the crisis isolated the government domestically and internationally.[90] As a renewed conflict with Turkey looked increasingly possible, Italy and France withdrew their troops from the neutral zone, not wishing to be drawn into another costly military campaign. Churchill, in announcing (without consultation) that the Empire would supply the troops needed, also alienated the white dominions and damaged imperial unity.[91]

British domestic reaction to the Chanak crisis had far-reaching effects on Iraqi-British relations. In spite of the coalition government's oft-repeated calls for a reduction of overseas spending, foreign and military commitments abroad were still accounting for £300 million out of an estimated government budget for 1922 of under £1000 million.[92] Bonar Law's critique of Lloyd George and the general imperial overreach, "we cannot alone act as the policeman of the world," well reflected public sentiment.[93] These general concerns about Britain's role overseas came together during the election campaign of November 1922 around the issue of Iraq. Law and the Conservative election campaign promised "tranquillity and freedom from adventures and commitments." [94] A vocal coalition, including the *Daily Mail, Daily Express* and a number of prospective MPs, managed to place the call for the evacuation of Iraq "bag and baggage" at the center of the election campaign.[95] Law, reacting to this concern, expressed the wish

> that we had never gone there . . . [and pledged that] . . . at the ear-
> liest possible moment consistent with statesmanship and honor . . .
> [the next government will] . . . reduce our commitments in
> Mesopotamia.[96]

Bonar Law, the victorious Prime Minister of the new Conservative government, was obliged to rethink Britain's role in Iraq and the wider Middle East.[97] The constraints placed upon him were both ideological and material. He was faced with a Parliament where "the overwhelming opinion . . . was against remaining in Mesopotamia indefinitely."[98] After the Chanak crisis Lloyd George's handling of foreign policy was widely viewed as reckless and counter-productive. The dividends of peace were still awaited by a long-suffering British public. The threat of another war rallied public opinion against the jingoistic rhetoric of the coalition government. Law was in part elected to reduce Britain's role overseas that were considered too risky or too peripheral to justify the burden on the already hard-pressed British tax payer.[99]

In December 1922, soon after having been elected, Law set up a cabinet committee to assess what was to be done with Iraq. Given the role that Iraq had played in the election and the general hostility of the House of Commons, it was not surprising that "during the early months of the Bonar Law ministry, the possible final evacuation of Iraq was seriously considered.'[100] Sir Percy Cox was recalled to London to testify before the committee. His testimony proved pivotal.[101] Cox set out to persuade the committee and with it the cabinet, that British policy in Iraq was working, would bear dividends great enough to justify its continuance, and that, if prematurely curtailed, the result would be disastrous. He claimed that the majority of Iraqis welcomed the British role and that withdrawal would lead inevitably to anarchy, a rise in Russian influence and ultimately the return of the Turks. If Britain turned its back on Iraq, he argued, the negative effects would be felt across the entire Muslim world.[102]

Cox was only partially successful. The demands for a "bag and baggage" evacuation of Iraq were avoided, but in the wake of the Chanak crisis the clamor for a speedy reduction in Britain's commitment to Iraq proved to have greater influence on the cabinet than Cox's eloquence.[103] He returned to Baghdad with a draft protocol which reduced the treaty of Alliance to a period of four years after a peace treaty had been signed with Turkey.

The conclusions reached by the cabinet committee on Iraq in 1923 marked the decisive shift in British policy. The treaty that Cox had worked so hard to impose on King Faisal and the Council of Ministers a few months earlier was effectively discarded. The Mandate ideal was dropped in favor of Britain exercising an advisory role, strictly limited by the time and money that could be expended on it. The Secretary of State for the Colonies summed up the approach:

> it may be taken as certain that His Majesty's Government has no intention of retaining mandatory responsibilities in respect to Iraq for a longer period than is absolutely necessary in order to secure the admission of the country to the League of Nations. It is not anticipated that this period will in any case exceed four years from the date of the ratification of peace with Turkey.[104]

From 1923 onwards, those making policy in London and implementing it in Baghdad faced the dilemma of conflicting objectives. How to retain influence with increasingly independent Iraqi politicians and civil servants while pursuing the medium- to long-term goals of the British state to disengage seemed to pose an insoluble conundrum. Overshadowing all decision-making was the unpopularity of the policy amongst the British press and Parliament. The dangers to British prestige of a British government being forced to sever its links with Iraq could be forestalled only by a steady reduction in the cost and manpower expended there. Economy and a drive towards higher Iraqi tax revenues came to dominate all official deliberations.

How was the British state to minimize its role in Iraq "while fulfilling its international obligations"? For those in the Colonial Office the only way to achieve this was to build a self-sustaining state as quickly as possible and convince the League of Nations that the duties awarded to Britain in 1920 had been discharged. Under these stringent conditions the long-term goal of a pliant Iraq safely within a British sphere of influence could be realized only by ties of mutual interest and common outlook between those who built the state and those who ran it after independence. The general goal was summarized in the letter of instruction given to Sir Henry Dobbs, the man chosen to replace Sir Percy Cox as High Commissioner for Iraq in 1923. Dobbs, trained in the Indian Civil Service, was sent to Iraq during the First World War. He went on to be the longest serving High Commissioner and became the dominant figure in the British attempt to build a sovereign but compliant Iraqi state:

> The basic principle underlying the relations between the two Governments is co-operation towards a common end, namely the progressive establishment of an independent Government of Iraq, friendly to and bound by gratitude and obligation to His Britannic Majesty's Government.[105]

From 1923 until 1926 the persistent problem faced by Sir Henry Dobbs and his staff in Baghdad was how to make use of their two main conduits of influence, the king and the Council of Ministers, without undermining the Iraqi government's credibility with the population.[106] Relations between Dobbs and King Faisal were critical. In 1923 the reduction of the Anglo-Iraq treaty to a period of four years and the appointment of Dobbs as High Commissioner marked a conscious decision to loosen the regulatory oversight by the High Commissioner over the king. Sir Henry

Dobbs, like Cox before him, questioned the king's character, his methods and ultimately his loyalty, but accepted that the fortunes of the Iraqi state rested to a large degree on his success or failure.[107] The king, argued Dobbs,

> has to keep his eye constantly fixed on possible developments after our departure and to guard above all against the allegation that he is a puppet king, propped up by our bayonets, who is willing to sacrifice the true interests of the country in order to keep in our good graces. He can hope to strike roots in the soil only by an attitude of independence and we must therefore look with indulgence upon any opposition on his part to our wishes, when those wishes run counter to popular clamor.[108]

To this end, during the first year of his appointment, Dobbs continually argued that Faisal and his government should be given more autonomy and that the financial strictures imposed from London were having a counter-productive effect on Britain's policy goals in Iraq.[109] It is indicative that by 1926 Colonial Office officials in London were sympathetic to Faisal's complaint that Dobbs himself was interfering too much in the running of government. In order to curb this, the expansion of Dobbs's staff was blocked and "the gradual "diplomatization" of the High Commissioner" was initiated as a policy objective.[110]

The change in the nature of Iraqi-British relations can be measured by the decrease in the number of British advisers in the employ of the Iraqi government.[111] Political debate in Baghdad between 1922 and 1927 centered around the inherent nonsequiter of executive Iraqi autonomy and sanctioned British advisory authority. [112] In fact, the power and role of the British advisers changed dramatically during this period.

In 1920, under the Mandate, the advisers were to be at the heart of the new state, acting as the eyes and ears of the High Commissioner and, through him, of the Colonial Office. But the job of advising the politicians of an increasingly independent state and simultaneously furthering British interests quickly became impossible. By the end of 1921, Hubert Young, on an extended trip to Iraq, warned that British advisers ran the danger of becoming "more native than the native himself." On returning to London in early 1922, Young noted further discord "between the two banks of the river," between the British advisers in the Ministries on the east side of the Tigris and the High Commission staff in the residency on the west.[113]

The conflict of interest inherent in the role of adviser claimed its first victim in 1924 with the dismissal of S.H. Slater, the Financial Adviser to the Iraqi government.[114] Colonel Slater had been involved in formulating Britain's policy towards Iraq from the Cairo Conference of 1921 onwards. By 1924 those in the Colonial Office were complaining that he was

> rather inclined to take up a contentious attitude and to assume that it was his business, as the representative of Iraq, to drive the hardest bargain that he could with His Majesty's Government.[115]

Slater later claimed that the position of adviser was "ignominious and odious," regarded with equal suspicion and hostility by both the Iraqi government and the Colonial Office.[116] Dobbs, in seeking a replacement for Slater, highlighted the difficulties of such a job. The Colonial Office recommended R.V. Vernon, its own financial adviser, but Dobbs saw his "previous identification with the Colonial Office point of view as likely to prejudice his chances of success in Iraq.'[117]

Slater's characterization of the perils of the job was borne out when, two years after the Colonial Office insisted on Vernon's appointment, Sir Hugh Trenchard, the Chief of the Air Staff, labeled him a Bolshevik. Trenchard's remark was made as part of a general attack on the Iraqi government's advisers in which he accussed the entire staff of disloyalty.[118]

On 3 January 1923, the Administrative Inspectorate Law was passed by the Council of Ministers changing the legal role of the British advisers. This legislation, passed before Cox was recalled to London in the aftermath of the Chanak crisis, was the product of pressure from the Council to obtain greater independence for the Iraqi personnel of the nascent state.[119] The legislation was presented as a positive codification of the British advisers' role. By changing their name to "inspectors," the law intended to emphasize the advisers' position as the final guarantors of administrative efficiency. But, under the terms of the new legislation, the inspectors, organized under the Ministry of the Interior and managed by the chief adviser to the minister, were to be based in Baghdad. The effect of the legislation was to withdraw British advisers from the

Iraqi hinterland, reducing their numbers and drastically curtailing their influence.[120] The consequence of the legislation was to give greater autonomy to the *mutasarrifs* and *qā'immaqam's*, the local government officials in Iraq.

The Administrative Inspectorate Law passed by the Council of Ministers, although obstructed by Dobbs, was not ultimately challenged by either the High Commissioner or the Colonial Office. With the change in policy represented by the 1923 protocol, there was a general realization that the new institutions of the Iraqi state, from local administrations to the Council of Ministers and the king, would have to bear the full weight of government much sooner than had been envisaged under the Mandate. For the High Commission staff, this rapid increase in autonomy would lead to a reduction in efficiency, but, as Cox and Dobbs agreed,

> The Iraqi Government must be allowed to make mistakes and learn by them during this probationary period, provided that such mistakes are not of a nature to lead to disaster and that British troops and officers are not forced to be instruments of misgovernment.[121]

In the wake of the Administrative Inspectorate Law and the signing of the Protocol, the Colonial Office sent to Baghdad a draft letter for all British officials in Iraq. The letter was an attempt to set terms of employment for the new era. It was also an attempt to overcome the problem of divided loyalties amongst British staff evident since 1921:

> We have to look forward to a four year period during which it will be essential that we should know at every stage what action the Iraqi Government is proposing to take, in case any question arises of authorizing the High Commissioner to take action under Article IV of the treaty.[122]

Both Cox and Dobbs objected to this, arguing that it was in contradiction to the overall direction and philosophy of the new approach. For Dobbs, the advisory period would work only if "the politically minded part of the Iraq people" were convinced "of the disinterested attitude of Great Britain." The Inspectorate Law "went a long way towards achieving this end. It made clear that the whole executive of the country has to be in the hands of Iraqi officials." Any attempt to water down that commitment would risk undermining it. This approach was accepted by the Colonial Office, which in 1925 vetoed the Air Ministry's attempt (in the name of greater efficiency) to appoint a British Commander-in-Chief of Iraqi forces. This would, it was argued, "be entirely opposed to our declared policy of disembarrassing ourselves of Iraq as soon as possible."[123]

The contradictions inherent in the British government's approach to Iraq came to a head during the last years of the Mandate from 1926 to 1932. The Mandate system had heralded a transformation of the international system. International relations were increasingly to be ordered through the universal unit of the sovereign state. For the British government, the difficulties this produced in the twenties and thirties (especially regarding its role in the Middle East) were a harbinger of the problems attending the dissolution of its empire after the Second World War. The rapid growth of well-organized and vibrant nationalism in Iraq exacerbated the conflict at the heart of the British policy. As the Mandate for Iraq progressed, Britain tried to be attentive to the Permanent Mandates Commission, which became increasingly assertive in its demands that the state being built be both efficient and liberal.[124] British public opinion, loudly expressed in the media and in Parliament, continued to denounce the extended commitment of resources to Iraq. The Colonial and Foreign Secretaries had the unenviable task of defending expenditure on Iraq in terms of the national interest without appearing to contradict the Mandate ideal too flagrantly.

British commitment to the League, despite the resentment of the British public, had, in turn, to face increasingly vocal Iraqi political opposition. For the Mandate to work, King Faisal and the small coterie of Iraqis who made up the political élite in Baghdad had to be satisfied and willing partners of the High Commissioner and the team of British advisers. The Iraqi political élite, mindful of the need to establish its own legitimacy and also of the promises won from the British in 1923, continually demanded greater autonomy and greater freedom to run the state on their own behalf. Their demands for entry into the League of Nations in 1928 brought relations to a new low. This demand immediately and violently exposed the clash between Britain's international commitments and its partnership with the Iraqi élite.

The violent and unstable results of Britain's contradictory responsibilities and goals set the pattern for the end of the European Empires. The irresoluble tensions inherent in British nation building produced, by 1932, the quasi-state of Iraq. When Iraq entered the League of Nations it was granted *de jure* independence as a self-determining nation state. But the reality was something quite different. Iraq was a territory inhabited by a diverse and divided population run by a small clique of mainly Sunni politicians who could not control the country without the help of British airplanes. Its government and economy were still financially dependent upon the British Exchequer. The commitments previously given to the League by both Britain and Iraq concerning the inclusion of and comity among the different ethnic and religious communities were discarded to achieve Iraq's formal independence as quickly as possible. The British state, in order to reduce her commitments to Iraq and meet her international obligations while retaining "ties of good will" to the Iraqi political élite, actively colluded to create the impression that Iraq had fulfilled the five conditions set down by the League for statehood. The League's demand that Iraq have a "settled" government and administration capable of operating essential services had in fact been met. But Iraq was nowhere near being able to fulfill the other four criteria of internationally sanctioned sovereignty: that the state be "capable of maintaining its territorial integrity and political independence," that it be "able to maintain the public peace throughout the whole territory," that it have "adequate financial resources to provide regularly for normal Government requirements," and that it have laws that afforded "equal and regular justice to all."[125]

The inevitable crisis arising from these failures was represented by the Mosul dispute and the way it was resolved in 1926. Sovereignty over the Ottoman *Vilayet* of Mosul was claimed by both the Turkish government and the Iraqi state. After the Turkish state had renounced the treaty of Sevres, the Mosul issue became the main stumbling block to a comprehensive peace treaty between Turkey and Britain. The dispute was eventually referred to the League of Nations for settlement and an international commission was sent to the area for three months in 1925. The conclusions of the commission's report (delivered to the League in July 1925 and accepted in July 1926) contained a blueprint outlining the steps necessary for Iraq's self-determination. More importantly, it exposed the distance between the Mandate ideal and the current real condition of the Iraqi state.

The commission's report recognized the "undeniable" progress made by the Iraqi government since the end of the First World War in security, public health and education. Nevertheless the report went on to say that even though the Iraqis running the state had "the best intentions," their "political experience is necessarily small." Overall, the commissioners found the situation "unstable," with the turbulent tribes and the tensions between Sunni and Shia, Arab and Kurd putting the very existence of the state at risk if the link with Britain were to be broken in four years, as had been agreed under the terms of the 1923 protocol.[126] The commission went on to conclude that, for the League to agree to ceding Mosul to Iraq, the Mandate relationship would have to be extended for "something like a generation in order to allow for the consolidation and development of the new state." This meant that Iraq and Britain would have to conclude a new treaty extending Mandatory role for twenty-five years.[127]

The British government's initial response attempted to square the circle of its commitments and interest. The Colonial Secretary, Leopold Amery, in order to secure the oil-rich area of Mosul for Iraq, immediately agreed to the Committee's conclusions and committed both Iraq and Britain to signing a new treaty to facilitate them.[128] But this commitment carried the caveat that the relationship could be terminated at an earlier date if, in the opinion of the League of Nations Council, Iraq qualified for admission to membership of the League.[129] So, although a new twenty-five-year Anglo-Iraqi treaty was signed in January 1926, it had as one of its clauses a provision for reviewing Iraq's case for joining the League and thus abrogating the mandatory relationship.[130] By the time of the first of these reviews, a mere eleven months after the new treaty was signed, the High Commissioner and key individuals within the Colonial Office in London were arguing that Britain should back Iraq's demands for entry in 1928.[131]

The reasons given by Sir Henry Dobbs for the indecent haste of this apparent *volte face* go to the heart of Anglo-Iraqi relations. Dobbs recognized that by putting Iraq forward for membership of the League in 1928 the British could be accused by the League itself and by other states of acting in bad faith. But weighed against this was the goodwill of the Iraqi political élite. For Dobbs this was by far the greatest concern. If this goodwill were lost,

> I am convinced that the whole political atmosphere would change and that Great Britain would soon experience in Iraq the same dreary disillusionment which she has had to bear in India and Egypt. . . . In no long time the students would be striking and parading, the king and his ministers suspicious and intriguing against us, the lawyers, as in the anti-treaty agitation of 1924, plotting assassination, and the Iraqi troops, the only forces left to guard our aerodromes, wavering. We should then have either to evacuate altogether or to bring back our troops and govern, whether with or without an Arab facade, a sullen people. We should have to abandon the hope expressed in the official letter addressed to all British Advisers that "The basic principle underlying the relations between the two Governments is co-operation towards a common end, namely the establishment of an independent Government in Iraq, friendly to and bound by gratitude and obligation to His Britannic Majesty's Government."[132]

Dobbs had identified the central imperative of Britain's policy in Iraq. The rhetoric of self-determination, combined with the pressing need for the economies to be gained by disengagement, meant that Britain had to devolve power to the Iraqi political élite. This élite might have been, as Dobbs suggested, unrepresentative of the country as a whole, but its "power for mischief" foreclosed any alternative policy of trying to foster "the solid classes' power of tranquillity" given such policy's uncertain chances of success, its costs, and the time it would inevitably take to achieve. The League's own vision of international order combined the ethic of self-determination with a strong commitment to the development of a sustainable and liberal state. Britain had come to accept the former, but, as the final years of the Mandate played out, it became convinced that it could not afford to devote the time and resources needed to obtain the latter. In the event, British employment of lethal, high-tech western military technology in the form of the newly-invented warplane became the only means of managing the violence created on the ground by the British Government's predicament.

The High Commissioner's analysis was quickly rejected as overly melodramatic by a Colonial Office dominated by the arch-imperialist Leo Amery. Instead Faisal was offered the sop of a renegotiated treaty.[133] But Dobbs's pessimistic prognosis proved to be accurate. When the king and the key politicians in Iraq, such men as Nuri Said, and the previously loyal Ja'far Pasha al Askari, realized that Iraq was not to be allowed to enter the League in 1928, they gradually brought the government in Baghdad to a standstill. These key members of the political élite deployed all means at their disposal to pressure the British into granting them control over Iraq's political and military affairs. From 1927 until 1929 politics in Baghdad were paralyzed.[134] Suspicion and anger mounted on both sides. Dobbs increasingly began to doubt the loyalty of the Iraqi army, while Nuri threatened to "pull down the Maude Statue, and turn the RAF out of Hinaidi." [135] In focusing on Maude and Hinaidi, Nuri accurately pointed to the twin concerns of the British. Maude had liberated Baghdad from Ottoman forces in 1917 and had died there of cholera shortly afterwards. For British ideology he represented the progressive nature of the British presence. Hinaidi, on the other hand, was the most important British air base in Iraq. The airplanes based there and the bombs they carried embodied the overwhelming violence the British Government relied upon in the last instance to make its will effective and enforce domestic order on a resentful population. Strategically, London regarded Hinaidi as a key staging point on the air route to India and thus crucial to Britain's global power.

Until 1929 the British government vacillated over what powers they would devolve to Iraqi politicians. The Colonial Office feared that to put Iraq forward for League membership so soon after agreeing to the League's request for a twenty-five-year Mandatory relationship would be seen as "sharp practice" in Geneva. Although progress had been made in state building since 1925, it seemed impossible to argue convincingly that the problems raised by the Commission's report had been dealt with in such a short period of time.[136] The Colonial Office itself thought the institutions of state were not efficient enough to function and protect British interests without continued oversight.[137] The Iraqi army, for example, was regarded as ineffectual and unable to maintain internal order without the support of the RAF. With the discovery of proven oil reserves and the input of large-scale investment to develop them, all British policymakers agreed that Britain could not put strategic and economic interests at risk by a premature loosening of control.[138]

It was recognized by the High Commissioner and the Colonial Office that a "contented Iraq" was essential to the success of Britain's policy. By choosing the king and the cabinet as its tools, the Colonial Office became increasingly dependent on active cooperation:

> The loss of his goodwill and co-operation (to say nothing of his covert hostility) would render our task almost impossible. We cannot, in fact, have a reasonably contented Iraq without a reasonably contented Faisal.[139]

Prolonged antagonism between the British and Iraqi governments would put Britain's position in Iraq, and ultimately her standing with the League of Nations, in jeopardy. International obligations, the weakness of the Iraqi state and Britain's own strategic and economic interests all contributed convincing incentives for preventing greater power from devolving to the Iraqi élite. But as Dobbs had seen, it was nevertheless crucial that some way be found to manage this devolution, otherwise the policy that kept Britain in Iraq ran the danger of unraveling.

As in 1922–23, it was an election and change of government in Britain that proved the decisive and final turning point in Anglo-Iraqi relations under the Mandate. When Leo Amery returned from his fact-finding tour of Iraq in 1925, he realized that if Britain were to build the type of Iraqi state that the League envisioned, while securing what he perceived to be Britain's national interests, a much longer-term commitment than the four years negotiated in 1922–3 was needed. Aware that British public opinion was unwilling to countenance this, he proposed recasting Britain's role in Iraq in terms of national and imperial interests:

> Iraq affords a splendid training ground for the Royal Air Force. Baghdad, so far as one can foresee, is likely to always be a pivotal point in our air communications with the East. In our own interests, quite apart from those of Iraq, we cannot afford to scrap the admirably efficient organization that has been set up. [140]

Unfortunately for Amery the Conservative Government had failed by 1927 to alter the long-running hostility of British public opinion towards maintaining an interest in Iraq. The Chancellor of the Duchy of Lancaster, Viscount Lord Robert Cecil, surveying public opinion in June of that year thought that the "overwhelming sentiment of the electorate at the present time is pacifist in the extreme." He pleaded with his cabinet colleagues that a reduction of "direct responsibilities" in Iraq would be

> a complete answer to those of our critics who allege that we are anxious to have a militarist or adventurous foreign policy. That charge has done us a great deal of harm already and may easily be fatal to our existence at the next election.[141]

Given the stakes of British involvement in Iraq, the cabinet felt this route was unavailable to them. As Cecil had predicted, the conservatives were turned out of office in May 1929.

The general election of May 1929 elected a Labour minority government that was not constrained by the imperial ideology of its predecessor.[142] With a new Colonial Secretary, Foreign Secretary and Prime Minister, the government found it easier to identify the contradictions at the heart of Britain's relations with Iraq and find ways to overcome them. A cabinet committee was set up under J.H. Thomas to scrutinize Britain's colonial expenditure. Its first task was an examination of policy towards Iraq.[143]

The new government in London was now willing to listen to the High Commissioner's advice and shape policy to take account of what was happening in Iraq. During the cabinet deliberations in the summer of 1929, the new High Commissioner, Sir Gilbert Clayton, suggested (as had Sir Henry Dobbs in 1927) that

> voluntary and unsolicited concessions . . . will do much to form those ties of gratitude and obligation with which it is hoped to bind Iraq to Great Britain; whereas, those same concessions, following upon lengthy, and perhaps acrimonious, negotiations, will be apt to produce the contrary effect and to be regarded as the successful result of bargaining with a crafty and unscrupulous opponent.[144]

Passfield, the new Secretary of State for the Colonies, unlike his predecessor, realized the extent to which Britain's influence in Iraq was dependent upon those Iraqi politicians who ran the state.[145] The "prolonged interruption of constitutional government . . . might well lead to disastrous results." So on September 11, 1929 the acting High Commissioner was given authority to tell the Iraqi government that Iraq would be unconditionally put forward to the League for membership in 1932.

The agreement of September 1929 to suspend the 1927 treaty and recommend unconditional entry into the League of Nations in 1932 was a result of the contradictory aims shared by both the Conservative government before 1929 and its Labour successor. Each government operated in an international system radically transformed by the rise of colonial nationalism and the demise of British hegemony. Ideologically, as well as practically, both were committed to building a state in Iraq under the international supervision of the Permanent Mandates Commission. Yet Britain's weakened financial and strategic position during the 1920s meant that this task had to be completed at the lowest possible cost. The heavy constraints upon the British state meant that sovereign power had to be devolved to the political élite of Baghdad — those who, by 1926, were in a position to run things. The short-lived Labour government could oversee this process relatively successfully because its officials were not as committed to the imperial thinking as their predecessors.[146]

The consequences of the September 1929 decision were far-reaching and not immediately recognized by those in the cabinet in London who made it. By unconditionally agreeing to recommend Iraq for League membership in 1932, the government sacrificed one of its professed central goals. The national interest would continue to be furthered, and the resources expended on Iraq would continue to be reduced, but the creation of a "modern" liberal state along the lines laid out in the 1925 League of Nations' Frontier Commission would be scuttled. This was the compromise needed to end the conflict with the Iraqi political élite in Baghdad. The 1929 decision in effect amounted to an announcement that Britain would abrogate its responsibilities under the Mandate and actively collude with her Iraqi partners in building a quasi-state:

My hope is that, even without our advice, Iraq may now be so well
established, that she may be able to rub along in a corrupt, inefficient, oriental sort of way, something better than she was under
Turkish rule . . . If this is the result, even though it be not a very
splendid one, we shall have built better than we knew.[147]

By unconditionally agreeing to support Iraq's entry into the League of
Nations, the British government succumbed to the pressure of its own
domestic public opinion as well as the demands of the Iraqi political élite.
To bring this policy to a successful conclusion however, the League of
Nations Permanent Mandates Commission (PMC) still had to be con-
vinced that Britain had discharged its duties under the Mandate.

Publicly, the Labour Government enjoyed extremely good relations
with the League. Following his appointment as Foreign Secretary in 1929,
Arthur Henderson became one of the most influential figures in
Geneva.[148] British public opinion, weary of war and foreign adventures,
enthusiastically backed the new government's role in the League, with its
professed commitment to disarmament and the prevention of war.[149] But
beneath the gloss of public relations the Labour administration had a
similar perception of the League to that of its Conservative predecessors.
At best they saw it as a useful addition to diplomacy:

but very few politicians when in power and almost no permanent
officials really believed it to be an efficacious instrument for the settlement of international problems.[150]

Britain's Mandatory obligations were based on Article 22 of the League of
Nations Covenant, which stated that a Mandate could be terminated
only when a "Community shall be able to stand alone without the ren-
dering of administrative advice and assistance by a Mandatory."[151] When
the Labour government decided to back Iraq's entry into the League,
their perception of the Permanent Mandates Commission was transformed. The Permanent Mandates Commission had been the personification of Britain's international obligations to Iraq, but, after 1929, it
became an obstacle to the government's goal of ridding itself of the costly
and potentially unending burden of turning Iraq into a liberal state of
international standing.

The development of a strategy to obtain Iraq's membership in the League by reducing the demands of the PMC began as early as February 1927. Henry Dobbs recognized the potential for a conflict of interpretations between the PMC and the British government. To gain entry for Iraq into the League, the British government would have to convince the PMC that Iraq had been brought to "a stage of political, social and economic evolution when it can reasonably be regarded as able to stand alone."[152] Dobbs first set out to limit which parts of the Iraqi state should be subject to the judgement of the PMC. Iraq should, he argued, be judged only on its ability to stand alone administratively, not on its economic or military capability.[153] Under this definition Iraq, although militarily unable to secure internal peace or external defense without British assistance, was administratively comparable to other states already recognized as independent by the League.[154] Secondly, Dobbs argued that the efficiency of the Iraqi state should be compared only to that of the weakest members of the League. In that case:

> Iraq is at least as stable as China, Portugal, Greece or Abyssinia . . . the complete cessation of consultation with Great Britain in foreign affairs and the complete withdrawal of the British Air Force would be very dangerous to the State; but even so it might be no worse than China or Greece.[155]

Dobbs's suggested tactic for tackling the PMC was to radically reinterpret the meaning of Article 22 of the Covenant. For Dobbs, Britain's task had never been to build in Iraq a state comparable to Britain itself or to other Western European states. Instead its function was to construct governmental institutions that could deliver the bare bones of de facto statehood within borders ultimately guaranteed by the international community itself. Implicitly, he was arguing for a two-tier League of Nations. An independent Iraq would be no worse off than any of the weak states in the second tier of membership. To ask for anything more from Britain would be highly unrealistic.

This tactic, first laid out by Dobbs in February 1927, was used to gain entrance for Iraq to the League in 1932. The report detailing the evolution of the Iraqi state demanded by the PMC opens by explicitly stating

Dobbs's thesis. The British government's conception of its mandatory responsibilities had never included the

> attainment of an ideal standard of administrative efficiency and sta-
> bility as a necessary condition either of the termination of the
> Mandatory regime or of the admission of Iraq to membership of
> the League of Nations. Nor has it been their conception that Iraq
> should from the first be able to challenge comparison with the most
> highly developed and civilized nations of the modern world.[156]

Testifying before the PMC in June 1931, Sir Francis Humphrys, the High Commissioner, developed this approach at some length. There were two types of state he argued: the "civilized nations of the modern world," and those like Iraq, where "the machinery of government . . . may not run quite so smoothly or so efficiently as in some more advanced and more highly developed State." A comparison between these two types of state was neither fair nor necessary. Both had the right to exist as independent states within the international community. Iraq, therefore, "given the support and inspiration of membership of the League, is now fit to stand alone; it is now capable of self-government, indeed for all practical purposes it is already governing itself."[157] This argument was deployed at the PMC and then at the full Council of the League of Nations. Backed by Britain's own "moral responsibility" and honor, it won Iraq membership in the League.[158]

The League's recognition in October 1932 of Iraq's full *de jure* independence brought to an end Britain's formal mandatory responsibilities. Institutionally, the League of Nations in the early part of the Mandate had acted as a patent restraint on the overt pursuit of British interests and prevented the annexation of Basra. But by the late 1920s, Britain's compliance with the League's requirements had turned into something very different. The type of state the PMC envisioned for Iraq was not the state the British government had the resources or patience to build. In 1932 Iraq could not have defended itself against its neighboring states, nor could it impose order unassisted across the whole of its territory. Ultimately it was dependent on the RAF as the guarantor of its internal and external sovereignty. Internationally, its *de jure* statehood rested not on the achievement of any "standard of civilization" nor on the ability to hold its own militarily, but only on its recognition as a state by the League. This recognition had been given because of pressure on the British government — from mass public opinion in Britain, from new international norms of self-determination, and from Iraqi nationalism. Recognition had not come about because of the successful creation of a modern liberal state through which a new, more just international order could work to the benefit of all.

Chapter Three

Corruption, Fragmentation, and Despotism

BRITISH VISIONS OF OTTOMAN IRAQ

B ritish actions in Iraq, undertaken within the framework of the "sacred trust" of the Mandate system, were a self-conscious attempt to build a modern state. How the British perceived the legacy of the Ottoman Empire profoundly shaped their interaction with Iraqi society and their reform of its governmental structures. These structures still operated largely as they had under Ottoman rule. The geographical area within which the state was to be constructed was not subjected to a detailed examination by any of the four British High Commissioners charged with the responsibility for its creation. This lack of knowledge was compounded after 1914 by the failure of the Indian General Staff to collate and distribute what information it held on the Ottoman *vilayets* that eventually made up Iraq.[1] The situation was exacerbated by the retreating Ottoman officials who took or destroyed many government records.[2] Financial constraints contributed to a general lack of empirical knowledge about Iraqi society and the old Ottoman system.[3]

Personnel sent from across the British Empire to build the new state interacted with the remnants of the Ottoman Empire on the basis of popular imaginative constructions influential in British and wider European society from the eighteenth century onwards. A lack of empirical data allowed a collective understanding of the nature and effect of Ottoman rule in Iraq to become dominant and to go unchallenged amongst the British staff charged with building the Mandated state.

This European vision of the world the British staff confronted was sustained by two central tenets. First, the Ottoman Empire in Iraq was conceived as an Oriental Despotism. Under this rubric it was unchanging and unable to escape the constraints of its inherent superstition, violence and corruption. Secondly, Iraq was perceived as fundamentally divided. For the British, the urban centers of Iraq were largely made up of *effendis*, remnants of the Ottoman Empire, who were tainted by training and working within corrupt institutions. Juxtaposed against the contaminated cities was the Arab countryside. Here the "true" Iraqi lived, unscathed by Ottoman influence

and in need of protection from the grasping *effendis*. The coherence and per-
vasiveness of this core vision had far-reaching effects.

The separation of state and society central to this vision of Oriental
Despotism supported the British Empire's clash with its Ottoman adver-
saries but hampered its interaction with the governing institutions the
Ottomans left behind. With the entry of the Ottoman Empire into the
First World War, British propaganda had begun to use Orientalist tropes
to portray "the Turk" as degenerate, slavish and brutal. As the war progressed, strategic thinking and public imagination focused on the role of
the Arab revolt and hence on the non-Turkish populations within the
Ottoman Empire. This conscious and subconscious separation of
Ottoman and Arab became more accentuated with the birth of the mandate ideal in 1919. The Arab populations of the Ottoman Empire were
now allies of the victorious powers. Free from Turkish oppression, they
were worthy candidates for states of their own, capable of benefiting from
European tutelage.

To give the Mandate ideal credibility, the pathological aspect of Orientalism was distinguished from the political "immaturity" in European
thinking. To this end, state and society in the non-Turkish Middle East
were prised apart. The corrupt Ottoman administration was separated
from the Arab populations who had suffered under it. The past role of
the "bad" Ottoman Empire could then unambiguously be contrasted
with the present and future role of the "good" British one. The selfless
British colonial administrator was then juxtaposed with the corrupt and
venal Turk. The Iraqi state constructed by the British was to be an occidental one, operating in a balanced and harmonious way with the Iraqi
people. It was to be defined in absolute ideological contrast to the
Ottoman state, seen as despotic, inefficient and tyrannical.

This stark vision intersected with the reality that the majority of those
with an education in the Arab Middle East in 1920 had gained it within
the Ottoman system. Those who were available to staff the new state's
institutions were, within the imagination of Oriental Despotism, tainted
by Turkish corruption. The state, staffed and then run by Ottoman-
educated Arabs, became an object of mistrust. In the British mindset, it
could easily return to type, developing despotic aspirations to dominate
the majority of the people living in the countryside.

This conception of the Ottoman Empire led the British to place their trust in those who inhabited the countryside, those identified as "tribal." The tribes, relatively untouched by Ottoman corruption, were to become the bulwark against the dangers of a new Iraqi despotism. Rural society was to be reinvigorated, organized to pose a virtuous counterweight to the inherently corrupt proclivities of the centralizing state. The focus of British hopes, and the key to rural organization, were the tribal shaikhs. It was they who would guard against the despotic tendencies of the *effendi* class. It was they who would mobilize society against the dangers of oriental despotism.

The European orientalist imagination was the means by which a normative vision of Europe was used as a standard by which to judge the non-European world. It allowed societies external to Europe to be divided into two broad categories: those judged to be immature and those condemned as pathological.[4] The immature were perceived to be on a unilinear historical path whose final destination would prove to be a European modernity. Those judged pathological were perceived to have deviated from that developmental path or had never been fit to join it. Why different parts of the Orient were classified at different historical moments reflected European developments and political preoccupations. These can be linked to sex and gender, but also to the dynamics of European social and political development. The essences that supposedly divide the Orient and the Oriental from the Occidental reflect the hopes and fears of western society. They provide little access to the historical or social truth of the societies they are meant so definitively to characterize.

In 1916, with the war in Europe bogged down in a bloody stalemate, there was a strategic and even ideological need to shift attention and effort elsewhere. This coincided in the Middle East theatre with the need to erase the humiliating defeats at Gallipoli and Kut from popular memory.[5]

Encouraging Sharif Husain to raise the standard of revolt against the Ottoman Empire at Mecca met several of these aims at once. By dividing the Turks from a larger Islamic *umma,* the danger of calls for a *jihad* against Britain spreading to India was reduced.[6] At the same time Britain's Red Sea communications were protected while tying up large numbers of Turkish troops. Once the Arab Revolt got under way its ideological portrayal also provided a heroic counterpoint to the mass mechanized killings on the Western Front.[7]

But the myth of the Arab Revolt ran counter to the general Orientalist portrayal of "eastern peoples." Large numbers of these apparently lazy, timid and ignorant Orientals had fought courageously against the Ottoman Empire alongside British troops. The distinction between pathology and immaturity within the western Orientalist imagination was used to allow these Arabs to be separated from their oppressive Ottoman rulers. Through this construction, the untainted, courageous, honest and pre-modern rural population of Arabia and Iraq came to be juxtaposed with the troublesome town dwellers, corrupted by close proximity to Ottoman culture and administration.

The influence of Oriental Despotism had clear policy implications for structuring the relationship between the new Iraqi state and society. The distinction between European feudalism and Oriental Despotism turned on the existence of autonomous European landlords.[8] In England the rural nobility, citing the "sacredness" of common law and ancient privilege had thwarted the Tudor monarchy's aspirations to absolutism.[9] The rural aristocracy defended the balance between Crown and Parliament, state and society, while retaining their parochial links to the peasantry and the land. When the British set about righting the perceived wrongs of Ottoman Despotism it made sense for them to try to strike a balance between state and society by recognizing the "loyal feudatories," the tribal shaikhs, as those who could act as society's guardians over the state.[10] The Administration Report for Basra Division in 1918 describes those of influence in the area in the following way: "These landlords are men of gentility and pride, occupying a position of influence and status reminiscent of that of the feudal landlords in English history."[11]

A history of Iraq first published in 1925, written by the British administrator and scholar Stephen Longrigg, captures perfectly the worldview of the British staff in Iraq.[12] Longrigg's views were considred authoritative. His first hand experience in Iraq was perhaps greater than that of any other non-Iraqi who served there. He first entered the country as a soldier with the British Expeditionary Force in the early stages of World War I and did not leave until 1931.[13]

Longrigg's books represent and reproduce the self-understanding of the community in which he spent a large part of his adult life. They accurately reflect the worldview held by the corps of British personnel, both military and civilian, charged with building and overseeing the Iraqi state. His first book, a detailed and influential account of the Ottoman influence in Iraq, was written as he served as a Political Officer in Hillah on the Euphrates south of Baghdad. It serves up a full-blown rendition of Oriental Despotism and applies its lessons without a moment's hesitation or doubt. According to Longrigg, Iraq had passed through 400 years of stagnant Ottoman rule with little or no change. Iraq's present may seem a "little less wild and ignorant," but it was certainly "not less corrupt."[14] The Ottomans had failed the Arab population in nearly every aspect. Despite the abundance and renown of Iraq's fabled resources they had gone undeveloped. The government had refused to recognize its "essential duties" of leading the country to progress and its "yet clearer task of securing liberty and rights to the governed (however backward)."[15] Longrigg's explanatory narrative was semi-official; his book was frequently cited as evidence in government reports.[16]

The highly ideological nature of Longrigg's perception of Ottoman Iraq becomes visible when its core themes are revisited in light of recent academic research based on Ottoman archives in Istanbul. Key to Longrigg's understanding of Ottoman domination was its static nature: Iraq under the Turks could not and did not change. In fact, Ottoman rule in Iraq and round the general periphery of Empire (especially during the nineteenth century) was active and dynamic. Government initiatives from the Sublime Porte in Istanbul were both reactive, attempting to counter or meet local events, and proactive, attempting to integrate Iraq fully into the governing structures and economy of the Empire while increasing its security and productivity.

The reign of Sultan Mahmud II, 1808–1839, for example, marked a conscious effort by government in Istanbul to strengthen its control over the provinces.[17] In Baghdad this meant the removal of Da'ud Pasha, the autonomous Mamluk *Vali*, and the occupation of the city by Ottoman troops.[18] The pace of change quickened after the promulgation of the *Tanzimat* reforms by Sultan 'Abd al-Majid. In 1848 a new military formation, the Army of Iraq and the Hijaz, was formed and by 1867 a new round of government initiatives, aimed at the periphery of Empire:

led to a series of transformations in the economic life of frontier districts. Enhanced security, regulation of weights and measures and growing monetarization encouraged the development of markets which, in turn, attracted merchant participation in the state's project of direct rule.[19]

Longrigg and the entire British staff, by accepting and deploying the frames of perception created by the cognitive schemata of Oriental Despotism, saw the Empire as constrained by its own nature. Internal reform was impossible. It was the intrusion of the British that would save the Iraqi population from the corrupt, "dead hand" of the Ottoman Empire. In fact, empirical evidence reveals a governing Ottoman élite, very much aware both of the Empire's weaknesses and the changing nature of the world's political and economic systems, attempting to meet these challenges.[20]

> The Turkish Government has never sanctioned any other system of administration in Arabia than one of oppression towards the weak and deceit towards the strong.[21]

The Ottoman Empire was understood to be hopelessly corrupt and unreformable. It was seen as being detached from the society it unsuccessfully sought to dominate. The unbridgable gap between corrupt state institutions and innocent society implied that those who staffed the Empire had little to do but effect western-style mannerisms and dress and perfect the exploitation of the subject races under their control.

Longrigg blames the emergence of the corrupt class of Ottoman officialdom in Iraq on the administrative reforms initiated by the Governor of Baghdad, Midhat Pasha from 1869. These, he thought, created a group of Iraqi civil servants who were detached from society. They were neither landlords, nor merchants nor religious figures. They constituted a distinctly secular, separate and parasitic middle class. They were, in British eyes, a fifth column, acting as a bridgehead between Turk and Arab: "the effendis formed a great part of the social element receptive of Turkish culture."[22] All that was wrong with the Ottoman Empire was embodied by this governing élite. First and foremost, they were "corrupt and remote from all spirit of public service"; but these weaknesses were part of a larger set of pathologies that included being "complacently urban," "barely literate," "persistent Turkish-speakers," "decorous in social habit" and, finally "uniform in their travesty of European dress."[23]

Descriptions of the "befezzed *effendi*," condemned as pathological because he sought to be modern, are telling. The trappings of modernity that the British saw him "flaunt" were the wrong type. The *effendis* were seen as impertinent. They had adopted the costumes of modern Europe without putting in the hard work of mastering its substance. By attempting to bypass the slow unilinear path to modernity, they had corrupted themselves and ran the danger of corrupting the society over which they asserted despotic control. Hubert Young, an influential civil servant in the Colonial Office, when discussing the possibility of Faisal being involved in plotting the murder of an Iraqi politician, explained that there was no need to harbor any illusions about his morality. "His early training at the court of Abdul Hamid in Constantinople would of itself be quite sufficient to qualify him for this unpleasant role."[24] Sir Henry Dobbs, in describing Abdul Muhsin Beg, the Prime Minister in 1928, began by positively noting his tribal origin but then lamented his education in Constantinople as having "infected him with a townsman's ideas."[25]

The potential corruption wrought by the *effendi* on the population was considered to have two sources: first, the pathological degeneracy associated with Turkish rule, morality and society; second, a bastardized modernity. The *effendi*, having come under a "foreign influence," might dabble in what he did not properly understand, the civilization and science of the west. This would then be flaunted as a sign of his superiority over the population from which he had been elevated. By bringing to bear the influence of modernity on Iraq too soon, the *effendi* would drag the population out of the natural order of things and force it to develop too quickly.[26]

The distinction between an oppressive and corrupt Ottoman administration and an oppressed and immature Iraqi society was a powerful organizing trope. The division between ruler and ruled explained the supposedly all-pervading corruption and neglect. But such a stark state-society divide was what the British needed to see and is not sustained by the historical evidence. Like that of all empires, Ottoman rule was dependent upon a close working relationship with key members of society. In a symbiotic interaction, the government's officials looked to notables to provide information, order and taxes. In return for this the notables had their social position recognized and enhanced.[27] But to view this relationship in purely instrumentalist terms would be to ignore the ideological commitment that ensured its smooth reproduction over generations. The *naqibs* of Baghdad, for example, had an independent source of wealth and prestige as the descendants of one of the most celebrated religious figures of the Sunni world. Pilgrimage from the Indian subcontinent meant that the family had a flow of income from outside the Empire. But from the 1870s, the *naqib's* family had consistently used their local, regional and international religious influence to bolster the divine and secular legitimacy of the Ottoman regime. During the Turko-Russian war, *Sayyid* Salam *Effendi* started a fund to raise money in India and Iraq for wounded Turkish soldiers. He visited Istanbul on at least two occasions and sat on a committee formed by the Sultan in November 1886 to investigate and attempt to stop a serious tribal uprising in Mosul and Baghdad *vilayets.*[28]

Examples such as these point towards a much more balanced, integrated and negotiated relationship between state and society in Ottoman Iraq than the discourse of Oriental Despotism allows. The Sultan frequently consulted Iraqi notables, appointed them to high position and listened to their grievances. Similarly, a more nuanced reality prevailed with regard to corruption and attempts to control it.

Evidence from both British colonial records and more recent academic literature shows that corruption was a problem amongst the lower levels of the administration in Iraq staffed by the *mutasarrifs* and *qd'immaqams.* But the influence of the ideology of Oriental Despotism on British colonial officials led them to see corruption as endemic to Ottoman rule, debasing it from top to bottom. One of the sources for this misunderstanding may have originated in the practice of *badal.* This was the sum each new *Vali* had to pay on being granted his office, in lieu of the estimated amount of revenue he could be expected to raise while he was in post. But the practice of *badal* was abolished with the appointment of Midhat Pasha as *Vali* of Baghdad in 1869.[29] Indeed Ottoman attitudes to corruption can be judged by the case of Namik Pasha. His time in office saw a rapid growth in maladministration and by January 1901 a special commission had been appointed to report on his alleged misdeeds. It requested that Namik Pasha and several other officials be removed for their misdeeds and their overtly favorable treatment of a specific notable family.[30]

Oriental Despotism informed British understanding of Ottoman law and administrator's attempts to reform the legal system. The Ottoman state was not only irrational and bound by Islam but structurally stagnant and weak. In effect, written law could be as rigid or liberal as the drafters desired because ultimately it would stand little chance of being enforced. For Gertrude Bell, by "their blind impulse to draw all authority into a single net, the Turks not only neglected but actively discouraged the delegation of power."[31] For Bonham Carter, the Iraqi government's Judicial Adviser, "the Ottoman Code as it now stands is unscientific, ill-arranged and incomplete."[32] For C. A. Hooper, under the influence of "western civilization" limited parts of the law had managed to break free of "pure Mohammedan jurisprudence." But because one of the central traits of Oriental Despotism was the lack of private property, general property law was beyond the influence of any external forces.[33]

By understanding Ottoman law as both a symptom and cause of Oriental Despotism, the British developed two approaches in their attempt to reform it. First, in the early years of the civilian administration, they set about attempting to systematize and unify the whole system.[34] The application of British logic could regularize it, while a new and rational governing system could fairly apply it. But as their role moved from Mandatory to advisory, and as they sought to create a more permanent and institutionalized government, they encountered a more subtle problem.

In 1922 a joint committee of Iraqi and British lawyers was convened in Baghdad under the chairmanship of Hubert Young to draft the Organic Law. This was to be presented to the League of Nations as evidence of the new state's liberal and progressive legal system. The overtly liberal and progressive appearance of the new Organic Law was of heightened importance, as it was negotiated under the shadow of Curzon's battle with the Turkish state about which government was best suited to take control of Mosul. Curzon's successful argument hinged on the modern and reasonable approach of the Iraqi state when compared with the harsh and undemocratic practices of their former rulers.

A problem arose when the two Iraqi drafters of the Organic Law, Sassoon *Effendi* and Naji Beg al-Suwaidi, complained that the Turkish Constitution, instigated after the Young Turks' revolution, was a more liberal document than that proposed by the British.[35] It was difficult to reconcile the self-understanding of the British role in Iraq with the drafting of an Organic Law less liberal than the Turkish one it was to replace. Yet the solution to this problem already presented itself from within the British understanding of Oriental Despotism. The Turkish Committee of Union and Progress, as part of a despotic regime, could afford to grant all the paper concessions it wanted. The power to rule, based as it was on the army and the use of unrestrained force, meant that "they could afford to disregard the Constitution whenever they thought that the stability of the State (to put their action on the highest level) required it." The new Iraqi state, on the other hand, being a democratic and liberal one, needed a stronger rule of law to keep the interests of state and society in equilibrium.[36]

Under the rubric of Oriental Despotism, Ottoman jurisprudence was bound to be driven by an adherence to Islam and therefore could not evolve rationally. The application of law, and the creation of order, were structured by two competing images of Turkish rule. First, influenced by the more general trope of orientalism, the Turkish personnel charged with keeping the peace and enforcing the law were classified as universally despotic, corrupt and violent. It was the job of the new liberal and western Iraqi state to overcome this legacy of ruthless oppression.[37]

But the dominant conception of the Ottoman state in Iraq simultaneously emphasized its overwhelming weakness. The state, hidebound as it was by stagnation and corruption, could not possibly project its power and influence to any great degree across the vast majority of the population it sought to oppress. The imagery that pervades British notions is that of a regime trapped within the city walls of Baghdad or in its outpost towns scattered across Iraq. Ottoman rule could and did order urban life, infecting it with negative pathologies, but the weak, cowardly and ineffectual instruments of rule had little influence beyond urban areas. Sir Ernest Dowson was the pre-eminent expert on land tenure in the British Empire. He arrived in Iraq in 1929 to advise on land reform.

His 1931 summary of Ottoman rule typifies the generally held perception:

It is evident that for several preceding centuries the officers of the Central Government were not in a position to exercise any system-

atic control over the large areas throughout the country. . . . Under
the conditions that commonly prevailed the authority of the Central Government ran slowly, while the effective local and social
units were tribes or sections of tribes.[38]

Ottoman law was written off because of its inability to evolve to meet the
changing needs of the Iraqi population. Once the legal system had been
reformed, any unfavorable comparison between Turkish codes and the
new state's record on law and order could be discounted on the grounds
that the Ottomans had never been able to impose law and order and so
could be as idealistic and liberal on paper as they wanted.

British attitudes to Iraqi land and its abuse under Ottoman rule throw
into stark relief the crucial leverage provided by the division at the heart
of the Orientalist vision between the corrupted Turkish state and virtuous traditional Arab society. This use of the Orientalist perspective was
played out in an interpretation of Iraq's history. Iraq, in the distant past,
according to this view, had been "one of the most prosperous tracts of
agricultural land in the world," an area of "untold wealth."[39] This prosperous land of yore stood in sharp contrast to present-day Iraq. Ancient
Iraq had been the province of specifically *Arab* tribes. The historic
renown of the fertile land between the two rivers had been due to the
hard work of the Arab population. The rot had set in with the arrival of
the Turks.[40] For Gertrude Bell the "Ottoman conquerors" had enforced
alien property rights upon the Arab tribes, claiming that all lands were
now to be owned by the state. For the Political Officer in the Samarra district, the Dujail plain could once again be restored to its legendary productivity when "the blasting and withering neglect" it had experienced
under the Turkish regime had been put right.

Upon the Turkish conquest the agricultural land of Iraq became
state property. In theory it would seem that the state was entitled
to their whole produce, and the Qanun al Aradhi definitely lays it
down—Articles 30 and 107—that forests and mines belong solely
to the state.[41]

But the Ottoman Empire, according to the narrative structure of Oriental Despotism, was both arbitrary and weak. The land and revenue staff

of the Empire were seen by the British as "feeble" and hence the "Ottoman Government were never in a position to exercise any systematic control of the large areas of miri land throughout the country."[42] The result of such pretensions to dominance combined with an inability to enforce them was a "hotch-potch of Turkish archaisms, puzzles, and caprices," with land tenure and practice apparently differing in each *liwa* depending on the level of Turkish power and the existing social practices they had to deal with.[43]

Muhammad Shafiq, Midhat Pasha, Ottoman Governor of Baghdad from 1869 to 1871, might have posed a challenge to this monolithic perception of the Ottoman Empire as a corrupt, stagnant and oppressive regime. Midhat Pasha set about attempting to instigate the reformist spirit of the *Tanzimat* movement.[44] As part of his overhaul of the governing system, he imposed the *vilayet* system and reformed the administration of land and revenue. He also enacted the 1858 Ottoman land decree under which *miri* land could now be granted to private individuals under a new system known as *nizam tapu*.[45] Indeed Sir Henry Dobbs recognized the three years of Midhat Pasha's reign as the most stable and secure period of Ottoman rule.[46] The motivation driving Midhat Pasha's innovations was seen by Dobbs and his colleagues through the prism of Oriental Despotism. The reform's aims, it was argued, were not primarily to increase government revenue and efficiency or the living standards of the population but to "break the power of the great tribes" and thus increase the dominion of the state over the society.[47]

Dobbs's and Longrigg's understanding of Midhat Pasha was based on a comparison with previous Ottoman governors. For the British, Midhat Pasha's reign was unique. His reforming zeal was seen as an aberration based on individual strength of personality. Those in the Mandate administration interpreting the results of his work saw them as preordained to fail. Those who took the time to study the detail of Midhat Pasha's work could not escape the analytical framework of Oriental Despotism or see Midhat's polices as a general Ottoman response to changing international circumstances. Midhat Pasha could not succeed given the inherently inefficient and corrupt nature of the state and the fractured and oppressed nature of society.

Midhat Pasha's imposition of *tapu* land tenure was a conscious attempt to modernize Iraqi landholding, but according to the British, an oriental state could only half-heartedly ape occidental rationality. Dobbs exemplifies this understanding of Midhat Pasha. He pours scorn on the "rigid land-laws" elaborated in text and law books.[48] For Dobbs it was typical of the Turks that idealistic and highly theoretical laws dreamt up for European Turkey, "a very different state of society, should be applied in such a doctrinaire fashion to a totally different geographic and social area." This misfounded attempt to be modern was compounded for Dobbs by a "faulty assessment and slipshod methods."[49] For Ernest Dowson attempts to apply the *Tanzimat* reforms were undermined by the lack of detailed investigation.[50] Longrigg had more sympathy with the logic of the *tapu* system. But he saw its failure in the Turks' inability to realize the "immense practical difficulties" in its imposition. With the state unable to enforce its will over the majority of the country, no cadastral survey was possible. A result was title deeds and records that were "incomplete and entirely inaccurate in respect of names, areas, and boundaries, sometimes forged, sometimes overlapping, sometimes duplicated in respect of identical properties."[51] Ultimately, "the tapu system could do little save create new disputes, bestow rights on parties powerless to exercise them, and destroy the best elements in the shaikh-tribesmen relationship."[52]

The modernizing aspirations of Midhat Pasha's reforms were, according to the British, unrealizable. The Ottoman system itself undermined this reformist ethic by its very "nature." The "corrupt" and "venal" approach of those Turks put in charge of the new land registry meant *tapu* rights would, irrespective of prescriptive rights, be bought by those with the money or influence to bribe the land registry.[53] Again, it is the motif of urban-based corruption spreading into the unspoiled countryside that structures this understanding of failed land reform. The "rich merchants" and "town dwelling speculators" bought up the land "over the heads of the tribes." For Dobbs the use of law, of an *iradah*, to grant *tapu* rights to the tribes would under the corrupt circumstances of the Ottoman state be a feeble instrument to stop "land-hunger of the rich city-men."[54] Instead land that had been farmed "for generations by the local tribes" was sold out from under them in the name of speculation and greed.[55]

The blame for the failure of the *Tanzimat* reforms in Iraq was mainly directed towards the pathological incompetence and venality of the Ottoman state. But the *tapu* rights were also understood not to have been taken up by an immature and fractured society that shunned their poten-

tially modernizing effect. Although a fear of conscription and government control deterred tribal society from utilizing *tapu* rights, the "other
evils" of "accessibility, toil, dependence on canals and markets" were large
incentives not to join the property-owning classes.[56]

There may have been a fundamental misunderstanding at the heart
of British notions of land ownership in Iraq. Timothy Mitchell argues
that, before the *Tanzimat* reforms, Ottoman understanding of landholding did not designate an absolute right of possession to land as an
object in itself.[57] Ottoman state claims to *miri* land were not as the
British supposed aspirations to absolutist control of the agricultural
means of production. Instead local representatives of government, legal-
religious authorities and the fellaheen themselves all had prescriptive
rights to the produce of the land. The Ottoman claim was for recognition that the government was due a proportion of the crop, not a
demand for ultimate control of the land. So several different groupings
at the local level all claimed a proportion of the produce, not by means
of abstract, externally imposed laws but through a negotiated and evolving ad hoc approach.

In this light, Midhat Pasha's reforms can be seen as an attempt to
impose a modern logic on existing land laws. He attempted to impose
abstract laws of single possession on shifting and diffuse local practices.
But again the motivation attributed to this policy has been misdescribed
by the British because it was seen through the paradigm of Oriental
Despotism. Midhat Pasha's explicit intention in implementing *tapu* legislation was to give individual cultivators more control over the land they
farmed.[58] His goal was to raise the productivity of the land. To this end
he actually cut the share of produce that the state demanded from the
producer. He went on to propose even greater reductions if the rural
population would not rebel against the state and would promise to pay
the revenues due. Ultimately his aim, much like that of the Mandate
administration itself, was to improve law and order and settle the
nomadic population. He set about achieving this aim with a mixture of
financial incentives and negotiations — not, as Dobbs would have it,
through double-dealing and the use of force.[59]

Ultimately Midhat Pasha's reforms did not achieve what he had
hoped, and he was removed from his post after three years. But to see
his time in office as an aberration in Ottoman rule, as Dobbs and Lon-

grigg did, is to misinterpret the agency behind Ottoman government policy in the late 1800s. Midhat Pasha was a product of a governing élite which clearly saw the profound crisis the Empire was in and the dire need for reform both at the center and the periphery. Midhat was one of a series of reforming *Valis* sent to Baghdad in an attempt to improve agricultural production and law and order. This conscious policy of modernization was instigated in the face of European economic and military encroachment and succeeded in increasing the prosperity and output of the area.

Midhat Pasha's reforms were actually similar in their nature and goals to the policy promoted by a section of the British officials dealing with land reform under the Mandate. He was attempting to impose a modern logic on landholding by solidifying personal ownership, thereby raising production. The British viewpoint, however, commited them to reject Midhat Pasha's attempts at land reform along with the wider Ottoman system. They were completely unable to derive from his efforts any lessons for their own policies.

The British projected simplistic but powerful notions of their own historic past on to the rural population of Iraq. The population was perceived as being largely tribal, but divided into competing and locally bound interests. These units were individually strong, warlike and militant in their resistance to the Turkish state, but because they were split and hostile to each other they could not collectively resist the corrupt and negative effects of Ottoman rule.

Tribal society, for the British officers encountering it in the wake of the Ottoman Empire's defeat in Iraq, was caught between two dynamics. On the one hand, it was simple and primitive. Remote from civilization, the tribal way of life and organization represented people as being as close to their natural state as could be encountered in the modern world.[60] The further away from government tribal society was, the stronger its tribal structures and the more powerful the individual's allegiance to the shaikh.[61] On the other hand, Iraqi tribal society was the victim of the disintegrating influences of enmeshment in the corrupt, devious, and despotic machinations of Ottoman power.

Ottoman policy was aimed at fracturing the society it sought to control. The Ottoman state, weak but devious, had planted the seeds of disunity amongst the once great tribal federations.

Instead of utilizing the power of the shaikhs, the Turks pursued their
classic policy of attempting to improve their own position by the
destruction of such native elements of order as were in existence . . .
To recognize local dominion and yoke it to his service was beyond
the conception of the Turk, and the best that can be said for his
uneasy seat upon the whirlwind was that he managed to retain it.[62]

The Ottoman Empire, personified by the "feeble Turkish tax gatherers,"
brought the contaminating effects of the pathological state to the weakened society. The results were "endless bickering" amongst the tribes and
"the tendency towards leveling, division, disunity."[63] For Longrigg this
led to the visible decline in the lifestyle and character of the tribesmen as
they struggled to adjust to the new and unfamiliar situation. The Turks'
attack on important tribal shaikhs became one of the central arguments
for explaining tribal disintegration for many years afterwards.

This perception of the Ottoman state as corrupting and fragmenting
Iraqi society is typified in Sir Henry Dobbs's understanding of the cause
of instability in the Muntafiq district. The problem of violent unrest
around issues of land ownership in the Muntafiq district had dogged the
British since the beginning of their involvement in Iraq. Dobbs first
investigated the sources of the trouble in 1915 and 1916 as head of the Revenue Office, with the issue still consuming his time in 1926 when he was
High Commissioner.

For Dobbs, Ottoman actions in this area personified their influence
over the whole of the country, "The Muntafiq agrarian troubles were
caused by the Turkish policy of divide and rule, a policy beloved by weak
oriental Governments."[64] They set about imposing the wholly unsuitable
tapu laws on the Muntafiq, unwilling and unable to see the radical difference between western Anatolia and southern Iraq.[65] In conjunction
with applying "their own Procrustean Tapu principles to the Muntafiq
tribal land system" they introduced to a previously "strong and healthy"
society a cause of conflict and degeneration.

For Dobbs, the Ottomans were the cause of Muntafiq's problems but
the Sa'dun family were the effect. This "purely non-tribal family" had previously played a secondary role to the tribal shaikhs. But the Turks had
granted them *tapu* rights over huge tracts of Shia tribal lands, over which
they had never had ownership or possession and which the Muntafiq

shaikhs and tribesmen would never even in their most subservient mood, have conceded to them.

Dobbs saw the Turks as having, by a devious stroke, changed the social relations of the Muntafiq area, "turning the Sunni Sa'dun city overlords into landowners," thereby sowing the seeds of inevitable conflict between them and the tribal shaikhs. In order to add to this source of instability the Ottoman government "artfully tempted the Sa'duns" into becoming the representatives of the Turkish government.

> The Sa'duns foolishly accepted, for, having fallen out with the Muntafiq Shaikhs over the land question, they felt that their position needed bolstering up, not realizing that they would lose the last vestige of their power and influence among the tribesmen, if they allowed themselves to be cunningly transformed from representatives and champions of the tribal confederation into representatives and bureaucrats of the Turks. That was their end. The rest was a welter of confusion.[66]

Turkish actions in Muntafiq according to Dobbs, esemplified the pathology of Oriental Despotism. Turkish administrators had to bolster their own power by destabilizing the Muntafiq and undermining its social structures. The great fault of the Turks had been to mix rural and urban in an effort to divide and rule. The Sa'duns were the personification of this policy, bringing Ottoman degeneration into the heart of the Muntafiq tribal society.

The role of the Sa'dun and the Muntafiq tribal confederation through the mid-1800s to the turn of the century was certainly one of decline and division. But this decline had as much to do with the growing military strength of Ottoman government in the south of Iraq as it did with a policy of divide and rule. Recent studies of the relationship between the Sa'duns and the Muntafiq confederation have them at the head of the confederation in the 1850s. Faced with the growing reach and strength of the state, the confederation's geographical influence was shrinking, forcing it to relinquish control to the state over Samawah, Suq ash-Shuyukh and the area between Shatra and Qalat Salih.[67]

From the 1850s until the 1900s the history of the Muntafiq region can be divided into two periods: that up until the 1880s, when key members of the Sa'dun family, in the face of increased Ottoman power, did indeed take up positions in the administration and that after 1880 (until the early 1900s), when the Sa'dun power was broken and the majority of the family left the area to live in the Syrian desert.[68]

The period after 1880 was marked by the armed conflict conducted by one arm of the Sa'dun family, led by Mansur Pasha and Farhad Pasha against the Ottoman administration. After falling out with a family of Baghdad notables, this branch attempted to raise a tribal revolt. In the resulting action by the Sublime Porte both branches were exiled to Baghdad and a large portion of the family left their lands in the area. This resulted in the growth in power of smaller "intermediate chiefs," who took over the organization of production and interaction with government.

It can be surmised that the unrest in the Muntafiq region that the British had to deal with when they took control was a result of the contest for power between the returning Sa'dun and these *sarkals*. The fact that the Ottoman army played a key role in breaking the power of the Sa'dun and exiling them is not mentioned in Dobbs's explanation. Under the rubric of Oriental Despotism, a weak state interfering in society had to be the cause of instability. The Sa'dun, then, were not rebellious leaders of a tribal confederation in decline but the tool with which the Ottoman state sought (with partial success) to corrupt a strong and vigorous society. The terms of the Oriental Despotic discourse ruled out an explanation that saw a comparatively strong state imposing order on rebellious sections of society. The British administration, by relying so heavily on their Orientalist vision, failed to appreciate the nature and extent of societal change already underway. Dobbs classified the Sa'dun and a despotic Ottoman state as the root cause of the problem. He was unable to recognize that the defeat of a much stronger Ottoman state in 1917 had created a vacuum that allowed the once vanquished Sa'duns to return.

For the British building the Iraqi state, the Ottoman Empire had become a distorted screen upon which to project and rework a deep unease about developments within English society stemming from the turn of the century.[69] The pathologies of the Ottoman state — the corruption of its sprawling administration, the contamination of the countryside, by its presence and propensity to absolutism — were projections in a bitter ongoing dispute about the imagined social trajectory of post-war Britain. The Ottoman Empire provided a useful external focus for these inner anxieties. Unfortunately for the future development of the Iraqi state, this internal English struggle had very real and far-reaching consequences over which Iraqis had no control. The vast majority of literate and educated people with whom the British Expeditionary Force and then the Mandate administration came into contact were subjected to the contempt reserved by the British for the Ottoman *effendi*. Those who would, in the end, staff the institutions of the Iraqi state were perceived under this label to be inherently corrupt and corrupting. The danger that the state built under British tutelage would revert to an Ottoman-like despotism dominated British fears. Like de Tocqueville surveying state-society relations in the aftermath of the French revolution, the British considered that the dangers of despotism could be avoided only by reconstituting society to act as an independent check over the state.[70] The British view of the Ottoman Empire led them to seek out a counterbalance to the new state they were building in rural society. The tribal Shaikhs were the group readily available to act as "loyal feudatories" of British imagining. They were given the role of the rural aristocracy in establishing and holding the balance between state and society — retaining their parochial links to the peasantry region, while ensuring the accountability of inherently corrupt state institutions.

Chapter Four

Rural and Urban

THE DIVIDED SOCIAL IMAGINATION

OF LATE COLONIALISM

History, for the British, has an ontological power in providing the
assumptions about how the real social and natural worlds are constituted. — *Bernard S. Cohn, Colonialism and Its Forms of Knowledge*[1]

The British forces, sent from India, that landed at the head of the Persian Gulf on November 6, 1914 had woefully little understanding of
the three *vilayets* of the Ottoman Empire that were to form the new state
of Iraq. This lack of empirical knowledge about Iraqi society had barely
improved by the time Britain accepted the Mandate for Iraq in 1920. The
"sacred trust" of the League of Nations demanded that Britain guide the
Iraqi people to statehood. But who were these people?

In an atmosphere of international change and ideological flux, Iraq
was perceived of in terms of the already known. British officials were
forced, individually and collectively, to fill the gap in their knowledge of
Iraq by drawing on previous professional experiences. To many this experience came from British India. That experience, combined with that of
the British Empire at large, structured perceptions of Iraq. Beyond this
English administrators were deeply influenced by competing European
philosophic traditions and by British understanding of European history.

The Iraqi polity was conceived of as being deeply split between urban
and rural forms of social organization. All the legal and democratic institutions of the new state were built with this division in mind. The
shaikh, as the personification of his tribe, became the pivotal indispensable figure in British conceptions. He was someone who could effectively serve as the point of contact between the state and the wider rural
population. It was the shaikh who was to reconcile the contradictions
between the modernity to be imposed by the apparatus of the liberal
state and the "immaturity" of Arab society within a colonial logic of historical development. This understanding simplified the task and cost of

administration. But it also meant that the structures of the new state did not reflect the realities on the ground. The British social vision of Iraqi society blinded them to a whole range of possible solutions to the problems they faced and severely limited any chance of successfully achieving a viable modern state for Iraq compatible with a new and more just international order.

At the end of the First World War there was a profound sense of uncertainty about the direction of British politics and Britain's place in the world. However, this did not displace the cultural attitudes that had driven the imperial mission forward. In Iraq, British officials' perceptions were still structured by an ensemble of prejudice and racism. The Orientalist discourse that influenced British thinking involved three basic elements. First, British officials juxtaposed their own selfless motives in offering advice and framing policy against the interest-driven actions of corrupt Iraqi politicians. Secondly, the urban Iraqi population was generally portrayed as being irrational and aggressive. Finally, Iraqi society was thought of as being hopelessly divided into rival religious and ethnic groups who were unable to overcome their mutual hatreds. The Shia community was perceived as backward-looking and prone to greater irrationality and violence than were the Sunnis.

The British in positions of power found that their means of control were limited. Colonial administrators knew what was best for those under their tutelage, but from 1920 Iraqis under the ebbing power of British instruction found ways of ignoring or circumventing their supposed tutors. As orders became advice responses were no longer demanded and could be tailored to suit identifiable British predilections and weaknesses.

The overt Orientalism of British personnel in the Middle East was generally deployed to justify their own position of superiority and influence. In 1907 Bell stated that "The Oriental is like a very old child . . . He is not practical in our acceptance of the word, any more than a child is practical, and his utility is not ours."[2] In the case of Iraq, Haldane, Head of the British Forces, again deployed the metaphor of immaturity to justify Britain's mandatory role but also to explain away the popular Iraqi dislike of its strictures as hypocritical:

They (the Iraqis) seem to me to resemble a child who, in its anxiety to display its power of walking, resents the nurse taking its hand, but submits, without loss of amour-propre and possibly with some gratitude, to support exerted less ostentatiously elsewhere.[3]

Through this construct of the Iraqi individual it was possible to deny any demands articulated by Iraqi public opinion. The population was "a mass of uninformed opinion with its natural propensity for 'backing the winner.'"[4] This allowed the British to place much of the responsibility and blame for growing dissent on the politically active, urban-based élite and outside forces who manipulated the mass of the population. "Arabs are too fickle, weak and uncivilized to rise against an organized Government, unless backed by some political or religious organization."[5] The logic of Orientalist understanding worked most brutally against those identified as urban and politically active. It was also used to understand the motives and actions of the king, his Hashemite retainers and the group of politicians that surrounded him. The king, who had been picked and installed by the British to be a pliant and "right-thinking" monarch, had by 1922 transmuted into something much more sinister. Cox argued that

he has in these recent episodes unmistakably displayed the cloven hoof. I have endeavored to be absolutely straightforward and frank with him, and to treat him like a brother, but there you are, when he is scratched deep enough the racial weakness displays itself.[6]

In the king's case the "cloven hoof" showed itself in his allegedly highly-strung nature, his moral weakness, his temper and his tenuous grip on sanity.[7] This moral weakness was exemplified in a classic Orientalist trope with reference to his sexual conduct, which, according to a report by Dobbs, was scandalizing polite society and further added to his untrustworthiness.[8]

Arabs who were in positions to act as historical agents were uniformly described in these terms. Such stereotypes were especially applied to all who were politically active. Nuri Said was described by the Chief Inspector of the Levies "as a man with the mind and morals of a monkey, who was an inveterate political intriguer."[9] Ja'far Pasha, one of the politicians closest to

Britain, was written off as "Obese and pathetic" and branded as duplicitous and insincere.[10] The Oriental's love of intrigue and scheming was deployed as a description and explanation of the political élite's actions.

The image that permeates British descriptions of the Iraqi governing group was of a small élite floating above society. "I do not suppose there is in the whole of history another example of a state with a representative government of a modern type, in which the only people who count are two or three hundred at the most. It is in fact a close[d] oligarchy."[11]

Although this can be seen as a fairly accurate empirical description of the size of the political élite, the explanation given for it by the British could hardly be more self-deceiving or revealing. The political élite was small and detached because the wider population, by its nature, could have little knowledge about or interest in high politics. The motivation of the unrepresentative élite involved in politics was bound to be that of self-aggrandizement and the furtherance of its personal interests. The inference that the British permitted themselves using the Orientalist explanation that only the informed and selfless British were capable of guiding the naive and uninformed Iraqi population safely to nationhood missed the point and the problem of Iraqi modernity entirely.

Under this rubric the hostility of the population towards the expansion of state control could be blamed on local government officials who were corrupt by their very nature, either because they had been trained under the Ottoman administration or because, as urban-based *effendis*, they had lost the innocence of the larger rural population. They "devote themselves entirely to the gratification of their own whims and ambitions to the entire disregard of the interests of the people committed to their charge."[12] A contributing factor was the character of Iraqis: honesty, punctuality, equality and the discouragement of corruption were "irritating and uncongenial to a Kurd or Arab. . . . we offer justice, he perhaps prefers a verdict of known price; we offer efficiency and speed, to him it is a set of annoying half-grasped rules to be kept at the cost of comfort and habit."[13]

The rise of a nationalist movement directed at the reduction of Britain's power in Iraq could be written off as unjustified in view of the selfless sacrifice of the British administrator. Those involved in agitation were doing so because it suited their pockets. When one of the Shia *Ulama* returned from his exile in Iran, his anti-British stance was explained by his inability to get a "big enough job in the Auqaf department."

This view of Iraq's politics was exploited and even encouraged by key Iraqi politicians. When, in 1924, the Iraqi cabinet and High Commissioner were having difficulties getting a new treaty ratified by the Assembly, the Prime Minister, Ja'far al-Askari, explained the problem to the High Commissioner: "You are trying to deal with these Arabs as if they were honest men. I know they are all rogues and villains and can only be won over by corruption."[14]

Orientalist discourse through which the British perceived Iraqi society robbed the majority of the Iraqi population of agency. Having escaped the grasping and inept clutches of Ottoman rule, they awaited British guidance to maturity. This construct allowed the politically active minority to be written off as aberrations, corrupted by exposure to Ottoman methods and driven by a selfish desire for money and power.

British understandings of Iraqi society were heavily dependent upon the rigid boundaries of its different ethnic, religious and social groupings.[15] Orientalism determined the way in which Islam was conceived. The religious divide was a major category through which British personnel understood the urban communities of Iraq. These groupings were ranked according to overlapping criteria at the heart of an Orientalist discourse: how rational and hardworking were they and how favorably disposed towards the British.

The Jews and the Christians . . . are the most progressive of the inhabitants of the country. Although they number only about 7 per cent of the population, the proportion of wealth in their hands must be very much greater. They are much more interested in the development of the country.[16]

The majority of the population, being Muslim, were generally dismissed, Islam being seen as a constraint upon the progressive development of the population. Longrigg sums this view up boldly by stating that "no Islamic state in modern times had reached the first rank of nations." The effect of Islam meant that "in the very air and aspect of the East there seems to lie an acquiescence, a lack of the forward impulse."[17]

Islam was a hindrance to development and, to the British Shia Islam, seen as more Islamic than Sunni Islam, was a metonym for all that was wrong with Iraq. A distinction was first made between the powerful clique of *Mujtahids* (the Shia religious hierarchy) and the Shia population itself. It was the *Mujtahids* who posed a direct challenge to British influence and to state building itself. Like the political élite, the *Mujtahids* were conceptually excluded from the larger Iraqi population. They were aliens, Persians, who owed neither loyalty nor commitment to Iraq.[18] Their interests were diametrically opposed to the process of centralizing governmental power. In a zero-sum game the state had to break the influence of the *Mujtahids*. Gertrude Bell repeatedly compared them to a group of "alien popes," "exercising real temporal authority . . . and obstructing the Government at every turn."[19]

The British saw the *Mujtahids*, who are at the core of Shia Islam, as having a philosophy opposed to progress of any kind. Their "authority . . . rests on an intimate acquaintance with accustomed knowledge entirely irrelevant to human affairs and worthless in any branch of human activity."[20] They were seen as being "arch conservatives" with a mastery of obscurantism. The *Mujtahids* attitude had been formed in the isolation of the claustrophobic towns of Najaf and Karbala, which were permeated with "a baneful atmosphere." Clerical attitude and its influence were considered as promoting bigotry and instability. The length and ferocity of the 1920 revolt was blamed on the *Mujtahids* influence, as they urged on the rebels hoping for the imposition of a theocratic state. Intelligence reports between 1920 and 1927 focus on the supposed role of the *Mujtahids* in formenting the violent uprising amongst the Shia tribes of the Euphrates.

The Shia population was viewed as being different from their religious leaders. British estimates of the *Mujtahids* influence over their congregation varied. After 1920 there was a feeling that tribal shaikhs from the Euphrates had learnt their lesson and would be less responsive to calls from the holy cities. But a negative view of the wider Shia population drove British thoughts and actions. Within the British unilinear view of development, it was assumed that the Shia community would slowly integrate into a wider Iraqi identity, yet despite British efforts they remained "self-consciously sectarian."[21] Within an Orientalist discourse this was explained in terms of the backwardness of the religion. The Shia were unable to break from their *Mujtahids* who kept them in a state of ignorance for their own selfish interests. The potential dangers of having a hostile group holding sway over a majority of the population had to be countered. This was one of the reasons, claimed Gertrude Bell, for keeping Sunni Mosul in Iraq and leaving the final authority with Sunni politicians. Otherwise Iraq would exist as "a mujtahid run, theocratic state, which is the very devil."[22]

It was the urban-rural divide, identified by the British, that structured their understanding of the emerging polity and determined the individual-collective tensions that emerged. The gulf between the urban-based *effendi* and the rural tribesmen was the assumed social fact around which the state was created. The *Ulama*, for example, were not only chastised for being Persian but also for being exclusively "town dwelling."[23] Najaf was described with an imagery that subconsciously alluded to the horrors of urbanization, one that would not have been out of place in one of Dickens's novels, in its description of the crowded towns where poverty and "oppressive wealth" lived side by side.[24]

This anti-urbanism can be partly explained by the fact that Baghdad was the main center of nationalism. But this demonizing of cities and their population can be traced back to England.[25] The rise of "ruralism" in popular British discourse in the 1800s and its great influence after World War I was the cultural background to Colonial Office employees harboring such a passionate distaste for urban Iraqis. This expanded into an active attempt to stop the commercialization of agriculture and the concomitant rise in power of large-scale urban-based landowners. We can identify similar attitudes and approaches in colonial discourse in both India and Africa.[26] The whole notion of the "martial races" is structured around the virile qualities of soldiers untouched by the emasculating effects of modernity and the city.[27] The notion of the "noble savage," deployed by Rousseau to rail against injustice in Europe, was easily adapted by those who saw the effects of modernity as undermining humanity's "natural" abilities, constraining them through complexity and regulation.[28] Although initially constructed as an internal critique of European society, it took on new resonance within British imperialist experience and helped determine British interactions with the rural population of Iraq. Fundamentally, capitalism was regarded as a negative force, destroying stability and tradition and entrapping the essence of humanity within a selfish and commodified world.[29] To the British the noble bedouin, untouched by all that was negative about the modern day, stood in stark contrast to those

who peopled the cities —— to those who had succumbed to the temptations of modernity. In Iraq this discourse predominated. Henry
Dobbs, when reviewing the principles that drove his approach, claimed
that Iraq was unique because

> the country men, including the inhabitants of the villages, are
> almost all tribal, unlike the cultivators of Egypt or India or even
> Persia . . . In this respect I doubt whether the conditions of any
> other country in the world, even of Afghanistan, resemble those of
> Iraq.[30]

For both Dobbs and his staff in Iraq, the prevalence of what they had
identified as tribes indicated a society only lightly touched by modernity.
The tribal system still held sway because capitalist penetration was limited. The notion of rural Iraq was therefore constituted to contrast with
the evils of urbanism. This polemical vision was sustained by stressing the
difference that separated the two spheres. The Iraqi population had no
national spirit because it was "split by an effendi-tribal breach."[31] This
was mutual and all-powerful, with the propertied and conservative classes
regarding the tribesmen as "little removed from savages"[32] and the tribesmen possessing an "almost instinctive hostility to Arab 'Effendis' in positions of authority."[33]

For the British the towns seemed to be populated solely by the *effendi*
class and the rural areas by tribespeople. Apart from the unsustainabil-
ity of such a caricature, there is strong evidence that the divide itself was
empirically false. With the rapid growth of Baghdad's population,
"many townsmen were of relatively recent tribal origin"[34] and some of
the tribespeople who migrated into the city "ignored urban laws and
entered into written compacts binding themselves to regulate their conduct and their disputes in accordance with their ancient tribal customs."[35] The relative speed and extent of Iraqi urbanization had led the
countryside to enter the town and hence blur any rigid distinction
between the two. Henry Dobbs's understanding of the nature of Iraq
(like that of many of his fellow administrators), could not countenance
this ambiguity. The towns were urban and so should be quantitatively
and qualitatively different from the tribal rural areas that accounted for
the majority of the population.

At the center of the British conception of Iraq and its social structures, therefore, was an unsustainable dichotomy between town dwellers and rural society built on a misinterpretation of both. Previous work on Iraq has noted this,[36] but it has been interpreted as a conscious effort to categorize and divide society, making it easier to dominate. A closer reading of the archival material, however, gives no support to this position. The officials concerned saw the division as real and continually worried about its effects on the present and future government of Iraq.[37] Many of their policy initiatives had the stated outcome of trying to lessen the ramifications of a fractured society. Far from consciously trying to create such divisions they saw them as a negative but pre-existing fact of social relations.

This view of an unbridgeable division between town and country was structured around a jaundiced construction of an uncivilized city with a biased view of the characteristics of urban populations. British discourse on urban Iraq developed the image of the young, politically aware Baghdadi as interest-driven and fighting for access to corruption. A standardized model of the effete urbanite, the "beffezed" and "tomato-eating" *effendi* began to develop in the minds of those based around the country.[38] He was young, loud, self-centered and self-seeking, and overly influenced by a half-formed understanding of European politics and culture.[39] This powerful image recurs in dispatches and letters with reference to the coffee-shop, an urban phenomenon that allowed the inactive dilettante to be seated amongst his own kind, commenting loudly on that which he knew little about.[40]

The politically active members of Baghdad's élite were negatively described at all levels of the colonial staff. Cox calls them "impecunious and backward," whereas Wingate, a Political Officer in Najaf, sought to isolate the rest of the country from the "half-fledged intelligence of Baghdad."[41] Tyler, a Political Officer in Hillah, also rails against "the low-born Baghdadi" and his hatred of the tribal system. The city, and especially Baghdad, carried the negative influence of modernity within it. The sons of shaikhs had to be isolated from townsmen to stop them being "corrupted by the manifold vices of the Iraq city" whose notables were described as being "spoilt by the acquisition of the worst European habits."[42]

The urban population was not only morally and intellectually defective it was also sub-standard physically. The long and acrimonious debate amongst British officials and between them and the Iraqi government over conscription and the size of the Iraqi army was greatly affected by the view that urban recruits were not up to the job of soldiering. Replicating the notion of martial races across the Empire, British officials argued that conscription would not produce the "viril" tribesmen required but instead would deliver weaker and less suitable townsmen.[43]

This class of urbanites was, in the British mind, synonymous with government administration and political activity. Any incursion of this separate and degenerate part of the population into the rural idyll constructed by the British could bring only negative effects. The division between these two sections of Iraq was so great, argued the British, that the town population could never understand rural life. Yet the tribesman had a "truer appreciation of what government entails than the average townsman."[44] In effect, any criticism of British actions in rural areas by Iraqi politicians must be driven by self-interest or ignorance.[45] The Iraqi administration, staffed by "corrupt and self seeking officialdom," created only resentment and instability as its influence grew among the rural population.[46]

This anti-urbanism at the core of British discourse was combined with a strong unease about the penetration of capitalism into rural areas. The vehicle for this was the commercial landowner, resident in the cities, motivated by profit and with no interest in the welfare of his *fallaheen*. These landlords were to be the tool which would eventually destroy the tribal structures that held sway over rural Iraq. For the Divisional Adviser in Dulaim, the major capitalists already established there were "parasites on society," positioned in opposition to the tribes. They "despised the work of the fallah."[47] An explanation for the constant unrest around land issues in the Muntafiq centered on the imposition of commercial property rights and landlords by Midhat Pasha. From 1920 these landlords "allied themselves with the extremists and with the merchants of the town known for their talent for intrigue."[48] Dobbs, in explaining why the Sa'duns were the core reason for the Muntafiq's instability, describes them as "never truly tribal," "urban dwelling" and, finally, Sunni "city overlords."[49]

Dominating the analysis that shaped British understandings of Iraq was the individual-collective and the urban-rural distinctions. The structure of this divisive social vision had its origins in the evolution of European development and social trends in Britain in the run up to and after the First World War. In Iraq it encouraged a conception of society that saw an unbridgeable gap between the *effendi* politician in urban centers and the rural tribesman. In effect, the urban-based minority of the population had been demonized as contaminated by both Ottoman rule and the negative aspects of capitalism. Outside these areas society was largely untouched, leaving the rural tribesman as the personification of prelapsarian man. The tribesman was certainly naïve, but he was honest, upstanding and ready to make the necessarily slow passage to a better, more authentic life under the modern liberal state.

British knowledge about Iraq was very inconsistent. In the archives of the Political Department of the Government of India there was a great deal of valuable information supplied by its officers who had been stationed across the region before the war. But this information was never distributed to British colonial commanders on the ground. British military forces were accompanied by officers from the Indian Political Service, as if British interest in Mesopotamia after the collapse of Ottoman rule could be handled through the administrative apparatus developed to run the Indian empire.

From the outset an atmosphere of uncertainty enveloped the administration of Iraq.[50] During an earlier more confident period or in a different, less demanding international context, the extension of British authority across Iraq would have involved mapping it geographically and ordering its population through scientific quantification.[51] That era of colonial penetration represented a time when the structures of European modernity were at their most visible, in contrast to the invisibility of older, non-European notions of order.

The colonial project of modernity was centered on disciplining the pre-modern individual and enframing him or her. This disciplinary power worked on the micro-level, restricting the individual by "entering into particular social processes, breaking them down into separate functions, rearranging the parts, increasing their efficiency and precision."[52] Colonialism was supposed to create a "modern" order through precise quantification, "enframing" and capturing the population by situating it within terms of reference of its own making. Some have argued, incorrectly, that the British did indeed succeed in using this approach "by means of their censuses and other methods of categorization."[53]

But there is ample evidence that the process of mapping and quantification identified as key to colonial power did not occur in Iraq. A.T. Wilson laments the Indian General Staff's neglect in failing to collate information about Mesopotamia in advance of the campaign and then failing to distribute what information it had.[54] The situation deteriorated further when Ottoman officials, retreating in the face of the British advance, took all the records they could with them.[55] This lack of knowledge was not corrected by either a universal cadastral survey or by a census. Ad hoc attempts were made at various locations to make assessments of land holdings and the population, but under the Mandate this was never coordinated across the country as a whole.[56]

British staff saw this lack of empirical knowledge of the country as a weakness in their attempts to control the population.[57] But the cost of a nationwide cadastral survey and the antipathy of the population towards a census, which they saw as a precursor to conscription, meant neither measure was enacted under the Mandate. The staff charged with creating the Iraqi state, who would previously have depended upon a vast quantity of reliable empirical knowledge, had limited data with which to work.

How the British understood the non-urban population of Iraq can be seen in their construction of tribal lists. This process began almost as soon as British troops moved up from Basra in November of 1914. Those involved realized they were beginning with almost no knowledge:

> It is easy to imagine that when we first took over the administration, the unraveling of this skein of tribes was quite a business in itself, with nothing more to help one than an odd name or so jotted down on a map, as often as not at the wrong point.[58]

In the absence of information, the importance of the lists to British understanding can be gauged by the time and effort expended in compiling and updating them throughout the Mandate period.[59]

These lists reveal the way the British thought rural society was structured. Each tribe was listed under its name with its history detailed at length. This involved tracing the origins of tribes back to the larger groupings from which they had split, with great importance placed on the "purity" of each tribe and the extent to which it was made up of peo-

ple who could rightfully claim direct descent from the original formation. The geographic area each tribe claimed as its own was delineated
along with the size and extent of its historic agricultural output. The core
of the list was the naming of key shaikhs within each tribe. They were the
only persons identified individually by the compilers. The character of
each tribe was gauged by the character of its leaders. The shaikh's personality, his lineage and, especially, how he came to obtain his authority
determined the authenticity, strength and cohesion assigned by the
British to his tribe.[60] No other unit of analysis was used to organize these
lists.

A. T. Wilson did recognize the "peculiar complexity" of Iraq, but he
described this complexity in terms of pastoral tribes, some partly
nomadic and some sedentary, but all organized along tribal lines.[61] Official estimates of the numbers of tribespeople in Iraq ranged from the
High Commissioner's estimate in 1919 of three-quarters of the population to Kinahan Cornwallis's statement in 1926 that "settled tribes . . .
constitute practically the whole of the rural population of Iraq" (Cornwallis was responsible for overseeing tribal policy at the Interior Ministry).[62]

The British approach to what was in fact a diverse and complex society was neatly summed up in a Land Revenue Report on Kirkuk written
in 1919:

> Political freedom cannot be attained except through a community.
> We must therefore look for some simple form of responsible com-
> munity on which to base our system. The simplest form of com-
> munity in the purely Kurdish area is the tribe or the section of tribe:
> elsewhere the village.[63]

Competing methods or categories of analysis were ignored or down-
played for the sake of simplicity. In this way, the homogeneous category
of "tribe" was violently superimposed over British ignorance and a complex and ambiguous social, political, religious and cultural reality. The
late-colonial imagination at work in Iraq injected the administrative
rationality of western enlightenment with more than a dose of romanticism. The tribe was conceived of in Lockean terms, as having been created by a state of democratic nature.

The ramifications of this approach were that those rural groups or individuals that did not fit well into the single all embracing category of "the tribe" were difficult to deal with. Their position had either to be violently distorted or overlooked. The High Commissioner, his staff and the advisers to the government in Baghdad, acknowledged variations in economic and social conditions across Iraq. But the rigid definition applied to "rural" social structures meant that those acknowledged variations would not enter into British policy. Although tribal disintegration had been identified and was a major point of debate, the rigid categorization of rural areas by tribe meant that it could not be understood as a prelude to an indigenous modernity. Until 1932, "tribal fragmentation" was seen by the majority of British officials not as leading to individualization and social modernity but to the creation of smaller tribal units and "petty shaikhs."[64]

The idea of the "tribe" was primarily defined by those outside it. As a unit it certainly existed, juxtaposed against non-rural sections of society and, more tangibly, against other tribes competing for land and government resources. But there was limited investigation into its internal coherence and dynamics as a structure of collective life.[65] Instead, the romantic theme of brotherhood and premodern mutual affective bonds ran through descriptions of tribal life and identity. A.T. Wilson strikes a familiar tone when he describes the "unsophisticated" Arab, Kurd or Persian's deeply held loyalty to family and tribe. Although practical, thorough and sustained until death, this loyalty appeared to Wilson to be beyond rationality, being "largely independent of admiration or affection for individuals", but giving, "unity and stability to their philosophy of life."[66]

Of all the colonial officials in Iraq, John Glubb had the most intense and extended exposure to the everyday life of both nomadic and sedentary Arabs. Glubb spent World War I fighting in Europe but volunteered to go to Iraq after the cease-fire. As a Special Services Officer he spent the 1920s stationed in rural Iraq many miles from the out-posts of the British Empire. He developed a very strong affinity with Iraqis, spending the vast majority of his time living amongst them, arguing for the protection of their way of life. Although his exposition of tribal cohesion was more detailed and anchored in experience than that of others, his understanding was still nevertheless permeated with romanticism. His written work can be read as an extended homily to the dying of a more noble way of life, one based on honor and virility.[67]

The tribe was described by the British as a democratic system of equality: leaders were naturally selected on the basis of strength of character;[68] the individual member gained his definition through the collective. When the organization broke down its members degenerated, becoming lesser beings. Assistant Political Officer Mylles, when comparing the members of the Dulaim to the Agadat, described the Dulaim as "twice the men . . . chiefly because the tribal organization is still strong." The Agadat suffered in comparison because the Turks had broken their "tribal spirit."[69]

The social plane upon which these tribes acted was seen by the British as one structured by anarchy. The internal life of the tribe exemplified respect and cooperation while the external world was Hobbesian. Inter-tribal relationships were defined by the lack of a sovereign-state structure to guarantee order. The feeble nature of the Ottoman government had left these groups to evolve in a violent atmosphere where internal collective security was the only guarantor of survival.[70] Thus, it was internal tribal cohesion that guaranteed the continued existence of authentic Iraqi society. The authentic Iraqi tribesman had been unencumbered by the state or any imposed notion of civilization. This had left him to rely on his natural abilities and the solidarity of his comrades.

In theory individual tribes were organized for purposes of defense into confederations grouped under a paramount shaikh. The tribes themselves were loose organizations within which "sub-tribes," with their own "sub-shaikhs," or headmen, appeared to be the final unit of analysis. D.G. Hogarth, who had been head of the Arab Bureau in Cairo during the First World War, attempted to clarify this with reference to the Anazeh tribe of the Syrian desert. They were not, he argued, a tribe but a people comparable in racial terms to Scandinavians. This racial whole, as with the Scandinavian people, could be sub-divided into smaller units: states for the Scandinavians tribes for the Anazeh. These units were politically independent yet bound together sentimentally by "a tradition of remote common origin." A pedantic and elaborate concern for blood traditions and genealogies, the veneration of their shaikhs, allowed them to remain loosely affiliated.[71]

Sir Henry Dobbs, the longest serving High Commissioner and a champion of this system of classification, was clearly uneasy about the smaller units. Before his appointment as High Commissioner, while still serving as Foreign Secretary to the Government of India, he wrote to the then acting High Commissioner, A.T. Wilson, to address the issue of the future political role for those exercising authority in the context of tribal subgroups. A committee discussing the future constitution had suggested that heads of the "sub-sections" should elect tribal representation. Dobbs argued that this method would be unworkable, as within tribes sub-sections were flexible and thus membership interchangeable. What was crucial, he argued, was to preserve the coherence of the tribes by bolstering the authority of the big shaikhs, which could not withstand the intrusion of "all kinds of petty headmen."[72]

The tribe, not the individual, became the unit of analysis through which this interpretation of Iraqi society gained its coherence. Tribal organization made other categories of analysis unnecessary. Such a clear understanding of how rural society functioned yielded a clear policy by which it could be controlled.

The centrality of the shaikh in the British imagination meant that those below him went unregistered as targets of policy. When it came to gauging the views of tribal populations, to ask the "rank and file of the tribesmen, shepherds, marsh dwellers, rice, barley, and date cultivators of the Euphrates and Tigris, whose experience of statecraft was confined to speculations, as to the performances of their next-door neighbors" would be ridiculous. Instead, Bell recommended consultations with their immediate chiefs, "in districts where the tribal system is still in force (and this includes much the greater part of the country)." This should be organized by election "by headmen of the tribal subsection."[73]

For the British, the "authentic," or ideal, tribe would be hierarchically divided into three categories the confederation, the tribe and the sub-tribe. At the very peak of tribal authority, and the point of contact with Baghdad, would be the paramount shaikh, who in theory controlled a whole tribal confederacy, someone like Ali Sulaiman, who ruled the Dulaim on the upper Euphrates, or Ibn Suwait, who was the paramount shaikh of the Dhafir. The position was supposed to have been inherited "in accordance to tribal tradition."[74]

In 1921 the Divisional Adviser of Muntafiq claimed there were only three such figures in his region: Salim al Khaiyun of the Bani Asad, Badr

al Rumaiyidh of the Albu Salih and Khaiyun of the Abudah tribe in the
Gharraf. Their authority over "unruly, turbulent and warlike tribesmen"
was dependent entirely on the support they could muster from within the
wider tribe. They were a "necessary evil" because of their role in providing social stability.[75] Glubb, in 1924, summed up the traditional powers
of office as the right to make war and peace on behalf of the tribe, while
emissaries from foreign tribes must dismount at the paramount's tent to
conclude treaties.[76]

Beneath the paramount leaders were the "big shaikhs," or shaikhs of
tribes that made up the confederacy, and below them the heads of the
tribal sub-sections (these two categories were somewhat flexible and not
always distinguishable). The High Commissioner went to great lengths
to discourage all but minor dealings between the British staff, the Iraqi
government and tribal sub-sections.

In this idealized framework of tribal organization a loose form of
democracy was thought to permeate the three levels of the tribe. The
shaikhs dominated and came to represent these democratic structures by
force of personality and natural intelligence. The British saw the whole
collective organized around a community of interest.[77] Shaikhs could
thus be identified and admired for their attainment of social position.
Bell, amongst others, frequently referred to this group as "great personalities" and "aristocrats," with the system generally being maintained in a
"natural equilibrium."[78]

The shaikh and his relatives became vehicles for the late colonial
romantic imagination. Captain Holt's description of Shaikh Mahmud's
surrender to British forces in May 1931 is instructive. As a long standing
Oriental Secretary to the High Commissioner (the post also held by
Gertrude Bell until her death), Holt had played a key role in forming policy and disseminating information across Iraq and back to Britain and
India. Shaikh Mahmud on the other hand had been the major challenge
to British and then Iraqi dominance of Kurdistan since 1920.[79] Upon
Mahmud's capture Holt wrote a note, detailing his history, which was
organized around romantic imagery and a lament for times past.

Holt describes the first engagement Mahmud had with Turkish forces
during the battle of Shu'aibah in April 1915. Mahmud, "like many other
tribal chiefs of ancient lineage," had arrived with his feudal levies to do
battle with the foreign invaders. Then, after prayers, "believing that the

age of chivalry was still with them, they swept forward on their gaily caparisoned horses to drive their enemies back into the sea which it was said was their home. Taunts and challenges were shouted at the still invisible enemy but only the shriek of shrapnel answered and a dozen saddles emptied and a score of horses fell. Ardour was daunted, home became dearer than glory and life on earth more blissful than the hope of Paradise and the hosts of chivalry melted away; each man the richer by at least two rifles taken from the Turkish wounded."

Describing Mahmud's final surrender to the British, Holt's admiration for the man and the passing of what he represented makes itself felt in gushing prose:

> As he rode to captivity after his surrender at Penjwin the Kurds streamed down from the villages on the hill sides to cluster round him and to kiss his hand and the eyes of many were filled with tears as they bid him farewell . . . His tyranny is the will of a tyrant but it is mellowed by the generosity of a prince. If he is cruel, where are the witnesses? Not among the villagers who press around to kiss his hand in the hour of his defeat, nor among the officers of the Royal Air Force who have fought against him (and of whom two have been his prisoners), who are all eager to say a cheery word of comfort to him . . . An outlaw brigand, let that be granted, so were Garibaldi and Mustafa Kamal. But when all has been said on both sides perhaps the wisest judgement is that his greatest fault is that he was born a century too late.[80]

In tandem with this romance of the shaikh was a continuing and sometimes bitter debate about whether authority and order could be transmitted through the tribal system. For some British staff, the office of the shaikh had failed to have any real political or social efficacy long before British troops landed in 1914. For others its weakness was personified by the 1920 revolt and the subsequent ignominious exit of some shaikhs from their supposed areas of influence to British-held towns. But the power of the British romantic vision meant that the version of Iraq's social realities championed by Sir Henry Dobbs — which fastened on to the shaikh as the linchpin of rural society— won out. The clash between this sociological romance and the problems of trying to rule Iraq through its categories led the British to adopt policies that can only be described as contradictory. Ultimately this clash sabotaged any successful realization of liberal modernity for the newly constructed Iraqi state. Dobbs's approach did however have the unintended consequence of restructuring Iraqi society.

Chapter Five

Using the Shaikhs

THE RATIONAL IMPOSITION OF

A ROMANTIC FIGURE

In trying to impose policy through the authority of the shaikh — an authority conceived of as consensual — the British inadvertently but radically changed the nature of the shaikh's actual relation to the rest of Iraqi society.[1] The irony was that the dominant, conservative British discourse of ruralism transformed Iraqi society in strikingly radical and "modern" ways. A romantically conceived "premodern" figure was used as the conduit for rational administrative methods, "successfully" imposed, finally, as we shall see, through the modern coercive technology of air power.

Sir Henry Dobbs clearly understood tribal structures in instrumental terms. When the main institutions of government were being built and state-society relations were being institutionalized, Dobbs had thought the state too weak to deal directly with rural individuals. The state apparatus, he said, could not go through Iraqi society with a "tooth comb."[2] Instead its relations with Iraq's population had to be mediated through a series of tribal shaikhs. But, crucially, Dobbs saw Iraqi state power as being necessarily limited by the very structures the shaikh ruled through. The approach he viewed as "common sense" was organized by the idea that Iraq was pre-modern and "rural," untainted by the negative and destabilizing effects of capitalism. The Shaikh and his tribe were therefore "naturally" the dominant institutions through which British policy aims were to be realized.

The tensions involved in being guided by this romantic discourse can be seen in the mechanics set up for recognition of tribal shaikhs and in the administration's efforts to secure their dominant position. Tribal shaikhs were divided by colonial officials into "nominal" and "recognized." Both categories were seen to possess the degree of social authority needed to control a given area. However, official recognition was conditional upon the suitability of the individual to rule in a manner that conformed with British notions of administration and upon a willingness to deliver guarantees of order on British terms.

For a shaikh, government recognition brought with it responsibility, reward and prestige. By guaranteeing the good behavior of the tribe or that of a particular section, he would receive a monthly subsidy and occasionally the right to regulate the movement of any bedouin from his designated area to markets and urban centers. Fahad Beg ibn Hadhdhal, for example, received a subsidy of Rs. 12,000 a month and

> In addition to this very large sum, he has the substantial privilege that no tribesmen of the Amarat or other nomads dependent on them can purchase supplies in Iraq without a pass signed by himself or his agents. It is hoped that the conditions now imposed may enable the Iraq Government to reap some advantage from its heavy expenditure on his barak.[3]

Official recognition of the shaikh clarified and strengthened his position. Nearest rivals would be ordered to submit to his authority under threat of state intervention. These rivals would gain recognition themselves and a place within this hierarchy only if they agreed to his authority:

> Jaid ibn Mijland of the Dahamshah . . . has been informed in the presence of Fahad Beg and his son Mahrut that Fahad has been recognized paramount Shaikh of the Amarat, of which the Dahamshah are part, and has the right to grant passes for the purchase of supplies, Jaid is expected to be loyal to the king, to recognize the paramountcy of Fahad, to have no dealings with Ibn Sa'ud and to help Fahad in carrying out his obligations to Government. Though he is to be treated as Shaikh of Dahamshah, he is not to be given official recognition until it is seen whether the reconciliation with Fahad is genuine.[4]

The state in Iraq, although ruling through what were perceived as indigenous institutions, had by that act, changed them. What had previously been "fuzzy" communities now became rigidly defined.[5] By imposing precisely defined requirements on the role of the shaikh, and by demanding an instrumental relationship between him and members of his tribe, the British decisively transformed the shaikh's place in Iraqi society and the character of his political role.

Where those individuals who had been identified as shaikhs became unruly or troublesome, they were replaced by more suitable candidates. Replacements had to come from the same social stratum given British understanding of authentic Arab authority. When Hamudah of the al Hasan became an outlaw, his nephew was placed on his land. A problem then arose when Hamudah wanted to make peace with the government:

> His character and record forbid his reinstatement in his old position, while to leave him at large, nursing a bitter grievance and dispossessed of his lands, would be to sow the seeds of certain trouble in the future. The same problem presents itself in the case of Faisal al Yasir, who is still at large.[6]

When, despite government recognition, shaikhs who proved unable to restrain the population under their control ran the risk of having their tribe de-recognized and its lands allotted to others.[7] In these circumstances, the British assumed that it was not the system of tribal organization or the use of shaikh's power that was at fault but individual personalities or the defective nature of the tribe. In fact, a radically new social order was being created. When populations identified as "tribal" failed to have an identifiable shaikh, trouble was sure to arise. For the Iraqis, it meant that they did not fit the government's understanding of rural Iraq and therefore lacked access to state mechanisms that distributed largesse. For the British, "tribal" groups without shaikhs appeared sinister, uncontrollable and a source of instability. One officer wrote in an intelligence report, : "Early in May a large band of miscellaneous tribesmen from the Muntafiq numbering about 5,000 tents crossed into the Sirah Nahiyan of the Kut Division. Trouble was anticipated as the tribesmen were armed and had no recognized headman."[8]

The fact that the groups concerned had no "recognized" leaders placed them beyond the British categories of order and so beyond their control. That no headman had been identified meant that they had not been documented, nor registered on the tribal lists. They had not been fixed in the rural order of things. An explanation of the state of affairs in this instructive case lies in the origin of these tribesmen, the Muntafiq. The Muntafiq, in British understanding, personified the instability of an area where categories could not be universally and unambiguously applied. The unrest that had plagued the British in Muntafiq was blamed on the Ottoman use of divide and rule. By introducing city-based landlords into the rural status quo, the Turks, so the British believed, had deliberately fragmented the "traditional" tribal structures that had preserved order. The result was a constant state of unrest, a "French Revolution in miniature." Any tribe that failed to have a shaikh of recognisable stature had slipped below British standards of acceptability. Any such population was too deficient to be treated as autonomous, and its capacity for collective action had to be a product of malignant outside forces.[9]

As the Iraqi state became more established and monetary pressure became greater, subsidies to recognized shaikhs were replaced by grants of land. The designated shaikhs themselves learned quickly what was required of them and how to manipulate the key concerns of the British. Ali Sulaiman, upon learning that his subsidy was under threat, argued that it was not the monetary reward that concerned him, but "he valued it for the prestige that it brought him in that he appeared to his tribes as a valued servant of Government:"

Taking a broader view he then went on to explain that the tribes judged by what they saw and that the fact that he ceased to draw an allowance without receiving any recognition for his past services would be taken to mean that he no longer retained the confidence of Government although of course he was satisfied that this was not the case. His prestige would suffer accordingly and his advice would not be listened to so readily. He presumed that Government was aware that many of the tribes were far from satisfied and that there was a considerable amount of talk abroad that a return of Turkish officials would be an improvement on the existing regime. The last thing in the world he wanted was *thaurah* and all his influence would be thrown into the scales to prevent this. He could not help feeling however that the Government forces in this area were small to cope with any disturbances which might arise and consequently anything which led to a reduction of his own influence he viewed with a certain amount of misgiving.[10]

The shallow foundations of the shaikh's authority became increasingly apparent after the chaos of the 1920 revolt subsided. The case of Ali Sulaiman not only highlighted a wider problem in Iraq but also the divisions within the Mandatory administration on perceptions of tribal cohesion. In 1922, Yetts, a divisional adviser, had seen Sulaiman as a potential pillar of government control, "if a place can be found in the body politic for the type which Shaikh Ali Sulaiman represents with their rights clearly defined the whole-hearted support of this class can be counted on."[11] But by 1924 it had become apparent that the ability of Ali Sulaiman to wield the type of influence amongst his fellow Dulaim tribesmen that the British needed was doubtful. After the 1920 uprising, several sectional leaders had recognized Sulaiman as their paramount shaikh in an attempt to avoid British retribution for their part in the disturbances. But four years later, he was personally unable to collect revenue from *sarkals*, requiring government support to do so. The Administrative Inspector in Dulaim saw Sulaiman as a hindrance to state control. He had little or no influence, it turned out.

Aly Sulaiman may be regarded in Baghdad as paramount shaikh of the Dulaim but to the Liwa authorities it is painfully obvious he relies more and more on Government support to keep up his position. One issue seems clear that with gradual disintegration of the tribal system it will be increasingly difficult to find room in the numerous constituencies of the Dulaim Confederacy for both the Shaikh and Sarkal. The Sarkal has long regarded the Shaikh as an incubus which he will sooner or later throw off. At present he is waiting for a sign from Government.[12]

Cornwallis, the adviser to the Ministry of the Interior, lent partial support to this view. Arguing against the position of the High Commissioner, Henry Dobbs, that Sulaiman was necessary for the preservation of order near the Syrian border, he stated that the main force for law and order in Dulaim had long since been the *Liwa* police.[13]

The High Commissioner responded to this interpretation of policy with great vigor:

The position which I take up is that it is essential to preserve the authority of Ali Sulaiman over the Badu portion of his tribe for the purpose of making the desert routes safe and that it is almost impossible to do so if his authority over the more settled portion of his tribe is undermined. He can't well become a mere "rentier" with regards to the settled portion, without losing his hold over the Badu portion also; for there is no very clear dividing line between them. Another reason for not lessening his authority over the settled portion is that we have no adequate machinery except the Shaikhship for controlling the Dulaim in their relations with the Aqaidat which are so important from the point of view of our relations with Syria. I gather Ali Sulaiman himself would be only too glad to become a "rentier" if Government would collect the profits due on his capital expended on the "Ali Sulaiman Canal" and also his dues on the *Karads* at Felujah and elsewhere. He would then practically abandon his position as Shaikh of the Badu portion of the tribe, which now brings him no profit and honor and a great deal of worry. But this would make him quite useless to the Government.[14]

For Dobbs Ali Sulaiman's power was a natural outcome of his position within his tribe. Any reduction in Sulaiman's power was, therefore, caused by external influences. In this case Dobbs saw it as a direct consequence of state interference. Therefore, he argued, the police should be kept out of Dulaim affairs in all cases but those of murder. Everything else should be referred to Sulaiman for resolution. His power as a tribal shaikh could then return to its natural level, unencumbered by the negative incursions of modernity in the shape of employees of the state.

The policy of subsidizing shaikhs came under repeated attack from the Iraqi cabinet. As Britain placed strict budgetary restraints on the Iraqi government, the money being spent on underwriting the shaikhs became a contentious issue.[15] Cornwallis was aware of this and the ramifications it had for policy:

The main point . . . is to maintain the authority of all the shaikhs and to use it to reinforce the Police. This is the policy which

Administrative Inspectors and I have always adopted. It is not a policy of which any Arab townsman approves and though it has been outwardly accepted as a necessity, one must always be on the lookout for attempts to run counter to it.[16]

The clash in perspectives between British advisers and urban politicians was in this and many other cases put down to the townspeople's ignorance and fear of anything outside their metropolitan domain. This itself sprung from a British collectivist social vision which had exaggerated the urban-rural divide. It allowed Cornwallis and Dobbs to override cabinet concerns about budgets or the power of sub-state actors.

The liberal international zeitgeist that had resulted in the award of Mandatory responsibility to Great Britain in 1920 enforced the notion that democratic accountability was to be included in the project of state building in Iraq. Yet, the "complete and necessarily rapid transformation of the facade of the existing administration from British to Arab" forced the creation of democratic institutions that were ill-conceived.[17] In the debates of 1920 on how to elect representatives, we can see the effect of these competing perceptions of Iraqi society. The central question was how best to structure state-society relations. The conscious instrumental use of the perceived authority of the shaikh is not apparent in the initial phase of building democratic structures. The original flurry of consultation around this subject produced four broad conceptions of how Iraqi representative institutions would be shaped. Those involved in the discussion were concerned with two sometimes mutually opposing questions: What was the largest degree of representation possible in a society like Iraq? How do we create the most efficient legislature, one immune from corruption? None of the four positions taken on building Iraqi democratic structures could resolve the tensions among democracy, efficiency and corruption.

The main forum for the discussion of these matters was the committee chaired in 1920 by the Judicial Secretary Edgar Bonham-Carter.[18] An appendix to the committee's concluding report details possible ways of electing a Legislative Assembly. In the country, where the population were thought to be tribal, the headmen of the smaller tribal units would elect representatives for the assembly. This was an idea based on a perception that tribal life was fully democratic: "They [the headmen] are themselves elected by the tribesmen under them, and they elect the Shaikh of the Tribe subject to confirmation by the authorities."[19]

This proposal brought an impassioned rejection from Sir Henry Dobbs, who argued that tribal representatives would use the assembly to question the actions and undermine the power of their shaikhs.[20] For Dobbs the elevation of headmen to an elected assembly (an urban-based one at that) would disturb the natural order of things. Also, for Dobbs the paramount shaikhs were the point of contact between a naturally well-ordered society and a rapidly changing world. So, he argued that the High Commissioner should instead grant the right for all important shaikhs to sit in the legislative assembly. Dobbs also argued that any law passed by a future assembly that affected rural areas and did not meet with the approval of tribal delegates should be automatically referred via the Council of Ministers to the High Commissioner. In this short telegram, sent from India in 1920, are to be found the themes that would come to dominate Dobbs's time as High Commissioner: the fear that corrupt and corrupting urban politicians would dominate the noble tribes of rural Iraq and the fear that the authority of the shaikh would be destroyed by rapid changes brought about by statehood.

E. L. Norton, the Secretary to the Committee of ex-Turkish Deputies, also discussing a possible electoral law under the auspices of the High Commissioner, advanced another view. For him, the right to vote carried corresponding responsibilities: the voter must make a rational, independent decision about what was best for himself. Tribesmen, being part of a collective, were easily manipulated by their shaikhs and could be sent to the ballot box in large numbers. This could allow "unscrupulous persons . . . to engineer the elections for their own ends." So, although the

> enormous majority of the population is tribal . . . it would clearly be impossible to have a tribal majority of electors, since nine-tenths of the questions which a national assembly has to determine do not concern the tribes, nor will the tribes willingly pay taxes or be liable to military service. I suggest that the tribes should be given no representation on the Assembly.[21]

For Norton, the tribesman (not an individual in the modern sense) could never act in a way that would sustain democracy. As an undistinguishable part of a collective, he could be marched to the ballot box to vote in any way the shaikh or his urban manipulator saw fit. It was because of this, he argued, that tribesmen should be excluded from voting altogether.

Finally, it was left up to a Political Officer, R. Marrs, in a rejoinder to Norton, to champion the unfashionable cause of the individual rights of the tribal *fallah*: "For while all other classes may be represented, it is improbable that the tribesmen, as opposed to his Shaikh, will be represented."[22] Marrs gently tried to debunk the notion of the tribe and that of collective responsibility that came with it. The *fallah*s, as fully formed individuals, were bound to have different and even conflicting interests to those of the shaikhs. If this was not recognized, the British Political Officer would have to act as their protector.

In the event, following interventions from the High Commissioner, the Council of Ministers decided to adopt both methods of election. The first Iraqi Assembly was based on direct elections by all those tribesmen who could write their name and were willing to register, with 20 per cent of the seats reserved for indirectly elected shaikhs.[23] The result was a Constitutional Assembly that had 34 shaikhs and *aghas* out of a total of 99 members.[24]

Explanations of the events surrounding the run up to and opening of the 1924 Constitutional Assembly became representative of British views of how Iraqi politics functioned. The conceptual division between the rural shaikhs—honorable, moderate and representative of the Iraqi populace—and the passionate, irrational, and often violent, urban "lawyer-politicians" was understood as the crucial dynamic.[25] As early as 1922 the tribal shaikhs were seen as the rallying point for moderate opinion. Their visits to Baghdad gave "more backbone" to the moderate element.[26] Again, the Dulaim Shaikh, Ali Sulaiman, was the personification of all that was right about tribal politics. He became the driving force behind the creation of a moderate party, registering 12,000 tribesmen as primary electors in his area. This, according to Bell, resulted in a jealous and threatened king forming a rival organization. Bell complained that

I know perfectly well that if the king's party (for before it has come into existence it is known by that name) is started by a group of

Young Arabs whom the country distrusts profoundly and rightly,
not a single man of the Ali Sulaiman type will join it.[27]

The moderate party faltered because of the shaikhs' inactivity, but this,
compared with the frenzied self-seeking activity of the Nationalist politicians, was taken as sign of moderation in itself.

The role of the Tribal Criminal and Civil Disputes Regulations
(TCCDR) in Iraq created a divided polity in a similar way to the electoral
system.[28] First drawn up by Henry Dobbs in February 1916, the TCCDR
was officially sanctioned by British occupying forces in July 1918 and
introduced into Iraqi law by Royal *Iradah* in 1924.[29] The regulations
explicitly divided the Iraqi population into two sections. Those dwelling
in the towns were subject to Iraqi civic law, originally based on Ottoman
codes. These legal codes were progressively reformed and tailored to match
the changing nature of Iraqi urban life as the state expanded its presence
and power over cities and towns. But those deemed "tribal," those external to the cities, were subject to a radically different legal code. This code
changed little over the eighteen years of the Mandate, as the society it pur-
ported to regulate was conceived of as pre-modern and static.

In its drafting and implementation, the TCCDR encapsulated the dominance of the romance of supposedly premodern collectivism through
which many colonial officials saw Iraq. The structure of the TCCDR was
taken almost unchanged from the colonial code used on the Indian North
West Frontier. The basic organizing principle underlying jurisprudence in
post-1916 Iraq was the dramatic and unbridgeable chasm between the corrupt cities with their tainted officials and lawyers and the rural areas with
their noble tribesmen. These regulations were given coherence and their
application made possible by the central role of the shaikh, used to understand Iraqi society, and to frame and organize the imposition of the regulations. Debates surrounding the application of the TCCDR also highlighted
clashing conceptions of Iraqi society and the modern state. It was left up to
successive Iraqi cabinets, lawyers and journalists (all labeled corrupt and
self-seeking by the British) to challenge the validity of the regulations and
criticize the effect they were having on the development of the Iraqi state.

The seemingly solid foundation of the TCCDR—that which anchored
it to rural society—was its conformity to and compatibility with ancient
custom.[30] For A.T. Wilson,

> It [the TCCDR] helped us all to a better understanding of the prin-
> ciples underlying tribal custom: these principles varied little from
> district to district, though in detail there were many differences;
> they were all based not on Islamic law, but on something much
> older, human nature, and on local conventions, some of which, it
> would not be difficult to show, were probably codified by Kham-
> murabi in 2000 BC or earlier.[31]

For juridical purposes, the rural population of Iraq—geographically, economically and religiously diverse as it was—was homogenized into one
bloc, with all its people assumed to react to "custom and law" in the same
way. All were subject to the application of the TCCDR because the regulations successfully reflected the premodern tribesman's eternal and
unchanging nature. For Bell, the need for extended police work and
detailed litigation was "largely abrogated by the almost disconcerting sincerity with which the accused will own up to his offence."[32] For Glubb,
"bedouin arbitrators are usually absolutely honest . . . Cases of bribing
the judges are well-nigh unknown . . . an oath is accepted as a final settlement of a case, and perjury is very rare."[33]

Tribal crime was considered to have a different character, one motivated by deeper, more passionate and "honorable" forces than mere greed
or politics. For example, in 1923 Dobbs defended the use of the TCCDR
by citing tribal "feeling and custom" in a case of adultery. Not only would
the tribesman not accept the ruling of a judicial court, but of "all cases
sexual cases are those which can be least considered offences against the
State or against the majesty of the law."[34] Dobbs further developed this
theme when testifying before the Permanent Mandates Commission of
the League of Nations. Running counter to many explanations of the
1920 Revolt, he told Lord Lugard that "Tribesmen considered crimes not
as offences against the state, but as "torts." To hang a tribesman for murder would be to miss the point; this was not a crime in the ordinary sense,
but an act carried out to avenge tribal honor; blood feuds would lead to
anarchy across Iraq if they were not dealt with on terms that met the
needs of timeless custom.[35]

This construction of an honest, but simple tribesman driven by
unchained passions was based on the belief that modernity, with all its
associated complexities and corruptions, had not penetrated rural Iraq.

These men were "entirely ignorant of a world that lay outside their swamps and pasturages, and entirely indifferent to its interests, and to the opportunities it offers."[36] This, then, helps to explain the conundrum posed by the use of an apparently far removed example (experiences of the North West Frontier) as the basis of the TCCDR. At first glance those advocating the use of the TCCDR did so because the majority of the population they had identified as tribal was distinctive and separated by its customs and laws. Yet Dobbs, when he tried to explain the basis of the tribal disputes law to Drower, the Adviser to the Ministry of Justice, had to refer to a totally different geographical area. He sent Drower the

> Baluchistan circular of 1907 on which I was largely brought up and which was originally circulated in 1916 to all Political officers here. It will explain to you my point of view (from the point of view of public security) better than reams of notes from me.[37]

The reason for the Indian example becomes clearer when Dobbs quotes his then boss, the Agent-General, Sir A.H. McMahon, for whom he worked as a Revenue and Judicial Commissioner in Baluchistan from 1909–1911. Customary and tribal law was

> based on the character, idiosyncrasies and prejudices of the people among whom it has originated and by whom it has been evolved during long periods of time to meet their own requirements and remedy their failings.[38]

So, the Baluchistan and Iraqi tribes were conceptually homogenised into one undifferentiated group. This was done within the "official mind" of colonialism because they were both perceived as unsullied by modernity, and they had both originated under a pre-modern system, with a different time-scale from that of these officials' own society. The tribesman, wherever British imperialism found him, could therefore be regulated under a much simpler code of law: his innate honesty and straightforward life would make this by far the best approach. For the TCCDR this lack of "development" meant that the rural population of Iraq had not been subjected to the selfish individualizing drives of modern life. They could be treated under its regulations as if both criminal motivation and the punishment for it were collective. Tribal criminal regulations operated "under the strict enforcement of tribal responsibility," and so the whole tribe should be punished for the acts of its members, with the strength of collective identity then acting on the recalcitrants to bring them into line.[39]

The TCCDR gained its coherence and its enforcement mechanism through the offices of the shaikh. The British knew relatively little about the internal functioning of the tribe, and, although the archives refer frequently to the unchanging nature of tribal custom and law, the vast amount of material on matters tribal is concerned with the actions, character and agency of the shaikh. The crucial issue of over whom the TCCDR had jurisdiction was left to the personal decisions of Political Officers and the High Commissioner and then to *Mutasarrifs* and *Qa'immaqams*.[40] The importance of the shaikh in underwriting the legitimacy of the divided legal jurisdiction can be judged by the TCCDR's official, if circular, definition of a tribesman:

"Tribesman" means a member of a generally recognized tribe or tribal section which has been accustomed to settle its disputes by recourse to the arbitration of elders or shaikhs and not by recourse to the Courts of the land as ordinarily constituted.[41]

The tribal disputes regulations worked by the assembling of an ad hoc *Majlis*, brought together for each separate dispute, that acted as judge and jury. It was staffed with neutral tribal arbitrators who could claim the respect of both parties involved in a dispute. These arbitrators were in effect the nearest shaikhs, paramount, or other senior personages.[42] The terms of law enforcement in rural Iraq, then, had the effect of giving to shaikhs judicial authority over the vast majority of the population. That this represented a large accrual of power to specific individuals was recognized by the likes of Bell and Dobbs, but it was seen both as a natural outcome of their prestige and a way of preserving the existing and favored tribal system.[43]

Opposition to the terms of the TCCDR and the effective division of the nascent Iraqi society into two distinct social formations came from several sources. First, Sir Edgar Bonham-Carter, the Judicial Secretary to the Iraqi government until 1921, and E.M. Drower, Adviser to the Ministry of Justice in 1923, both voiced deep concern with the terms of the regulations as they stood. Bonham-Carter's critique attacked the core logic at the heart of the TCCDR, the notion of tribal custom, collective responsibility and punishment. In cases of murder, he argued, the practice of extracting blood money would be an adequate deterrent when levied on the individual but when the punishment was extracted from the whole tribe it was no deterrent to the individual.[44] He went on to argue that, far from being the application of tribal custom, the disputes regulations were in fact an unsatisfactory combination of both tribal and civic law—a combination that omitted their most powerful sanctions, the levying of fines on the individual and the death penalty.[45] Finally, he argued, the application of the regulations to settled tribesmen was wrong: "one finds that when tribes whether Arabs or others settled down to agricultural conditions they tend to give up their tribal customs, and this is a necessary step on the road of progress." That is, settled tribesmen would break away from their shaikhs, a process that Bonham-Carter thought should be encouraged.[46]

E. M. Drower, acting as adviser to the Minister of Justice, revisited these themes when he clashed with Henry Dobbs over a proposal to redraft the TCCDR. Like Bonham-Carter he was unhappy that Iraqi society had been judicially divided in two. Empirically, he saw this division as "difficult to define."[47] Juridicially, he was concerned that, by having given the *Mutasarrif* the power to judge who and who was not tribal, the division between the executive and judiciary had been in effect dissolved. This would undermine the credibility of the legal system and weaken the power of the state. The responsibility for the punishment of crime should, argued Drower, be solely that of government. It should not be delegated to tribal shaikhs. If the TCCDR had a role, it was to temper the central application of justice to the circumstances of the tribes. Tribal settlement should alleviate punishment when the crimes were "purely personal wrongs, for example, the last act in a feud." But the full force of the law should be applied in an equal and regulated fashion when crime disturbed "public tranquillity."[48]

Both Bonham-Carter and Drower implicitly challenged the alleged underlying dominance of collective premodern social cohesion that gave the TCCDR its rationality. They both saw Iraqi society as relatively unexceptional. Like other countries heading down the road of modernization, the Iraqi polity had to be tied to the state with rights and responsibilities clearly and unambiguously set out in the legal codes of the land. These two legal experts saw the TCCDR as an unjustifiable anomaly. The law should apply equally to all rational individuals. To argue that some sections of society were fundamentally different was illogical and dangerous. To have two sets of legal codes, two starkly different conceptions of how society was meant to work, struck at the very heart of their training and their perception of how the law functioned in regulating a civilized society.

Debates about the strengths and weaknesses of the TCCDR dominated Iraqi political circles. The newspaper *Al Sha'ab* championed the guaranteeing of a separate legal code for the tribal population. It argued that, as the tribal population formed the majority in Iraq, their interests should be protected in the Organic Law passing through Parliament.[49] This brought a series of criticisms along lines similar to those of Bonham-Carter and Drower. *Al Iraq* argued that the demand to be tried according to tribal custom was

> contrary to the fundamental principles of democracy and conflicts with the principles of the sovereignty of the State. Indeed it is disgraceful such a matter should be even discussed in a country which is demanding liberty and independence and which hopes to base its government on the practices of democratic nations.[50]

The best constitutions, *Al Iraq* argued, those of progressive nations, did their utmost to give no special rights to any person or class. To go along with such anti-progressive measures, it concluded, would be to invite both internal and external political interference.

This theme was taken up later in the year by the avowedly nationalist and anti-British newspaper *Al Istiqlal*. For Ali Mahmud Al Mahami, who wrote the detailed article, the continued use of the TCCDR was a stain on Iraq's claim to be a modern and progressive state. The TCCDR was "fit to be deposited in a museum so that the world may see in what era Iraq is living; in the twentieth century or in the dark ages: and may know how far the intelligence of her sons has advanced."[51] Al Mahami argued that the law was divisive because all Iraqis were not equal before it. It had also increased crime because it offered no deterrent to murder. Tribesmen were merely fined a small sum of money for any murders they committed. Most worryingly of all, though, it gave excessive powers to the *Mutasarrifs*, who had become both judge and administrator in the tribal areas. Al Mahami concluded that the continuation of such a law could lead to absolutism.

This debate was driven by politicians both in cabinet and in Parliament. As early as 1921, King Faisal expressed the desire to institutionalize the execution of tribal law by establishing standing tribal courts.[52] In 1923, Naji al Suwaydi, the Justice Minister, and in 1926, Abdullah al Muhsin al-Sa'dun, the Prime Minister, tried to have the TCCDR reformed to bring the administration of justice to tribes further under the control of central government. Both sets of proposals aimed to bring the system for trying and punishing "tribal" crimes more fully into the mainstream legal system. Under their proposals, the only dispensation for crimes considered tribal would be the length of sentencing.[53]

So, the clamor for the reform or abolition of the TCCDR came from British legal professionals appointed to advise Iraqi politicians, from the politicians themselves and from the wider political circles represented by the nationalist journalists writing in the Arabic newspapers in Baghdad. Iraqi and British critics alike, most often lawyers, had a clear vision of the role a unified and coherent legal system would play in binding Iraqi society together and to the state.

Sir Henry Dobbs (and by implication the other British staff overseeing the Mandate administration), on the other hand, could not possibly accept this analysis of either the shortcomings of the TCCDR or, implicitly, the nature of Iraqi society. To do so would have been profoundly threatening. They would have had to discard the way they understood not only Iraq but all non-Western societies with which they came in contact. Instead, Sir Henry fought tenaciously (and ultimately successfully) to defend the TCCDR. The tropes he deployed to win the debate were the now-familiar ones, organized around the urban-rural divide. The personification of urban modern degeneration now became the Iraqi lawyer. Dobbs portrayed a Baghdad that was full of self-seeking, young, semi-educated solicitors. As with the majority of the Arab town dwellers, their motivations were suspect and their influence pernicious.

[T]he whole campaign against the tribal system is a plot of the lawyers, who have been cheaply manufactured by the Law School in excessive numbers and now find themselves starving for want of work. They cannot bear to see important disputes, which might be comfortably aggravated and afford pickings for hordes of pleaders, if brought to the regular courts, settled by tribal arbitration. The result of such arbitration is that both the number of judicial appointments (which are filled by lawyers) is kept low and also the employment of pleaders is less than it would otherwise be. There is no genuine dislike of tribal law and customs as a barbarous system. It is merely a pounds, shillings and pence dislike of an arbitration system which deprives the lawyers of bread. The lawyers would like to force all tribesmen to settle their disputes or have their offences tried in regular courts, to see tribal rising result and tribal outlaws filling the mountains, to suppress these by help of the British power and then to indulge in extra-legal assassination of troublesome tribal leaders, such as the lawyers party attempted during the anti-treaty agitation. For it is a paradox of the East that the lawyer can never bear legalized strengthening of the executive authority, such as is to be found in the Tribal Disputes Regulations, but is quite indifferent to, and in fact applauds, extra-legal violence and administrative tyranny against his opponents outside the sphere of law.[54]

As with the Iraqi electoral system, the TCCDR was the outcome of the dominant frame for understanding Iraqi society. Urban Iraq, already transformed by the forces of modernity, was now subject to a civic law that dealt directly with individuals and evolved to meet the challenges of continued change. The TCCDR was, however, structured to meet the perceived needs of rural Iraq, which, being predominantly tribal in nature, needed protection from the urban minority. The honest and simple tribespeople of rural Iraq had to be protected from the corruption of modernity.

Once the Mandated state had been established, it became obvious to the British officials that the onward march of modernity was unstoppable. Their very presence, the order and stability which they brought, would eventually change Iraqi society. Although there was a broad agreement that this was bound to happen, attitudes towards the process and estimates of how long it would take were far from uniform. As he traveled through Iraq compiling his report on land tenure regimes, Sir Ernest

Dowson identified a general process of increased tribal sedentariness and decreased tribal cohesion and authority. He linked this to the spread of government authority. "[E]verywhere I was advised tribal disintegration was accelerating, everywhere the tribesman was becoming an individualist and wanting his individual holding."[55] For Dowson this was a positive process: the rational individual, liberated from the constraints of the tribal system, could now pursue his life with all the freedom that a modern state and civilization allowed him. All that had happened was that the restraints of the pre-modern world had been lifted from the shoulders of the individual, leaving him to flourish. [56]

The opposition to Dowson was represented by John Glubb, who, although recognizing a tribal system in decline, considered the cause of its terminal ill health to be the arrival of technology. It was the car and the airplane that had killed the tribal system.[57] But far from seeing this as the welcome effect of "progress," Glubb lamented the passing of what he labeled the "patriarchal system."Although patriarchy was referred to with "contempt" by Europeans, "it had many advantages. Basically it was founded on the mutual love of the governor and the governed."[58]

Glubb, like many of his colleagues, was deeply uneasy about the disruption he was causing. In a diary entry in April 1923, he rails against Woodrow Wilson, the British press and politicians, who "continue to demand that the nations of Asia and Africa should make a clean cut with their past, and at one fell stroke, adopt the mentality and traditions of the Western democracies." He concludes: "Would it not be more practical, as well as more polite, if we left these nations to govern themselves in their own way?"[59]

Chapter Six

The Social Meaning of Land

STATE, SHAIKH, AND PEASANT

Ought we to aim at a "bureaucratic" form of administration, such as that in force in Turkey and in Egypt, involving direct control by a central government, and the replacement of the powerful tribal confederation by the smaller tribal or sub-tribal unit, as a prelude to individual in place of communal ownership of land, or should our aim be to retain, and subject to official safeguards, to strengthen, the authority of tribal chiefs, and to make them the agents and official representatives of Government, within their respective areas? The latter policy had been already adopted, in default of a better one, in Basra wilayat, and especially in the Muntafiq division: was it wise to apply it to the Baghdad wilayat? Both policies had their advocates.[1]

No policy debate was more important for the making of the Iraqi state than that over the system of land tenure and revenue. No other issue revealed so starkly the ways British conceptions of Iraqi society influenced the shape the state and society assumed at the moment of Iraq's entrance onto the world stage. There was a broad consensus about the goals of any prospective land policy. It had to maximize the revenue extracted from agricultural production in the form of taxation while posing no threat to the state's ability to guarantee order. But the use of land policy to achieve these goals brought the differing social conceptions among British colonial officials in Iraq into stark relief. The intense and often angry debate revolved around the role and appropriate strength of the newly formed state in relation to the society it was designed to order and administer. Were the institutions of the evolving state strong enough to penetrate society and transform it? The competing social visions understood rural society as being constructed around shaikhs and peasants; the debate focused on the nature of state interaction with each. Was the peasant an individual, rational maximizer constrained by the despotic rule of his shaikh? Or were peasants members of a collective economic and social unit best represented by the shaikh? This debate defined and ultimately decided the way Iraq's modernity evolved.

As the British consolidated their position in Iraq, it became widely acknowledged that the Turkish system of land tenure had been badly conceived and haphazardly applied.[2] In the aftermath of the 1920 revolt, the remnants of the Turkish system were in a state of collapse, and disputes over land ownership and revenue were the major cause of social unrest. The proposals for reform highlighted the two conflicting visions of Iraqi society: the collectivist and the individualist. As these two approaches became polarized, lesser officials found themselves caught between them and under increasing pressure to choose one or the other. The divisions within British approaches to land policy can be examined by comparing the different categories deployed to understand rural society. The three main units of analysis, shaikh, *sarkal*, and *mallak*, had distinct meanings, and their use carried ideological as well as practical consequences. By examining how these three categories were used in different areas of central and southern Iraq, the Muntafiq, Amarah, and the Dulaim, the fault lines within the British social conceptions informing the making of Iraq can be better understood.

The three main protagonists in the debate surrounding the land issue, Steven Longrigg, Ernest Dowson, and Henry Dobbs, deployed different understandings of state and social structures and the effects of modernity upon both. Longrigg had risen through the ranks of the Mandate administration to become the Revenue Secretary to the Ministry of Finance. Sir Ernest Dowson had become the preeminent colonial land expert. Having occupied the posts of Surveyor General, Under Secretary of State for Finance, and Financial Adviser to the Egyptian government, he went on to write a major report on the land problem in Palestine. Finally, the figure of Henry Dobbs dominates the issue of land and revenue in Iraq from 1915 to at least 1929, when he retired as High Commissioner. In 1914 he had been transferred from the Government of India to become a Political Officer with British forces in the Middle East. From January 1915 until 31 July 1916 he was the First Revenue Officer for the British Expeditionary Force in Iraq. It was Dobbs who carried out the most thorough investigation into the basis of the Ottoman land system in Iraq and formulated British regulations designed to reform and replace the Turkish system.[3] How these three British experts on land deployed social categories to understand Iraqi society reveals the different social assumptions and conceptions behind the British attempt to create a modern and liberal Iraqi state.

Land, Colonialism, and the Consequences of Modernity

No administrative system is capable of representing any existing social community except through a heroic and greatly schematized process of abstraction and simplification.[4]

The British sought to make society socially comprehensible and hence controllable by regulating and reforming land tenure and revenue. These reforms were designed to impose a modern homogeneous order. Policy making involved the application of a universal unit of analysis to the understanding of landowning. The British aimed to provide a reliable and quantifiable answer to the question of land entitlement. Although this application of modern method strove by its very nature to impose a unitary standard upon landholding, arguments immediately arose over what the precise units of ownership were to be. These debates, although centered on three specific individuals, represented much wider divisions in the social imagination of modernity. The dispute between Dobbs, Dowson, and Longrigg was expressed in terms of personal preference and professional experience. But the conceptual structures that shaped the terms in which these arguments unfolded had their roots in the evolution of European land-tenure regimes and the divided discourse of modernity that underlay them.

The process of centralization and governmental reform had begun during the later period of Ottoman rule in Iraq. But it was the British army's seizure of territory after November 1914 and then the British-administered mandated state that instigated the far-reaching transformation of Iraqi society—with the country's full involvement in the dynamics of global markets—and, hence, its modernity.[5]

The enframing rationalism of a "high modernist ideology" peaked in confidence, coherence, and reach on the eve of World War I. It was seen by its advocates as granting the state the power to dominate and transform society.[6] This ability to understand and therefore transform society was ensured by the state's capacity to make society intelligible and hence accessible to its functionaries and institutions. The basis of this power was the creation and imposition of social units of analysis that were at once simple and unambiguous. Driven by a limited number of objectives, officials took exceptionally complex, illegible, and local social practices, such as land tenure customs or naming customs, and created a standard grid whereby it could be centrally recorded and monitored. . . . They did not successfully represent the actual activity of the society they depicted, nor were they intended to; they represented only that slice of it that interested the official observer.[7]

The effect of this transformation was to impose solidity upon the units of social analysis the state was using to understand the society it sought to dominate. Communities and social groupings that were, under premodern conditions, "fuzzy," or socially overdetermined became enumerated, simple, and precise. The state's rationalist demands for precision transformed in its own image the society it sought to understand.[8]

This modernizing process had begun to transform property rights in the aftermath of the Enlightenment. "Facts" were standardized so that they could be enumerated, collated, and compared without ambiguity.[9] The creation of a neutral and enumerated space was imposed by and then mediated through the institutions of the state. In Europe, the rediscovery of Roman law had made the unqualified possession of land a commonsensical article of faith. John Locke legitimized this notion by claiming private ownership as a law of nature.[10]

The state, in order to efficiently extract wealth from agricultural production, set about attaching all taxable land to an individual or institution it had identified as responsible for the land's taxable value. The result was the imposition of a land-tenure system that was conceptually coherent for the state. Units of land had to be delineated and their possession legally enforceable. This process, by its very nature, imposed homogeneity within the state's boundaries, forcing local landholding practices to conform to the universal norm that suited the state's fiscal and administrative concerns:

categories that may have begun as the artificial inventions of cadastral surveyors, census takers, or police officers can end by becoming categories that organize people's daily experience precisely because they are embedded in state-created institutions that structure that experience.[11]

This model of state-driven modernization that would transform property rights was exported along with everything else that colonial modernization entailed.[12] In effect the "heroic simplification" inherent in modern state institutions was so hegemonic that the alien societies encountered by colonial administrators could not be viewed in any other fashion.[13] The precision of analysis and the imposition of enumerated units of understanding was certainly transformative. Yet both society and land were ordered in this way not because this template fitted Iraq's state and society but because it was the only one available.

For British colonial administrators across the Empire, property rights were seen as universal and applicable to all territories they controlled no matter what the superficial differences between them appeared to be.[14] The imposition of European notions of land tenure brought order to rural societies but also an ideological coherence to the colonizing mission.[15] This order was imposed in two stages. First, all land had to be owned, and it was the administrator's job to find out who that owner was—to formalize and then protect his rights of possession. Then the proprietor was encouraged to farm the land as efficiently as possible.[16]

Although the imposition of European notions of land tenure was interpreted by its colonial administrators as merely codifying what was already in existence, it had profoundly transformative effects. By its very nature, this system of solidification and homogenization could not countenance or even recognize local differences in approach to social organization.[17] The far-reaching effects of this can be gauged when it is realized that although all capitalist societies share a similar structural logic, all precapitalist societies are "traditional" in their own very specific ways.[18] So the imposition of unambiguous European notions of unqualified possession ignored other more complex and flexible attitudes to land use. Across the precolonial world, individual ownership was often an alien concept. Instead, the produce of a given section of land was shared out on the basis of mutual obligation and input to the production process.[19]

Social-scientific study of the imposition of modern forms of land tenure in Europe and their globalization through colonialism rightly stresses the instrumental rationality at the heart of their conception and implementation. The rationalism of high modernism led to the imposition of a simplified social map of unambiguous units of analysis and comparison. But for many scholars studying this shift, the hegemonic unit of analysis imposed on societies was that of the rational individual. This is especially true in the case of land tenure. In tracing the rise of the European concept of the rational, unencumbered individual from the Enlightenment onward, we find that this argument places the individual property owner at the center of modern land tenure in Europe and later in the colonized world.[20] Although many (and perhaps most) land-tenure regimes came to be based on this model of economic man, to concentrate upon this to the exclusion of all else is itself a reductive simplification. A closer examination of the development of European social thought in the aftermath of the Enlightenment identifies a hard-fought struggle between two competing conceptions of society and the units that composed it. The discourse of modernity is more accurately theorized not as the hegemonic dominance of one system of thought over all others but as a series of competing systems struggling to gain ascendance. The ideals of the Enlightenment were forcefully challenged as rational individualism competed for dominance with more collective visions of society. [21]

The arguments around land tenure in Iraq were representative of this division within the discourse of modernity. The conceptions and approaches of Dobbs and Dowson most starkly represented this dichotomy. Rational instrumentalism as a method of grasping and ordering society was certainly deployed by both of them. Their disagreement focused on whether the vehicle of instrumentalism would be the individual or the tribe. In each case, once the unit had been selected, its "nature" was then "heroically simplified." It was universalized across the territory of the state, and then, by channeling the power of the state through it, it was imposed on the whole of society.

Land Policy in Iraq

The problem of land and its control was central for the Mandate, but the lack of a coherent British approach led to an inconsistent and piecemeal policy. Throughout the period of the Mandate, British officials acknowledged that "the land problem" was the most important issue to be dealt with once the state's nascent institutions had been put in place.

The reasons for this urgency were twofold: revenue and order. In Westminster, most prominent amongst the British government's concerns was the expenditure devoted to underwriting the administration in Iraq.[22] As the vast majority of Iraq's population lived on the land and earned its livelihood from it, the only feasible route to financial self-sufficiency for the emerging state was to dramatically raise the tax extracted from the rural population.[23] Also, it was quickly realized that the disorganized and unstable condition of land tenure was the single greatest cause of social instability. There was a strong concern running through official documents from 1914 until 1932 that the continuous conflict caused by disputed land ownership undermined the imposition of law and order.[24] Despite its acknowledged importance, British land policy from 1914 until 1932 was confused and contradictory, lacking any overall coherence or direction.[25] The predisposition of land-department officials to impose common law led them to undertake a sustained investigation into existing tenurial procedures on which to base their own approach.[26] This resulted in the one and only overall directive issued on land policy, which was to maintain, as far as possible, the existing Ottoman procedures.[27] This edict was issued despite the writing off of Ottoman land policy by British administrators as hopelessly idealistic, ambitious, and, in practice, thoroughly corrupt. This confusion was compounded by the government's failure to carry out a successful cadastral survey or a census.[28]

The result of applying the Ottoman land code to the whole of Iraq was that the state continued theoretically to be the landlord of two-thirds of the cultivable land. So, with the increased efficiency and power of government, a degree of homogeneity was imposed upon a set of previously diverse approaches to land. However, because "survey and registration are so incomplete," the appearance of a powerful arbitrator increased the disputation surrounding land tenure.[29] By 1926, government officials from the Interior Ministry were

> compelled to spend a great portion of their time in dealing with disputes and cases arising from rights of tenancy. In view of the fact that these rights are not based on clear principles or laws, a just and satisfactory solution of the dispute and differences arising therefrom becomes almost impossible. This state of affairs places the

Government officials in an awkward position on the one hand and increases the number of discontented people on the other.[30]

Yet although British attitudes to the problem of Iraqi land were confused and contradictory throughout the period of the Mandate, from 1926 onwards a concerted but ultimately unsuccessful attempt was made to develop a consistent and effective land policy.[31] The causes of this new concern with land tenure can be found both in the Iraqi economy and in the international environment. Internally, the possible impact of large-scale commercial exploitation of Iraqi oil fields was beginning to be understood. Although agriculture was still seen as the main source of the country's future prosperity, those in the High Commission and the Revenue and Interior Ministries began to think about the effect cheap oil would have on irrigation. By bringing down the price of pumps used to water the land, the availability of cheap oil would rapidly increase the profitability of farming. Internationally, the settling of the Mosul dispute with Turkey and the signing of the twenty-five year Anglo-Iraqi treaty appeared to provide for a new era of economic stability and therefore increased opportunity for investment.[32] The areas most suited for the boom in agricultural production and the commercial scramble for land were on the Tigris and Euphrates below Baghdad, governed mainly by the *miri* system of tenure. The land had not been alienated to any officially recognized private owner and was therefore legally controlled by the Iraqi government. It was also farmed by what the government understood to be settled tribal communities.[33]

Attempts by Henry Dobbs and Steven Longrigg (then Director of State Domains) to construct a policy to regularize land tenure across the whole of Iraq brought to the surface their differing conceptions of the nature and evolution of Iraqi society and its relationship to the state. These disputes were exacerbated when Ernest Dowson arrived in Iraq in 1929 to write a report on land tenure. An individualist framework that celebrated rational action and the positive role of the state confronted a more collectivist one. The opposing conception doubted the market's ability to transform social structures and the power of the state to bypass traditional social arrangements and influence the individual directly—as well as the desirability of its doing so.

The Ordering of Rural Society: Shaikh and Tribe or Mallak and Sarkal

The maximization of revenue and the preservation of order became the dual obsessions of the Mandate's land policy. Amongst Mandate staff there was a clear division about how these twin goals were to be realized, which centered on two broad sets of social categories deployed to understand Iraqi society: one group focused on the role of the shaikh; the other on the role of the *sarkal*. The tensions between the holders of these two categories structured the debate surrounding land policy. The two broad sets of categories through which Iraqi society was perceived can be separated into an economic-rational approach, on the one hand, and one viewed by its adherents as traditional, on the other. Those categories understood to be traditional came to dominate conceptions of Iraqi society and so came to dominate policy toward land. The relationship between shaikhs and tribesmen was viewed by those who promoted this position as being bound by custom and the mutual bonds of community. These bonds had evolved over many hundreds of years and acted as a powerful constraint on all those subjected to them.

The competing category perceived Iraqi society in rational-economic terms. Although more recent in origin, those who promoted this view felt it to be the product of the inexorable rise of market forces. These categories, the direct result of market relations, would come to dominate all aspects of rural life. They represented not only the future but ultimately the only logical way that a modern society could be organized. From this viewpoint, the figures of the *mallak* and *sarkal* were seen as being primarily involved in organizing the agricultural production of the peasantry. The *mallak* was the landlord, with legal possession of the land and a right to demand *mallakiyah*, or rent. The *sarkal* was comparable to a tenant or foreman and was responsible for organizing the planting and harvesting of the crop. Below both categories was a rational peasantry continually trying to maximize output.

Both sets of categories, one broadly communal, the other based on the individual, were in part underpinned and reinforced by differing perceptions of the capabilities and nature of the state. When the main institutions of government were being built, and state-society relations being institutionalized, the "communal" perception, as represented by Henry Dobbs, was that the state would be too weak to deal directly with individuals in rural Iraq.[34] Instead, its relations with the mass of the population had to be mediated through a series of tribal shaikhs. Dobbs's perceptions of state and society were mutually reinforcing. A society collectively organized in tribal groupings was easy to administer but also too strong to be broken or reshaped by state intervention. Added to this, Dobbs was haunted by the fear of a new, neo-Ottoman despotic regime. For Dobbs, the state was weak for financial and social reasons but also because of belief in the desirable configuration of state-society relations.[35] Traditional societal bonds between shaikh and tribe would be a better guarantee of personal liberty than a relationship between the individual and the state only theoretically and tenuously safeguarded by civil society. Yet in this understanding, the coldly instrumental relations between *mallak*, *sarkal*, and peasant were shifting, unreliable, and hence unable to deliver order or guarantee equity.

The second broad understanding of Iraqi society was that used by Ernest Dowson. The categories he deployed to order Iraqi society were rational and economic. From Dowson's perspective, the objective of a state's agrarian policy was to form direct links with the individual cultivator. Societies universally consisted of little more than individual members of a population. They had no inherent strength beyond the actions of individuals. This conception saw the forging of direct links between the state and the individual in practical terms as a task of efficient administration. This had been possible in Egypt and was certainly so in Iraq. The categories of *mallak* and *sarkal* had been created by the workings of the agricultural market and the needs of production in Iraq. They were both logical and desirable. Any other approach, such as one based on an alternative understanding of community and trust, was idealistic, wasteful, and ultimately anachronistic.

Of Shaikh, Tribe, and Land

The understanding of the harmony between the shaikh and his tribe formed the basis of land policy from the occupation onwards. It was in the Amarah *liwa* that the policy had its most unfettered application.

British revenue officers with the expeditionary forces attempted to order land settlement in Amarah by placing large estates on two-year rolling leases "in the hands of a strong and capable shaikh." The shaikhs were felt to possess leadership and influence over a large constituency and were the ideal interlocutor for government-society relations. The First Revenue Officer of the Expeditionary Force, C. C. Garbett, described how in 1918, in Abu Hallana, he had reallocated the land of a "non-tribal 'farmer,' " giving it instead to a man whom he had identified as a tribal shaikh.[36]

The British made a conscious decision once shaikhs had been either established on the land or had had their position recognized to deal only with them, refusing to "go behind" their backs and deal with the *sarkals* directly involved with production. The *sarkals* were then left to make their own terms with the shaikhs: "If we interfere between the Shaikh-farmer and his Sarkals-sub-farmers, the result to my mind will be bad."[37] As leader of his community, the shaikh created order. From within this conception, the *sarkal* was a minor and ultimately unimportant figure. Recognition, power, and resources would be devolved through the shaikh and no one else.

It was freely admitted from 1919 onward that this approach had its basis in political rather than revenue objectives. The shaikhs, through their relationship with the wider agricultural community, were seen as being able to enforce law and order. By 1922, after the authority of government had increased in Amarah, there was an attempt to improve revenue extraction by a fresh redistribution of land on the large estates of Chahalah. It was proposed that the lands of Shaikh Muhammad al Araibi be reduced because it had become apparent that he did not possess the skills to administer all of them efficiently. But the strength of the collective framework was such that the category of the shaikh (to the exclusion of other possibilities) was still used to administer this redistribution. A percentage of Shaikh Muhammad's lands was reallocated to another shaikh of the Albu Muhammad, Falih al Saihud.[38]

Although it could be argued that Amarah represented an extreme case of British policy favoring shaikhs above all other groups in society,[39] the same social conceptions underlying land and revenue policies can be found in more turbulent and heterogeneous areas. In Dulaim, for example, the perceived impossibility and undesirability of the state's forging direct links with the "inchoate mass of cultivators" led to the government's reliance on the authority and "tribal status" of the shaikhs to carry out "manifold administrative duties." By depending on these figures of authority, the British administrators believed they were merely recognizing social practices that had been in existence since the tribes of the Dulaim had moved from nomadic pasturalism to settled agricultural production.[40]

For those enforcing policy, the shaikh had kept order before the British arrival and continued to do so. Hence the *mashaikha* of between 10 to 12.5 percent of the crop that the shaikh took from "his" cultivators was a practice structured by social relations and independent of the state's actions. In harnessing the shaikh's power, the state simply added on the collection of its own taxation to the *mashaikha*, thereby creating a three-tiered revenue system. So, along with *mashaikha*, the *fallah* paid tax due to government to the *sarkal*, who in turn handed the revenue to the paramount shaikh, who finally delivered it to the government after extracting a percentage for himself.[41]

In the wake of the chaos caused by the 1920 uprising, the state went a step further and sought to institutionalize the influence of the Dulaim shaikhs by demanding that several minor and previously rebellious shaikhs sign pledges of allegiance to Ali Sulaiman, officially agreeing to pay him *mashaikha*, that is, shaikhly dues.[42] At the time this did not appear to be a change in policy. Ali Sulaiman, because of his perceived social position at the head of a collectively structured society, was seen as the only man capable of delivering revenue and order.

As paramount shaikh of the Dulaim, Sulaiman came to personify the positive role such a figure could play in agricultural life. In early 1921 he organized the digging of a canal at the Saqlawiyah, a tributary of the Euphrates below Ramadi.[43] When completed, the canal would bring an extra 100,000 acres of land between the Tigris and Euphrates under cultivation.[44] By deploying his prestige and influence amongst his own tribe, he secured extensive free labor to dig the canal, and the new land brought into cultivation allowed him to settle hitherto landless members of his tribe. It was then a logical step to grant his request for the *tapu sanads* on the newly fertile land to be given to him personally. He represented the pinnacle of the tribe. It was his social position that got the canal dug in the first place, and it was he who was best placed to serve the interests of the Dulaim newly settled on the land.[45]

Ali Sulaiman became a central figure in the debates surrounding the nature and utility of the shaikh in rural Iraq. His strengths or weaknesses became a pivot around which the wider policy was either championed or attacked. His collection of tax, his digging of what became known as the Ali Sulaiman Canal, and his role at the head of a tribal federation that guaranteed the stability of the Dulaim area all appeared to support the argument for a collective understanding of Iraqi society. He was an ally of the British army but also a figure of influence in his own right. As the personification of a strong society, he was part of the reason why the state was weak—but he was also the solution to its weakness.

There is clear evidence to suggest that in Muntafiq, one of the most turbulent areas in the country, the categories of shaikh and tribe were deployed not only to order society but also to explain the persistence of social turmoil and violence. For the British, Muntafiq had a reputation for agrarian turmoil that had long predated their involvement in Iraq. Once British forces had secured control over the Muntafiq area, their perception of society became the key to how they imposed order on it.[46] The shaikhs and their tribes were a force for good, representing social stability and equality. The cause of British problems were Sa'dun landlords. Within this understanding, the landlords by their very nature could not be authentic; they could not have originated organically from within traditional Iraqi society. Instead, their imposition by the Ottoman government and their origin in the urban areas of Iraq meant that they were a corrupting influence, bringing with them all the woes of the cities, including extremism and self-interested violence. In contrast the tribes—and by sponsoring and validating them, the British—were authentic, moral, and noble.

As they had in Amarah with its shaikhs, British forces during the Mesopotamian campaign used the influence of the Muntafiq shaikhs to keep the area quiet during the war. Responsibility for the land, its tax, and its produce were concentrated in the hands of those who were identified as tribal shaikhs.[47] This resulted in the marginalization of other categories and social actors who were seen as superfluous to Muntafiq society.

The dominant collective social imagination of the British administrators ordering Muntafiq came to the fore when they sought to understand the battles over land that had continued to destabilize the area long after their arrival. They assumed that because the tribes of the Muntafiq had exercised rights over the land they had farmed "from time immemorial,"[48] the cause of conflict had to be located elsewhere, outside Muntafiq society. The conflict that had been destabilizing the region since the 1880s was understood to be between the Sa'dun, classified as landlords, and their tenants, classified as tribespeople. British policy, structured by this collective understanding of Muntafiq society, took the side of the tribespeople over that of the Sa'dun. However, the British were ideologically committed to the rule of law and the defense of property rights, so this apparent negation of a landlord's rights had to be justified. Accordingly, in this case the landlord's "right" of possession was not what it seemed. The corrupting presence of landlords in Muntafiq was the result of devious Ottoman practices.[49] Hence, this ownership of property was conceived of as illegitimate and indefensible. These landlords had not purchased the land from the tribes; it had been given to them by Ottoman dictate. Therefore, for the British, the Sa'dun had no legal right to this land; they could not even substantiate their ownership by physical possession.[50]

For the British, the landlords' legitimacy had been undermined by the very act of their creation by the Ottoman government. Their actions under the Mandate had confirmed the corrupting influence of their presence in the Muntafiq. The landlords, reflecting their urban lineage, "allied themselves with the extremists and with the merchants of the town known for their talent for intrigue."[51] They came to be seen as fifth columnists, a conduit for all that made Baghdad the epitome of what was wrong with Iraq.

The Sa'dun, as the conduit for urban influence into the countryside, were seen by the British as natural allies of the Iraqi politicians in Baghdad. Indeed, at times, "the landlord class" and the political elite were merged into one category to explain the causes and effects of the Muntafiq violence. As Faisal grew in power and began to appoint civil servants, it was assumed by the British that their urban origins would lead them to favor the landlords' interests.[52] There was "little sympathy with tribal grievances in the highest official circles in Baghdad." This resulted in local government officers being forced to collect rent on behalf of the Sa'dun, thus focusing tribal resentment on state institutions.[53]

The innate bias of urban politicians allowed British staff to discount all criticism of British land policy in Muntafiq. In April 1921, at Percy Cox's request, the Iraqi cabinet formed a committee to look into the unrest and advise on possible solutions. The report produced by the Mallakiyah Committee was condemned as "jejune" and its recommendation that the government should protect landlords' rights and return land taken from them by force was written off as the observations of "the landlord class."[54] The same applied to the interventions of the Iraqi Chamber of Deputies. In September 1925 and January 1927, debates were held in Parliament and bills were drafted in an attempt to shape policy toward Muntafiq land reform. These were dismissed by British commentators as biased to "the Sa'dun point of view."[55] For British officials defending their policy on land in the Muntafiq, the personification of a self-interested politician was Abdul al Mushin Beg al Sa'dun himself. As Prime Minister from November 1922 to November 1923, he was constantly accused in reports and telegrams of favoring the Sa'dun cause for personal or family reasons.[56]

Ultimately, then, the long-running problem of disorder in the Muntafiq, which was to plague the Iraqi state for the whole of the Mandate, was blamed upon the introduction of a foreign body, the landlord, into Muntafiq society.

Of Sarkals, Mallaks, and Markets

Both the logic and success of the policy of ruling through tribal shaikhs and the collectivist vision that underpinned it were challenged by a minority of the British staff working in Iraq, as well as by Iraqi politicians in cabinet and Parliament. Their critique of allowing the rule of shaikhs was based on the efficacy, morality, and legality of channeling state power through the person of the shaikh. In Amarah, Major S. E. Hedgcock, the Political Officer in 1920, wrote a damning indictment, challenging the whole policy of supporting the shaikhs to the exclusion of all other sections of society. The shaikh, he argued, stripped of government support, "is more or less a figurehead, with very little power." He continued:

We have fallen into the error of over-rating his value and consulting him too much, to the exclusion of educated and far-seeing men of other classes. . . . We have somewhat lost sight of the fact that the shaikh does not represent agricultural interests from the point of view of either the sarkal or the fallah; on the contrary, he is usually ignorant, narrow-minded, and unprogressive, extremely selfish and possessed of an inordinate greed for money.[57]

Hedgcock challenged the very basis of the policy and the social perception it rested upon. The shaikh, far from being tied to a collectively organized rural society by bonds of mutual trust, was in fact a throwback, hindering progress and restraining individual productivity. Hedgcock therefore recommended elevating the *sarkal* to the position of owner-occupier. By removing his insecurity of tenure, the British would encourage the *sarkal* to act as a rational economic being who would undertake expensive improvements, thereby hoping "to gain from his own industry and forethought."[58]

In Dulaim, greater weight was being added to this argument by the increasing difficulties that Ali Sulaiman had in collecting his *mashaikha* from 1923 onward. In 1924, the *Mutasarrif* of Ramadi imprisoned ten "sub-shaikhs" of the Albu Fahad section of the Dulaim for allegedly refusing to pay their *mashaikha* and tax to Ali Sulaiman. In their defense, the men claimed that they were obeying government orders to recognize Ali Sulaiman as paramount shaikh. Yet Sulaiman was using his authority to extort three times the amount of money that he and the government were due.[59] From 1923 on, an increasing number of such reports began to portray Sulaiman not as a paragon of his community but as a resented exploiter of the *fallah* he ruled over in the name of the government.

By 1924 Sulaiman's ability to collect his own *mashaikha*, let alone the government's tax, was being questioned. In November 1924, the Dulaim Administrative Inspector described the four paramount shaikhs of the division—Sulaiman, Mushin al Harsan, Shoukah al Mutluq, and Aftan al Sherji—as "a real hindrance to Government from the point of view of revenue collection." From the perspective of Baghdad, Sulaiman might have been seen as a paramount, but to the *liwa* authorities it was "painfully obvious he relies more and more on Government support to keep up his position." The inspector clearly saw the *sarkal* as being the most efficient and hence most useful figure in organizing agricultural production. There was simply not enough room for both the shaikh and the *sarkal*, and the inspector saw the *sarkal*'s eventual triumph as inevitable.[60]

Sulaiman's inability to collect revenue without government assistance became a political issue when Mahmud Ramiz drew attention to it in the Chamber of Deputies. Was it true, he asked the Minister of Finance, that the *Mutasarrif* of Dulaim was collecting *mashaikha* from cultivators? Such collection would, he argued, be illegal under Iraqi law.[61] Here we see that some Iraqi politicians were actively challenging the theory and practice arising from the collective ontology that underpinned British land and revenue policy. In this case, Ramiz was highlighting the contradictory position of the Dulaim shaikhs under the law. In theory it was their social standing that allowed them to collect taxes; in practice it was the state's power.

The mounting problems surrounding Ali Sulaiman led the adviser to the Ministry of the Interior, Kinahan Cornwallis, to review his position. From October 1925 until February 1926, Cornwallis consulted a range of British officials in Dulaim and Baghdad. It became apparent that Sulaiman could not fulfil his tax-collecting duties; Cornwallis sought to discover the reason. He considered himself "a strong supporter of Shaikh Ali and all other Shaikhs of the Dulaim,"[62] but even from this vantage point it was apparent that Sulaiman's influence was in decline. Cornwallis identified problems within the shaikh's tribal constituency. He discovered that in the aftermath of the 1920 rebellion some of the shaikhs who swore allegiance to Sulaiman, at the bidding of the British, were not even members of his own tribe.[63] This had clearly made it difficult for him to sustain his influence. Ultimately, however, the extreme weakness of Sulaiman's position forced Cornwallis to speculate that changing economic and political circumstances had reduced the shaikh's influence and role in the everyday lives of his tribe.[64]

The ideological challenge to British policy in the Muntafiq came primarily from Iraqi politicians in the Chamber of Deputies. In September 1925, a member of the chamber, Ahmad Daud, introduced a resolution that challenged the theory and practice of the Mandate officials' approach to the Muntafiq. Daud argued that "military necessity" had forced certain measures on the Government of Occupation. But now, in times of peace and stability, government actions were depriving the landlords of the Muntafiq of revenues from their property. Daud went on to argue that this policy directly contravened the British-drafted constitution (the Organic Law). Daud cited Article 6, which guaranteed equal rights for all Iraqis, and Article 10, which protected the right to property. In his speech Daud defended the "sacred rights of property and ownership," declaring that policy in the Muntafiq violated the very basis of Iraqi democracy.[65] In appealing to constitutional law and democratic principle, Ahmad Daud was attacking the ideological legitimacy of Britain's involvement in Iraq. If the state created under the Mandate did not defend property rights and democracy, then on what basis did the British claim to be in Iraq and what type of state were they building? In response, the colonial staff tried to deflect the logic of his attack. First, as with all parliamentary assaults on British policy, the selfless approach of the Mandate staff was contrasted with Daud's self-interested parliamentary support, allegedly made up of those with land in the area. Secondly, Daud was portrayed as an eccentric fool who declaimed at length but whose "limited knowledge of modern economic doctrines" meant that he had no real understanding of the greater issues at stake.[66]

Not so easily dismissed, and hence the most damning critique of the use of the shaikh as the key organizing category in land policy, was Steven Longrigg's assessment of the unrest in Muntafiq. Although his critical remarks consisted of only one line in a wide-ranging thirty-one page report on land reform in Iraq, they were a direct attack on British land policy in general and especially as applied to the specific problems of the Muntafiq. The context in which Longrigg mentioned Muntafiq was the much broader issue of how the government should use the large amount of *tapu* land that it owned. Longrigg accepted the existing view of shaikhs as being figures of influence within their tribes and wider Iraqi society, but he disagreed with the policy of "the artificial reinforcement of the tribal influence of the Shaikh . . . by the conferment upon him of the function of landlord or capitalist."[67] To do so would not only be "unjust to the individual tribesmen" but would also be "fatal to security and progress and yet not destructive to tribalism—as seen in the Muntafiq."[68] Thus, Longrigg, in 1926, was placing the blame for the continuing violence in Muntafiq not on the legacy of the Ottoman Empire but on the British policy of bolstering the power of the shaikhs with personal grants of land. He considered that this policy denied individual tribesmen the responsibility of owning land and was therefore unfair. More importantly, because it gave "artificial reinforcement" to a shaikh's position, it was the cause of instability in the Muntafiq. In effect, then, Longrigg was attacking the collectivist mentality underpinning the dominant British view of rural society. A tribal shaikh "must find his level upon purely tribal lines." The tribal system itself was slowly but inexorably degenerating and releasing tribesmen to become individual cultivators in their own right. Government policy to date had hindered this process and as a result was driving the unrest in the Muntafiq.

Such a damning (if brief) indictment of the effects of government policy in the Muntafiq could not go unchallenged. This one-line reference to Muntafiq resulted in two letters from Henry Dobbs, who tried over six pages to refute Longrigg's argument. The High Commissioner's aggressive and pedantic rebuttal only serves to highlight the challenge to government policy encapsulated in Longrigg's explanation of Muntafiq's instability.[69]

Those British officials arguing against collective and "traditional" notions of social organization looked beyond the shaikh into the wider agricultural society of Iraq and tended to use economic and instrumental language to describe what they found. It was the economically defined figure of the *sarkal* who was held up as a rational replacement for the anachronistic figure of the shaikh. It was recognized that to encourage the *sarkal* to form direct links with government would place the role of the paramount shaikh under direct threat. But under this perception of Iraqi society, the *sarkal* was seen as the more rational figure. As his role and position were primarily economic, by his very nature he would be open to the influence of the market. The language of voluntarism was deployed to describe the role of the *sarkal* and his relationship with the *fallah*. The *fallah* as a rational producer was concerned with little else but crop production. He would choose the *sarkal* over the shaikh because the *sarkal* was active, organized, and was forced by the economics of his position to minister to the *fallah*'s needs. The *sarkal* kept open house, organized loans for seed, and generally supplied what the *fallah* needed to produce his crops.[70] The *sarkal*'s own "industry and forethought" could be deployed to increase the productivity of the land.[71] Under this understanding of Iraqi society, order would be secured by ministering to people's individual needs, aiding their prosperity, and convincing them of the benefit of direct government.

Unlike that of the shaikh, the more recently formed and malleable nature of the *sarkal*'s position was seen as having a distinct advantage. The government could recognize and encourage useful *sarkals*, transferring them to different sections of land or undermining their position depending on policy requirements.[72] The *sarkal*'s attachment to different tribal groupings would also be instrumental, based as it was on the economic needs of production.[73]

Ultimately, the strength of the *sarkal* as a figure of rural control also proved to be its weakness. When compared with the figure of the paramount shaikh, the perceived economic basis of the *sarkal*'s position was felt to be too weak to provide a stable footing from which to order rural Iraq. Unlike the supposed bonds of community and solidarity binding the shaikh to his tribespeople, with the *sarkal*, relations of production and self-interest were seen as more problematic and unreliable.[74] This opinion was summed up by an Air Service Intelligence report of 1931. Neither on the "grounds of equity nor expediency," the author felt, should the *sarkal*'s authority and role be encouraged as a replacement for the shaikh. To do so would encourage the "obsession for breaking the power of the bigger shaikhs" held by the urban politicians in Baghdad. These politicians, cut off by education and demeanor, could not understand "the difficulties and danger of removing all the intermediaries between the Government and the inchoate mass of cultivators." To do so might lead to "a complete social revolution."[75]

This debate amongst British officials about the utility of the shaikh as opposed to the *sarkal* was ultimately resolved in favor of the shaikh. The effect of this decision profoundly transformed the social system as it was being ordered. The channeling of state power and resources through the shaikhs meant that their relationship with society had to change. The state's "heroic simplification" of the rural population could not tolerate ambiguity. The units it used to order society were solidified, enumerated, and universalized simply by their deployment. In favoring the shaikh, the British modernized his interaction with society based on revenue collection and land ownership, so imposing a new utilitarian dynamic between state and shaikh and between shaikh and *fallah*.

Dobbs, Dowson, and Longrigg: State, Tenure, and Tribe

Sir Henry Dobbs was heavily influenced by policy developed on the North-West Frontier of colonial India at the end of the nineteenth century. It was here that Sir Robert Sandeman had developed his policy of "humane imperialism," which recognized the dominion of tribal shaikhs and ruled through them. Dowson, on the other hand, spent much of his working life in Egypt and clearly had a different experience and approach. Dowson's main influence was Lord Cromer, with the individual self-interest of small cultivators being the main organizing concept. The general influence of colonial India on those serving in Iraq is hard to overestimate.[76] On a personal level, throughout the files, reports, memoirs, and letters home concerning Iraq, concrete examples from India were given to explain the writer's new experiences.[77] But the Indian examples being deployed were far from homogeneous, riven as they were with the very conceptual tensions and ambiguities that would come to structure perceptions of Iraqi society. Indian policy was split between

two divergent or even contradictory theories of rule: one which sought to maintain India as a feudal order, and the other looking towards changes which would inevitably lead to the destruction of this feudal order. Each of these theories about British rule incorporated ideas about the sociology of India, and the relationship of the rulers to individuals and groups in Indian society. If India were to be ruled in a feudal mode, then an Indian aristocracy had to be recognized and/or created, which could play the part of "loyal feudatories" to their British queen. If India were to be ruled by the British in a "modernist" mode, then principles which looked to a new kind of civic or public order had to be developed.[78]

It was the influence of a geographically peripheral area of British India, "whose inhabitants were the most recalcitrant of all the Empire's ungrateful subjects,"[79] that proved to be the greatest influence on Dobbs and, after him, Sir Francis Humphrys. Both were India Frontier officers in the early part of their careers before becoming High Commissioners for Iraq.[80] Dobbs's experience on the North-West Frontier and in Baluchistan provided the model for his general policy towards tribes and for his attitudes to land tenure. Dobbs's approach was dominated specifically by the policy of Colonel Sir Robert Sandeman, improvised from 1868 onwards, when the latter was appointed Deputy Commissioner of the

Dara Ghazi Khan district in Baluchistan, and increasingly formalized after 1875.[81] Sandeman's model of "humane imperialism" became the touchstone of Iraqi tribal policy.[82] More directly, Henry Dobbs's experience of working under one of Sandeman's successors, Sir H. McMahon, Chief Agent-General for Baluchistan, was cited on numerous occasions in the formation of policy.[83]

The unit that dominated Sandeman's approach was the tribe. For him it was the primary way in which Pathan and Baluch society could be understood. Sandeman's conception of tribal structure was one of vertical transmission of authority: "in every Pathan or Baluch tribe, however democratic, there does exist headmen of more or less influence and a system of tribal authority."[84] Subsidies were allocated to these headmen and they were encouraged to offer men for service in the tribal levies that Sandeman raised.[85] British use of their office to impose law and order further strengthened the authority of these tribal heads.

Dowson's experience in Egypt stood in stark contrast to Dobbs's in India. In his recommendations on land reform in both Palestine and Iraq, Dowson was to reproduce Lord Cromer's model. Cromer had come to personify the imperial mission during his twenty-five year tenure as British representative in Egypt. Through his strength of personality and copious writings, he codified an influential philosophy of rule. Cromer's successful application of this approach allowed him to "emerge as the paramount consul-general in England's empire."[86] Both T. E. Lawrence and A. T. Wilson, when discussing Iraq, cited Cromer's example as the basis on which Iraq should be run.[87]

For Cromer (in contrast to Sandeman and Dobbs), society was not collectively structured: the individual was the defining category. Therefore, individual self-interest was at the center of his attempt to keep the peace while he arranged the restructuring of the state. Cromer argued that imperial administrators forgot this factor at their peril. "If we are not to adopt a policy based on securing the contentment of the subject race by ministering to their material interests, we must of necessity make a distinct approach to the counter policy of governing by the sword alone."[88] So the central plank of Cromer's approach was low taxation; government departments saw their budgets cut as fiscal relief became policy. Subject peoples should financially benefit from European rule. Through providing tangible help, both by tax relief and improvements in the country's infrastructure, Cromer hoped to build an indigenous class of small landowners. This group, which would form the basis of social stability, was to be protected from losing its holdings to large landowners, whether Egyptian or foreign. They would not love British rule but would at least see its benefits and so provide a stable base for it. Thus, Cromer argued, the nationalists' natural constituency would be placated: "In spite of outward appearances to the contrary, the whole nationalist movement in Egypt has been a mere splutter on the surface. It never extended deep down in the social ranks."[89]

In his advice on land tenure in Iraq, Dowson also deployed this individualist social vision. Giving the example of Egypt between 1905 and 1912, he argued that the state should strive to establish and maintain direct links with individual cultivators.[90] As with Egypt, individual legal title should be guaranteed so that the cultivator would be driven to invest in his land and improve its productivity.[91]

The other issue that defined the stance that Dobbs, Dowson, and Longrigg took on land tenure was their understanding of the state. For Dobbs the issue was divided into two related arguments: how much power the state should have and also what its correct role in society should be. Dobbs had a very pessimistic view of state capabilities under the British, even more so once the timetable for independence was set. For Dobbs, "The country is too vast and unmanageable and the population too scattered for the Government to attempt direct arrangements with cultivators." The machinery of government was too "hopelessly inadequate" even to contemplate such a policy.[92]

The relative weakness of the state meant that tax collection could be enforced only through "the terror of the Air Force." But even this appearance of power was deceptive; it encouraged government officials to extract unrealistic levels of tax, which caused resentment and anger. As Dobbs noted,

I have little doubt that attempts to enforce such claims [enormously enhanced taxation] in the Euphrates areas, where larger amounts were collected during 1919 and the beginning of 1920 than have ever been collected before or since, was one of the main causes of the great rebellion of 1920.[93]

This understanding of the potential disadvantages of enforcing state power was underpinned by an ideological rejection of its excessive use. When Dobbs criticized Longrigg's detailed plans for a government land policy in 1926, he began by alleging that it was based on the presupposition of government omnipotence and societal subservience. Longrigg's note was flawed, he argued, because it took the side of government without paying attention to the rights of the *fallah*. For Dobbs, the rights of the cultivators should have been given at least equal standing. He developed this theme when assessing what should be done to deal with the growth in land prices. The "theory" inherited from Ottoman rule, that the government was landlord of the vast majority of land in Iraq, was doubtful and should not be encouraged. In reviewing the draft form of leases to be signed between cultivators and government, Dobbs went out of his way to reduce the state's rights vis-à-vis those who farmed the land.

> From the point of view which I am taking up, agreements should now be executed, not with the object of establishing the rights of Government as landlord (the main object suggested by Mr. Longrigg), but with the object of assuring the present occupiers of security of tenure sufficient to enable them to invest in pumps and develop their lands, without depriving them of any rights of permanent occupancy on tapu tenure which may have accrued to them under the Law and which they will be at liberty at any time to seek to establish.[94]

The reason for this antipathy towards the state and the dangers of its sinking into despotism lay within Dobbs's conception of Iraqi rural society as primarily tribal and collectively organized:

> the tribal landlord with tribal cultivators below him is much more effectively restrained by tribal custom from oppression and exactions than can ordinarily be managed by regular laws . . . he [the shaikh] . . . cannot afford to oppress or rack rent them beyond a certain limit.[95]

For Dobbs the bonds of community between the shaikh and his tribespeople were more effective than any law that the state could enact. The shaikh, owing his position to tribal support, had to listen and take account of his tribe's opinions. The state, on the other hand, armed with terror-inducing airplanes, could enforce its will on a cowed and subservient population. Dobbs, then, set out to reduce the state's intervention in society and to minimize potential misuse of power.

Longrigg and Dowson, though, had much less ambivalent and broadly similar attitudes toward what the state could and should do. For Longrigg, the state's rights as landlord had long been accepted by society. Even "the wildest tribesman," when involved in a land dispute would admit that the government owned the property concerned: "he claims nothing but the superior right to occupy [it] . . . the 'academic' claim that all unalienated land belongs to Government is a claim conceded by every tribal litigant."[96] Suddenly dropping the idea of the state as landlord would have been revolutionary; it would have upset the established order and ignored the precedent of centuries. Instead, Longrigg saw the state's role as that of an honest arbiter, one who would oversee the fair distribution of land, gradually "breaking up privilege" and "substituting economic or logically calculated demands for traditional demands."[97]

Dowson saw the ideal goal of any state-driven land reform as being the establishment of a direct link between the state and the individual cultivator. With this in mind, the object of land reform for Dowson was to break down old procedures and use the power of the state to "establish land tenure progressively throughout the country . . . on a firm foundation of legal right determined in a judicial manner on the spot with reference to actual parcels of land that are precisely defined at the same time."[98] The difference of approach caused by the opposing social visions of Dobbs, Longrigg, and Dowson became most apparent when the question of who should be granted the right of tenure arose. Dobbs's fear of state domination led him to fight against recognition of the state's ownership of land. Both Longrigg and Dowson, on the other hand, saw the potential economic benefits of having a powerful role for the state as the freeholder of *miri* land. All three claimed as their ultimate goal the protection of indigenous cultivators across Iraq. However, their different understandings of who these cultivators were and their place within rural society opened up the crucial space of policy debate.

For Dobbs the tribe's centrality meant that little in the way of social organization existed outside its bounds. His main concern was to protect what he termed the "prescriptive tribal right" to remain in possession of the land its members farmed. Dobbs had identified the greatest threat to the land rights of the tribes as being "the greedy grasp of the city-men."[99] As a Revenue Commissioner in 1916 and as High Commissioner in 1925, he strove to restrict the commercial market for land. He did this by rec-ommending that foreign ownership of land be banned and then by striv-ing to protect tribal property rights.[100]

In a 1928 letter to the Secretary of State for the Colonies, Dobbs listed the defense of these prescriptive rights as one of his fundamental policy aims.[101] When the Government of Iraq moved to draft a law of land pos-session in 1926, Dobbs argued that this should be based not on an inquiry into titles but on "actual possession."[102] The extent of the landholdings of a particular tribe should be assessed on the basis of the area that the tribe had been in the habit of cultivating, irrespective of their ability at any spe-cific time to farm it all.[103]

Dobbs hoped that the result of this policy would be the establishment of 4,000-acre units of land. These would be held by a specific tribe on semipermanent tenure.[104] As he saw the tribe as being personified by the shaikh, Dobbs considered that the shaikh's role of protecting and organ-izing the tribe should be recognized by the government's granting him large sections of land, along with the task of collecting government rev-enue.[105] This would be recognition of the shaikh's efforts towards tribal management and mediation.

Dowson's understanding of rural society and his advice on land reform stood in contrast to that of Dobbs. Dowson saw rural Iraq as being com-posed of rational individual cultivators. Having followed the debate on land tenure from 1926, he took exception to both Dobbs's and Longrigg's ideas: "I do not myself think that either simplification, or public peace or economic advance are to be realized by a deliberate policy of establishing a series of large holders as intermediaries in dealing with the mass of smaller holders." [106]

Dowson saw a direct and instrumental link between a growth in tribal strength and a weak government. Under a feeble Ottoman Empire, the tribe, as a corporate entity, had imposed its will on the individual culti-vator, allotting land to them but also taking it away when it wanted to.[107] But with the end of the First World War and the rise of a stronger state, the individual cultivators had managed to assert their rights to the land they farmed:[108]

In many liwas I was afforded evidence of the numbers of smaller men paying their land revenue directly to provincial officials and occupying the position of smallholders, either as heads (sirakil) of minor tribal or other farming groups, or even on a more individual footing. And everywhere I was advised tribal disintegration was accelerating, everywhere the tribesman was becoming an individualist and wanting his individual holding.[109]

His conclusion on land-tenure reform was, interestingly, that the British administration should avoid the imposition of any stereotyped uniformity. Large landholders should be recognized when found to be protecting the smaller cultivators' rights. Where "genuine" tribal tenure still survived and was favored by the tribe, it should be acknowledged. But his impression was that such cases were rare. The society he encountered in Iraq was one increasingly made up of individual cultivators whose rights should be protected above all else and who would eventually form direct links with the government.

In a more ambiguous position—between that of Dowson and Dobbs—was Longrigg, whose approach was heavily criticized by both men. In trying to understand and reform the land registration system Longrigg did not want to totally abandon the Turkish approach. Instead, his aim was to inject a degree of precision and uniformity. For Longrigg, the population of rural Iraq and the land it farmed could be divided into two categories, tribal and nontribal. For those cultivators who were nontribal, Longrigg's prescription was similar to Dowson's: incremental measures should be imposed to establish rights, with title deeds being granted to individuals who were already in possession of the land.[110]

Of the tribal system itself, Longrigg thought, "it would be foolish to take unheeded steps to support or perpetuate it." But he understood its power to be such that "the formulation of a Land Policy . . . will, nevertheless, realize the actual potency and probable persistence of the tribal and social system in Iraq, and will endeavor to cooperate with or utilize it rather than clash with or prematurely . . . suppress it."[111] To this end, Longrigg thought it essential to recognize long-standing tribal occupation of land and use it as a reason for granting such tribes the legal right to cultivate this land.

Longrigg's main dispute with Dobbs centered on the internal structure of the tribe. Unlike the High Commissioner, Longrigg had no faith in tribal custom restraining shaikhs.

> The conferment of a Tapu sanad upon the Shaikh of the occupying tribe or even upon the various sarkals of sections, would be unjust to the individual tribesmen and contrary also to the general tribal policy of Government. . . . When this has been attempted, it has resulted either in the excessive and abused power of the Shaikhs, or in such conditions fatal to security and progress and yet not destructive to tribalism as are seen in the Muntafiq.[112]

Longrigg concluded that neither the shaikh nor the *sarkal* was responsible enough to own land. However, bringing in outside landowners could have potentially disastrous effects. His conclusion, though similar to Dowson's, was arrived at quite differently: the state was to remain as landlord of the majority of agricultural land, while the tribal system moved slowly towards disintegration.[113]

From 1914 until 1932 there was little or no difference between the goals set out for land policy by the British government in London and those of the British staff working in Iraq. Land policy sought to maximize revenue and support order. But until at least 1926 British attempts to achieve those goals were confused and dislocated. Having begun by agreeing to rule through Ottoman structures, they held to this improvised policy until a scramble for land subverted it. Yet, even after 1926, no dominant state-sanctioned policy was resolutely applied throughout Iraq.

The opposing sides of the land-tenure debate placed different explanatory weight on three different categories: the shaikh, the *sarkal,* and the *fallah.* The nature of the modern state that all the Mandate officials were actively involved in building meant that the units they deployed to understand Iraqi society had a profoundly homogenizing effect despite their important differences. By arguing for the place of the shaikh at the heart of Iraqi society, officials like Dobbs were transforming the relationship between the shaikh and members of the tribe. The act of quantifying what had previously been a nebulous relationship between shaikh and tribe institutionalized it, and large amounts of power were given to the shaikh. If the conception of society promoted by Dowson had in fact won out, similar homogenizing processes would have occurred. The social unit of the rational individual would have been imposed across Iraq in order to embody and enforce the state's understanding of society.

The uncompromising imposition of either category, the shaikh or the individual, did ontological violence to Iraqi society. This society had previously been made up of diverse social practices dependent on geographic, economic, and historical differences across the territory of what was to become Iraq.[114] Hence, the various interpretations of "shaikh" or "*sarkal*" were dependent on local specificities. The terms would therefore have had large variations in social and economic meaning across Iraq. The imposition of a modern state, with its modern method of social organization, meant that the terms shaikh, *sarkal*, or *fallah* would have to carry the same meaning across the whole country. The state could countenance no variations in category or land-tenure system however much administrators might disagree among themselves about the most desirable model of political and social development.

Chapter Seven

The Imposition of Order

SOCIAL PERCEPTION AND THE
"DESPOTIC" POWER OF AIRPLANES

With regard to military forces, the Royal Air Force . . . is the backbone of the whole organization. If the writ of King Faisal runs effectively through his kingdom, it is entirely due to the British airplanes.
It would be idle to affect any doubt on that point. If the airplanes
were removed tomorrow, the whole structure would inevitably fall to
pieces. Any locally raised forces without assistance from the air could
not maintain internal order nor resist external aggression. I do not
think that there can be any doubt whatever on that point. Owing to
difficulties of transport and communications, ground troops however
efficient cannot replace air control. —*Leopold Amery, 1925¹*

[T]here are only two things to fear—Allah and the *Hakumat al tayarrat*
[government by aircraft] —*A tribesman speaking to a Special Services
Officer, 1924²*

Colonial officials sent to build the Iraqi state under the Mandate
had limited coercive and financial resources with which to order
society. By the time Britain had been awarded the Mandate, her Empire
was in crisis, beset by upheavals and strapped for cash.³ This meant
coercive resources, the use of British and Indian army troops, were from
1920 onwards a sensitive political issue, subject to increasing press and
parliamentary hostility in London. After the 1920 revolt, the campaign
against British involvement reached such a height that cabinet discussions in London revolved around only two options: either a drastic
reduction in the costs of administration or complete withdrawal would
be necessary.

Winston Churchill's plan was to stop criticism while continuing
Britain's involvement in Iraq. His plan for controlling Iraq hinged on the
replacement of costly imperial troops by the newly formed Royal Air
Force (RAF). The interaction between the new, technological nature of

state control and the resulting perceptions of state officials revolutionized state-society relations in an unforeseen way.

Anthony Giddens has written that "All types of rule . . . rest upon the institutional mediation of power."[4] Recent social theory views the state as the handmaiden of a powerful modernity. For some theorists the essence of the modern state's power to discipline its population is the move from "wholesale" to "retail."[5] Individuals become specific targets of the state's power. They are inserted into the "micro-physics of power" where the panoptical ability of the state and its allied human sciences force him or her to internalize the rules governing personal behavior. This allows the state to dispense with the costly spectacle of violence and rely on subtler, more pervasive ways of exercising its power.

This move from wholesale to retail, crucial for understanding the modern European state, never happened under the Mandate. The nature and extent of the state's power, constrained by time, international opinion and most of all by lack of resources, never allowed for this concentration of administrative power. In order to understand the type and effect of the state's power in Iraq, then, a different understanding of state-society relations is needed. The political sociologist Michael Mann analyzes state power by breaking it down into three related aspects : ideological, economic, and military.[6] The making of the state in Iraq depended upon its ability to dispense largesse and upon the legitimacy conferred by the international promise to honor the principle of self-determination. Both of these attributes of the successful state, in the case of Iraq, were heavily underpinned and ultimately guaranteed by the overt and frequent deployment of organized violence. For Anthony Giddens a state's power is either allocative or authoritative.[7] Allocative power concerns the control of resources whereas authoritative power is the deployment of coercion to control the activities of the state's subjects. In the case of state-society relations under the Mandate, it was the state's ability to deploy violence simultaneously with the influence given to it by the exercise of largesse that defined the nature of its relations with the Iraqi population. More important still is Giddens's point that all power has to be mediated through state institutions and is transformed by the essence of this mediation. In Iraq, after 1921, the main institution mediating the application of state power was the RAF. The control of the population by airplane, although comparatively cheap and superficially attractive, had a profound effect on the way the state ruled Iraq and heightened a particular understanding of society.

Mann further distinguishes between infrastructural and despotic power.[8] Infrastructural power is based on the "the capacity of the state to actually penetrate civil society, and to implement logistically political decisions throughout the realm." It needs coherent and efficient state institutions that reach across the whole extent of a state's territory. The state also needs legitimacy to negotiate with civil society and have its presence and the extraction of resources seen as justifiable. Despotic power, on the other hand, involves "the range of actions which the élite is empowered to undertake without routine, institutionalized negotiations with civil society groups."[9] This can involve the extraction of resources from society without consent and the arbitrary but frequent deployment of violence to facilitate the state's survival.

The financial constraints that the mandated state worked under from 1920 until 1932 meant that it did not have the resources to deploy state-wide armed forces in great numbers or with any degree of permanence. Nor did it have the ideological legitimacy or bureaucratic institutions to extract greater military manpower from society by the enforcement of a conscription law. It was forced instead to rely on bombing to guarantee the collection of taxation and the enforcement of some kind of order. This had two consequences. First, it gave the British administration an overwhelming technological advantage over the population it was seeking to dominate. The start of the First World War had seen the Middle East flooded with modern, accurate and efficient rifles. This had greatly narrowed the weapons gap between British forces and what had become a heavily armed population and had made military domination a costly business in terms of lives and resources. The use of air power, represented a reversal of the weapons balance, with the state once again gaining and retaining the upper hand.[10]

The second consequence of the reliance on airplanes was that the power of the state in Iraq came to resemble that of Mann's definition of despotic power. The coercive manifestations of the state that carried the most weight were the fleeting visits of government airplanes. They regulated the broad parameters of permissible behavior by bombing tribes who were "out," rebelling against the government, or those which refused to pay taxation. This dependence upon air power led to the neglect of other state institutions. Power—counter to Michel Foucault's description of it— became largely symbolic, based on the demonstration of aircraft above recalcitrant tribes or the use of punitive bombing raids against tribes as an example to others.[11] The state through its dependence upon air power not only became detached from society but also hung two hundred feet above it, bombing people when they did not behave in the way the state wanted.

The triumphalism within the British cabinet that resulted from the signing of the armistice of Mudros on October 30, 1918 was replaced relatively quickly by the stark realization that Britain's newly-achieved predominance in the Middle East had to be secured and sustained within strict financial limits.[12] In 1918 the government's spending deficit was running at £1,690 million a year, with British exports failing to recover their prewar levels.[13] It had also become clear that attempts to lure the United States into the Middle East to share the burden of controlling the area were not going to succeed.[14]

With the rising specter of industrial and political unrest at home, domestic demands for speedy demobilization and the continuing problem of Ireland, the already stretched deployment of British troops became unmanageable. In July 1920, the Chief of the imperial General Staff summed up the situation:

> In no single theatre are we strong enough, not in Ireland, not in England, not on the Rhine, not in Constantinople, nor Batoum, nor Egypt, nor Palestine, nor Mesopotamia, nor Persia, nor India.

To add to this problem, the defense budget was cut in half each year between 1919 and 1923.[15] Before the First World War, the Empire had been controlled by the use of Indian troops, and Indian tax to pay for them, but political instability on the sub-continent had made this no longer feasible. The head of the military, as early as 1919, had sought an answer to these problems by suggesting the concentration of troops in the "coming storm centers" of the Empire: Ireland, Egypt and India. His advice had little effect on his political masters.[16]

The precarious nature of the armed forces' control in the Middle East was brought home to those in Baghdad and London alike by the 1920 revolt in Iraq. The incoherence of British policy towards Iraq from the end of the war until 1920 had allowed A.T. Wilson, the acting High Commissioner, to pursue his own vision of how Iraq should be run. By the end of Ramadan in June 1920, his insensitivity to the politically active in the Iraqi population, the increasing desperation of Faisal and his entourage to capture British attention and the disgruntlement of the heavily taxed tribes in southern Iraq, had exploded into a widespread revolt against the British presence in the country.[17] The revolt lasted through July, August and September, with British control firmly re-established only in February 1921. At its peak the rebels managed to field an estimated 131,000 men across Iraq. Of these the British army estimated that 17,000 had modern rifles comparable in accuracy, speed and reliability to those of the imperial troops they were fighting against.[18]

The 1920 revolt had the immediate effect of focusing the British government's collective mind. How could order be maintained in such a turbulent area, in the face of drastic budgetary restrictions, while the international responsibilities of the Mandate were being fulfilled? Churchill (possibly with the public humiliation of the campaign in the Dardanelles still fresh in his mind) forced both the cabinet and the administration in Iraq to focus on the unsustainable nature of the current situation. From May 1920 onwards he began suggesting drastic policy solutions in cabinet, recommending the evacuation of outlying regions and then arguing that, by pulling British forces all the way back to Basra, the cost of occupation could be cut from £30 million to a more sustainable £8 million.[19] He coupled this with direct threats addressed to the administration in Iraq, stressing that the continuation of the British presence hung in the balance.[20]

The combined result of the revolt and the rise of a new realism in London about British capabilities in the Middle East resulted in the convening of the Cairo Conference in March 1921. Churchill assembled over forty military and civilian experts for a week in Cairo to determine the best way forward for British policy in the region.[21] The overall conclusions of the conference were that the emphasis of British policy should be shifted in an attempt to rely more on ideological and economic power than on force. Resources previously expended on military control would be drastically reduced in favor of subsidies paid to indigenous rulers, who, in theory, were to reign with the consent of the population.[22] Militarily, the success of the plan rested on a speedy and thorough reduction of imperial troops stationed in Iraq. The imperial garrison was reduced to twelve battalions by 1 October 1921, and then to just four battalions by a year later.[23]

The success of the Cairo Conference scheme and the continued British presence in Iraq depended on the ability of the Mandated state to maintain order while simultaneously reducing the cost of Iraq to the British exchequer. Order and economy were to dominate British concerns until the end of the Mandate in 1932.[24] These apparently contradictory aims could be achieved only by the massive technological innovation represented by the development of air policing. The airplane became "the backbone of the whole organization."[25] Air power was the "midwife" in the birth of the Iraqi state. Without it, the whole Mandate project would have been in jeopardy.[26]

The Cairo Conference plan not only launched the air-policing scheme but also set about creating indigenous armies in the hope that they would eventually take over responsibility for the creation of internal order and, ultimately, external defense. This, it was hoped, would assist in the speedy reduction of imperial troops and cut the defense budget. But the post-Versailles international system under which these armies were being created complicated this task. At the heart of Churchill's plan was the creation of indigenously run states with native armies under the banner of Wilsonian self-determination. The Iraqi army was to be staffed, run and funded by Iraqis. This division of control between a shrinking imperial power and a growing yet untried indigenous élite was a constant source of tension between Iraq and Britain. Combined with the acute shortage of financial resources, this tension stifled the growth of the army, leading to it becoming an appendage of a planned Iraqi air force.

The decision to create an indigenous army unleashed a struggle among competing constituencies revealing different interests in, and disagreements about, every aspect of the new Iraqi army. The two constituencies based in London were the Colonial Office, primarily concerned with Britain's international responsibilities and the cost of the Iraqi Mandate, and the Air Ministry, which was responsible for British imperial forces in Iraq and for Britain's overall strategic interests in the Middle East. Yet, although there were clear tensions between the Colonial Office and the Air Ministry in London, the main battle, over the nature and size of the army to be built in Iraq, was fought out in Baghdad.

The main group in Iraq, who would ultimately inherit the state and its army, consisted of King Faisal and the Hashemite officers he had brought with him from Syria. There was also the British Mandate administration in Iraq, officials employed by the Colonial Office to oversee the creation of the state. The violent disagreements between these two groups about the growth and use of the Iraqi army had their roots in differing conceptions of the role and nature of the state they were building, its relation to Iraqi society, and, ultimately, what the Iraqi nation was and what it should become. Faisal and his Hashemite officers wanted to build an army that would be the personification and instrument of a strong Arab state. To this end they favored a mass conscript army that would act as an institution of, and weapon for, the imposition of national unity. They wanted to build an army through which young Iraqi conscripts would learn Arabic and a Hashemite vision of Iraqi nationalism. Such an army would become a powerful symbol of an independent Hashemite state.

The British High Commissioner and his staff saw the army in very different terms. Their approach was dominated by what they saw as strict financial, but also social, constraints within which the new state would be forced to work. The Mandate staff wanted to build a small and efficient army that would guarantee internal order without bankrupting the state. Dobbs especially feared the possibility of a larger army becoming the tool of a government with despotic aspirations. Those British advisers with influence on the growth of the army chose for the rank and file those they considered the most representative and efficient.

How was the army to achieve the level of efficiency and strength it needed to replace imperial troops and guarantee order across the country? How and where would the personnel for this army be found? Could the state afford a professional volunteer army or was it strong enough to enforce conscription on an unwilling and well-armed society? The financial and ideological impasse created by these questions was overcome only when all sides agreed on the creation of an Iraqi air force.

From within the Iraqi political class, the most active, vocal and homogeneous group concerned with the issue of the army were those who can be usefully classified as Hashemites.[27] Their positions of power, expertise in military matters and close links to the Palace led them to become the major pressure group from within the Iraqi élite — one which scrutinized British attitudes towards defense and demanded change. Aside from King Faisal, Nuri Said and Ja'far al Askari were two of the most prominent and powerful of this circle.[28] Before Faisal's arrival in Iraq, Ja'far had actively promoted his kingship and by the mid-twenties Nuri had in effect become Faisal's right-hand man.[29]

Both Ja'far and Nuri had had wide-ranging experience and had fully formed opinions on the role of the military in society. They had both studied at the Military Academy and Staff College of the Ottoman army in Istanbul. The leading authority on these men notes that there was something of a "martial temper" about them; a "partiality for a forced social change, for a push from above."[30]

From the early days the issue of the Iraqi army had deeply divided Iraqi politicians. Certainly Ja'far and Nuri were overly concerned with military matters, constantly pushing for the expansion of the army to the exclusion of wider issues of socio-economic development.[31] For them the first step in state building was the creation of a strong and autonomous army. This fuelled a series of clashes between the Hashemites and more established urban notables in the nascent cabinet. At a meeting of the Council of Ministers in May 1921, the proposed appointment of Nuri as head of the army caused unease among those present. The *naqib*, with a prescient reference to the Committee of Union and Progress and Faisal's short reign in Syria, warned of the dangers inherent in building an army unrestrained by the rules and regulations of civilian government. The Council, then, instead of agreeing to appoint a largely autonomous head of the army, demanded to see a general program for the building of a national defense force before they would countenance Nuri's appointment.[32]

In response to the bitterness that this debate fuelled, the High Commissioner wrote to the Council taking the Hashemites' side. He pointed out that the British Government regarded the making of speedy progress with the creation of the army as the most important and urgent problem which lay before the Arab Government, and he asked that army questions should be given precedence over all other business in the council.

At the same time he wrote privately to the *naqib* promoting the Hashemite cause, stressing that Nuri and Ja'far were regarded by the British as trustworthy allies, that their skills and experience made them indispensable to the Iraqi army and that the government should rely on them as much as possible.[33]

This clash of opinions over the position of the armed forces in the new Iraq caused the fall of the first cabinet appointed after Faisal's coronation. Against the background of increasing violence and raiding across the southern desert from Saudi Arabia, Faisal demanded that a much larger proportion of government expenditure be devoted to defense. Sasun Hesqel, the Minister of Finance, and also an important Jewish Baghdadi merchant, refused to stop development projects in education and irrigation to pump money into the army instead. The ensuing trial of strength resulted in the fall of the government.[34]

This dispute was ultimately resolved in two ways. As the king and the Hashemites began to gain ascendancy over other political groupings within Iraq, it became less of an issue. More importantly, Nuri, Ja'far and the king set about building a specifically Hashemite army, loyal to the king and his retainers and not to the wider Iraqi government. Indeed, by July 1922, when the *naqib* asked Ja'far whether the army was loyal enough to be used to suppress internal uprisings, Ja'far could reply that "Arabs could not be relied upon to fight against Arabs." When asked the same question shortly afterwards in private by the king, his answer was that "the Iraqi Army would obey his [the king's] orders to a man."[35]

Throughout the Mandate period, the king used the army as the ultimate symbol of national pride and dignity, tenderly nurtured by Hashemite hands and easily trampled upon by British insensitivity or mendacity. In this guise the extent to which the High Commissioner and Colonial Office would acquiesce in the king's military plans became the personification of British sincerity and the primary test of the degree to which they would deliver the long-promised independence. British Ministers for the Colonies and Air suggested in 1925 that the efficiency of the Iraqi army would be increased by the appointment of British officers in positions of executive control. This was seen by the king and the Prime Minister as an unmasking of Britain's true intent. The Prime Minister saw this as "the thin end of the wedge" designed to safeguard British investments by keeping the army small and powerless. For the king this was part of a general British policy used throughout the region to deprive Arab armies of all power and secure the air-route to India.[36]

It was over the issue of conscription that the themes of state power, army efficiency and the lack of mutual trust between Britain and Iraq came to dominate the interaction among the Mandate officials, the king and his Hashemite courtiers. For the Hashemites conscription eclipsed all other military matters. Ja'far had been Minister of Defense in the first Iraqi cabinet for less than a month when he suggested it as the only way to build an efficient army. The Hashemite vision of the role of the state and the character of the nation therefore fused over the issue of conscription. Ja'far saw compulsion as the only way to transform ordinary people into satisfactory soldiers. The only suitable candidates for this transformation were those with "a certain stake in the country." [37] These people were not the "homeless wandering" Kurds and Bedouin, but those property owners who were tied to the soil of the Iraqi nation.[38] Obviously, the state could not afford to tempt such people into a volunteer army and so had to resort to conscription. The bias towards townspeople by the Hashemites was written off by the High Commissioner as a manifestation of the weakness of the state. But consistent with Ja'far's first musings on the subject, this commitment to an urban social base for the army represented the Hashemite ideal of the Iraqi nation, one comprised of the urban lower and middle classes—much the same as the Hashemites themselves—not of the majority tribal population favored by the British.

The Hashemite vision of a mass conscripted army mirrored their conception of the state and nation. Conscription of the urban population into the army would forcibly create a homogeneous and loyal nation through state action. The army was to be the primary tool of education and state building. In the early 1920s, the Hashemites saw reliance on an air force as being misplaced as it did not allow nation-building to happen. When Nuri was struggling to build a mass conscript army, the resources diverted into the air force were a distraction. Although it could exact revenge through bombing, the air force could not hold territory or impress the government's propaganda on the population.[39]

The British were philosophically opposed to the state vision of the Hashemites. The High Commissioner, as the personification of British power and responsibility in Iraq, embodied British opposition. He represented the overwhelming advantage in military power that Mandate officials had over Iraqi politicians. Dobbs summed up his power by claiming that "the sheet anchor" of the British role in the country was the threat to withhold military assistance to the Iraqi government.[40] Institutionalized by formal agreement, this meant that any decisions taken by the Iraqi government against the High Commissioner's advice which resulted in social unrest or violence would not be supported by the intervention of imperial forces. This veto, although overshadowing the whole Anglo-Iraqi relationship, was overtly threatened only on military matters, specifically the issue of conscription.

Throughout the Mandate period, the High Commissioners were aware of the constraints within which they were working. The conflict was between furthering the strategic interests of Britain whilst meeting the demands from London for a rapid reduction in expenditure. The primary and constant goal of those in London was to reduce the costs of the Mandate by forcing the Iraqi government to take greater financial and strategic responsibility for its own defense as soon as it could. But juxtaposed against this was the contradictory goal of securing and furthering Britain's strategic interests in Iraq and the wider Middle East. These tensions caused an incoherent and frequently changing policy towards the Iraqi army.[41]

Added to these competing aims were the contradictory goals of Henry Dobbs. Following the 1920 revolt, High Commissioners had been acutely aware of the potential strength of tribal society in comparison to that of the state. But, with his perception of the legacy of Ottoman despotism, Dobbs was equally concerned by the ability and perceived desire of Baghdad's politicians to use the army to dominate and oppress the largely rural society. This series of contradictions between power and economy and state and society all came together over the Hashemites' demands for a large conscript army.

The creation of an effective Iraqi army was at the core of the Cairo Conference plan but was always a major focus of dispute. By 1926 it was listed in intelligence reports as the "first chief problem" remaining to be addressed.[42] Even then it remained unclear to the High Commissioner and his staff just what type of army Iraq should have and how they should get it. After the Mosul dispute with Turkey had been settled, Dobbs saw little chance of an invasion from either Iran or Turkey. This left internal security as the principal problem. Dobbs worried about the heavily armed rural population, but, unlike the Hashemites, he believed that economic expansion and minimum taxation were essential for a quiescent society. The military was the main draw on government resources and Dobbs saw a rapid expansion of the army as the most likely cause of an armed uprising.[43] The army thus became for him not a tool of stability and national integration but a cause of instability and potential mass rebellion. This clash of outlook with the Hashemites sprang partly from Dobbs's conception of state weakness, but also from a set of beliefs about an attainable balance of power between state and society.

Faced with the continuing battle of wills and the shortage of funds, Dobbs concluded by the mid-1920s that the creation of an Iraqi air force was the only realistic way of guaranteeing internal order. A 10,000-man army would act as the air force's appendage. For Dobbs, accepting the Air Ministry's propaganda, the reach of the state would be limited only by the role and utility of aircraft. The Hashemites would be denied the ability of bankrupting the state and dominating society through the creation of the all-encompassing institution of a mass army.[44]

If the Hashemite ideal for the Iraqi army mirrored their vision of what the Iraqi state and nation should look like, then Dobbs's understanding of the military equally reflected his own conception of Iraqi society and his wishes for the state. Mirroring imperial cultural constructions of the "martial races," Dobbs saw the urban classes favored by the Hashemites as being effete.[45] He therefore constantly encouraged the recruitment of tribal soldiers for the rank and file and sons of shaikhs for the officer class.[46] This was reflected in recruitment for the military college, with the enlistment forms sent to each *liwa* stating that recruits had to be verifiably the sons of a shaikh or head of a tribe.[47]

The results of this developing battle of wills over the social composition of the army were mixed. At the creation of the army, 640 ex-Ottoman and ex-Sharifian officers were inducted into it. This largely urban bias remained, with only 25 per cent of officers having a tribal origin. But amongst the rank and file the picture was more mixed, with anything from 37 per cent to 74 per cent of each regiments' troops being drawn from the tribes, mainly those based between the Tigris and Euphrates south of Baghdad.[48] It was conscription that revealed the true depth of the fault lines dividing the Hashemites and the British.

From the early 1920s, both Henry Dobbs and Cornwallis, the Adviser to the Ministry of Interior, saw that conscription would arouse the intense hostility of the rural population across Iraq. Dobbs understood this potential hostility as having its roots in Ottoman rule, when, he thought, a general fear of the state was all-pervading. But this adamant opposition to conscription did not subside throughout the 1920s. In 1925, the conscription bill was drafted for application in 1928. Dobbs argued that Britain would have few imperial forces left in the country by then. If the High Commissioner was asked to help impose the unpopular conscription law across rural Iraq, it would have to be done by aircraft. By bombing the tribes to enforce a widely-resisted law, "the popular dislike of it would concentrate itself on the British, and there would be every kind of misrepresentation of British intentions." [49]

The British administration would be helping to enforce an unpopular law at a time when the forces it had at its disposal would be at their weakest. Dobbs warned that not only would this focus discontent on the few remaining British troops in the country, but

> failure would be followed by a widespread tribal combination and rising which might easily bring about a return of the conditions of 1920, conditions which *ex hypothesi* the Iraq Army would have to attempt to suppress without any aid from British forces.[50]

As the debate surrounding conscription developed, both sides recognized that the Iraqi state was not strong enough to conscript the tribal sections of the population. This left the urban and suburban sections of society as the only source of possible recruits. For Dobbs and Cornwallis this presented another set of problems. On a practical level, the removal of a large section of the workforce would have a negative effect on "sub-urban agriculture."[51] The supposed qualities of these potential recruits fuelled British unease with the scheme. Cornwallis argued that the scheme would fail to produce the "virile . . . tribal element so necessary for the army" and was hardly worth pursuing.[52] Dobbs agreed, believing that even the "best townsmen" would not match the fighting skills and courage of the "ordinary tribesman." [53]

The British position resulting from these concerns created a policy hostile to conscription. But because the Hashemites had made the army, and by extension conscription, the touchstone of British sincerity, it could not be actively opposed. Dobbs and Cornwallis recognized that conscription offered a solution to the desperately needed expansion of the armed forces, although they favored a volunteer army recruited on the basis of attractive rates of pay. In the end, it was decided to let the Iraqi government proceed with conscription if and when they believed their own armed forces were strong enough to enforce it independently of any British support.[54]

The fiercely contested nature of military policy in Iraq, the growing power of the Iraqi political élite, British indecision and the general scarcity of finance all combined to undermine the growth of the Iraqi army. Recruitment, training and deployment all suffered from changing policy priorities and the confusion inherent in having two separate military forces, two separate chains of command and two sets of objectives, Iraqi and British, competing to administer order. It is hardly surprising that as early as 1923, Iraqi politicians were pressing for the creation of their own air force. In addition to citing the same argument that had made air policing so attractive to Churchill in Cairo in 1921— the economic efficiency it gave state control— Iraqi politicians added a new element. Air control developed as a way to defend state violence from negative press coverage in Britain. Air policing, the Iraqi Prime Minister stated, was "extremely efficient" and "a merciful instrument of government." The answer to the defense problems of the new Iraqi state would be to equip it with airplanes.[55] With the primary goal of the Colonial Office in London being the reduction of both direct military spending and the subsidies needed to support the Iraqi state, the logic of the position was undeniable. By the end of 1923, the High Commissioner, whilst fearful of the new power airplanes would give to the Iraqi state, was persuaded of their value and began to push for the creation of an Iraqi air force.[56] Despite opposition from the Air Ministry, fearful of nationalist reaction in India and Egypt, the Military agreement drafted in 1924 and attached to the new Anglo-Iraqi treaty, foresaw the building of an Iraqi air force. Iraqi pilots would be trained in England taking over responsibility for the preservation of order once Iraq had entered the League of Nations.[57]

The political contest over military policy from 1920 until 1932 effectively stymied the development of a state-wide military force capable of creating and preserving order. As the Hashemite political élite gained greater power over the creation of the army, their goals for the nation, and the military's position within it, came increasingly into direct conflict with British intentions. Ultimately, neither side in Baghdad had the resources to create an efficient army. Reliance upon the air force remained the state's means of enforcing its will. Unlike that of the army, airplanes enabled the rapid deployment of retribution against rebels. This power was necessarily a blunt instrument, however, mediating state-society relations in a one-dimensional way. By relying on aircraft, the Iraqi state developed a modern but nonetheless despotic state power. State institutions did not penetrate society, and therefore the state's presence became neither permanent nor legitimate to the Iraqi people. It was fleeting and violent with a limited and extractive purpose.

> The development of the military aircraft created a weapon with the near-miraculous property of lengthening the arm of government whilst shortening its purse. —*Charles Townsend*[58]

The development of a new strategy of air power and the use of Iraq as its laboratory were not immediately popular amongst military and political circles. For institutional reasons, it is not surprising that the main criticism came from the army, the service it was designed to replace. Although the scheme had been devised to meet Henry Wilson's charge of imperial overreach, the Chief of the imperial General Staff was not initially supportive of the scheme.[59]

The very novelty of the new technology meant that its utility and methods were doubted by those not directly involved in its development and application. There was a need from the outset to construct an ideology surrounding air power that would explain its use and promote its effectiveness. The ideology first stressed air power's uniqueness. The airplane gained a military identity by claiming to be everything that the army was not. With the horrors of the static and bloody trench warfare of the Western Front still very much in the public mind, the airplane was sold as a break with the past, drawing a line separating the present from past mistakes. For its promoters, it was cheap, precise and quick. It involved small numbers of people on both sides, its effects were immediate, in contrast to the drawn out stalemate of ground war. Above all, its targets were material not human. The strategy governing this new military tool was to have an entirely different logic, one governed by RAF personnel and distinct from anything that had preceded it.[60]

The ideology of air power bore all the hallmarks of its age. It was explicitly developed as a technology of control not occupation. Whereas at the height of imperial conquest large armies had stamped the character of Britain on the center of seized territory, the airplane's effects were diffuse. It was also to be deployed against a new category of the world's population, that of the "semi-civilized." Linked to the philosophy of the Mandate ideal, the "semi-civilized" were involved in a process of evolution, with a recognized and respected material and cultural civilization that needed the distant discipline of the airplane, not the ever-present occupation of the army.

Key to the promotion of air power was its definition as being an explicitly moral instrument of social control. Those championing it against charges that bombing was "hunnish" and unsportsmanlike contrasted it with the effects of sending a column of troops to subdue an area. British public disquiet about this novel war technology was blamed on a general lack of education. In 1920 A.T. Wilson argued that the people of Iraq, being fully acquainted with the pros and cons of air power, viewed it as "a legitimate and proper form of warfare." Hence it was only a matter of time before the British public would do the same. Air power was novel not brutish.[61] The morality of using air power lay in its alleged mercy. Although, if given full rein, its effects could be "very severe," this was rarely if ever necessary.[62] Instead, it was claimed, casualties were usually "remarkably small," even "negligible." [63] Air strategy made a virtue out of technological shortcomings. The chief targets of air action were not the miscreants themselves but their property. Bombing would target the livelihoods of those tribes that were misbehaving; it attacked livestock, grain and fuel stores and the houses of those communities it wanted to punish. Because complete surprise "was impossible"

> the real weight of air action lies in the daily interruption of normal life which it can inflict, if necessary for an indefinite period, while offering negligible chance of loot or hitting back.[64]

The target was thus transformed. This was not a conventional attack on individual life and limb, but a

> moral attack upon the nerves, the habits, and the means of livelihood of the peoples against whom it is necessary to take action, and its moral effect is obviously enhanced in the case of semi-civilized

people by the fact that it is a weapon against which they cannot effectively retaliate.[65]

The symbolic effect of the planes themselves further expanded the theme of the moral and comparatively cost-free nature of air power. In reverse of Foucault's dictum that modern power involves the move from spectacle to intrusion, those developing the ideological promotion of airplanes claimed their mere presence in the air above a trouble spot was usually more than enough to halt a potential insurrection. The power of "demonstrations" as opposed to actual bombing was first noted by A.T. Wilson as early as 1918 and was again cited by him and Sir A. Haldane, the Commander in Chief of British forces in Iraq, as a reason why certain areas of Southern Iraq did not join the 1920 revolt.[66]

The "moral" use of the airplane in contrast to its capacity for violence was stressed throughout the 1920s and integrated into a theory of state-building. Government could "show the flag" and emphasize its capacity for influence in areas too inaccessible for regular administration by directing airplanes to patrol the area. This faith in the symbolic power of planes appears to have sprung from the idea that the tribesmen appreciated the awesome destructive potential of bombing and the unbridgeable gap in technology between them and the state the planes represented. If this appreciation began to fade with familiarity, then a bombing mission or the threat of one would soon restore it.[67]

The disciplinary impact of planes was extended to their power of surveillance. In March 1920 the Air Staff claimed that

It must be remembered that from the ground every inhabitant of a village is under the impression that the occupant of the airplane is looking at *him*, and the frequent, and perhaps daily appearance of aircraft apparently overhead will do much towards establishing the impression that all their movements are being watched and reported.[68]

This allowed supporters to claim a highly centralized but detailed intelligence system as another benefit of the air-policing scheme.[69] The moral defense of air policing lay in the limited effect it had as a weapon on humans. Its real attraction in the 1920s and 1930s was the economy of the control it delivered. Crucial to this was the rapidity with which an air operation could be launched:

> almost before the would-be rebel has formulated his plans, the droning of the airplanes is heard overhead, and in the majority of cases their mere appearance is enough.[70]

Retribution for misdeeds could fall from the skies within twelve to twenty-four hours of the act. In military terms, this allowed an almost immediate response to challenges to government authority taking place hundreds of miles from Baghdad.

The construction of the ideology surrounding air power gained its coherence and strength from drawing a stark contrast with the use of armed troops. With the horrors of the First World War still weighing on the British population, the wasteful destructiveness of infantry was easily contrasted with the clean and efficient deployment of airplanes. In the time it took to organize a punitive expedition of troops, the rebels would have had the space to find allies for their cause. Planes, on the other hand, could be there in hours. By marching into an area troops offered a target to well-armed rebels who wanted to strike out against a recognized government institution. By removing the target for retaliation, planes also removed the chances of potential booty and so undermined one of the alleged main incentives to revolt.

> [A]ir action rapidly taken at the focus of trouble, and before it has a chance to spread, and discriminating in its incidence, is in every way a less severe and yet a more powerful corrective than the visit of a column of troops to a then extended area of trouble, with its inevitable accompaniment of destruction and tribal retaliation, and casualties to both sides and long-remaining misery in the area visited.[71]

Trenchard, the Chief of Air Staff from 1919, and Churchill, Minister for the Colonies from 1921, sought to promote air power as a solution to the "crisis of empire" in the Middle East for their own reasons.[72] But they both agreed on the way it was to be promoted and defended. The vulnerability of the army as an instrument and the drawbacks of mass and unpredictable slaughter were to be escaped through deployment of a clean, efficient and moral technology. Airplanes, as a new form of coercion, combined with the Mandates as a new form of government, would allow order to be brought to the Middle East in a time of British austerity. What was not appreciated in the Colonial Office, the Air Ministry or amongst the governing classes of Baghdad, however, was how the efficiency and economy of air policing would directly influence the process of state-building in ways no one quite imagined.

British perception of Iraqi society, the comparative weakness of both British imperial forces and the nascent Iraqi army, and the ideological climate all united to structure the way in which air power was used in Iraq. The planes' bombs and machine-guns were blunt instruments and therefore dependent for their effect on a readily available intermediary on the ground. The shaikh, as the dominant figure of the tribe, would be the enforcer and guarantor of the order deployed by the state's airplanes.

Three dominant themes emerged as air power was tentatively tested in the early years of the 1920s, institutionalized after 1923 and then used as the main instrument for providing order until 1932. First, efficiency: it could get to places troops could not or should not go. Secondly, knowledge: the maps planes provided confirmed and consolidated the dominant understanding of rural Iraq. Third, triumphalism: the destructive force of the new weapon was widely celebrated as a vindicating testament to western superiority over the world's backward peoples.

The first period during which air power was used ran from the First World War to October 1922 when the RAF took over responsibility for the provision of order in Iraq. Internationally this was a period of great turmoil and political uncertainty. The British government's attitude to Iraq underwent a profound change and policy, both political and military, had to change with it. Until October 1922 air power was not the main coercive tool used to enforce order across Iraq. It acted as a useful and novel ancillary to the army. However, its utility became increasingly apparent. In Kurdistan, around Rowanduz, and in the south of Iraq, in the marshes around Suq and Hammar Lake, the British army struggled with the geography as it attempted to impose the will of central government on the more peripheral areas of Iraq. In both these areas it quickly became apparent that the utility of airplanes greatly outweighed that of ground troops. Casualties were minimized and the novelty of the new technology startled its adversaries.[73]

Although the rationale for the deployment of air power was not fully articulated until 1923, the dominant discourse concerning Iraqi society structured the use of airplanes from the beginning. It was tribal shaikhs who felt the full force of the bombing. They were the targets of the airplanes and it was their guarantees that would result in the order to stop the planes from returning to bomb again.[74] The initial success of airplanes led the Commander in Chief in 1921, General Haldane, to make the bold claim that "had I sufficient aircraft last year I might have prevented the insurrection spreading from beyond the first incident at Rumaitha."[75]

From the moment the Royal Air Force took over formal responsibility for military order in Iraq from the army in October 1922,the need for a large-scale operation against an unruly section of the population was clear.[76] It would enable the much trumpeted theory of air power to be put into practice, silencing those skeptics who thought it unworkable. It would also further refine the regular use of air power so that eventually it could be perfected and exported to the rest of the Empire.

The first large-scale deployment of air power was against the Barkat and Sufran sections of the Bani Huchaim confederation at Samawah on the Euphrates. This early example of concerted air policing underscores the way the social vision of the Colonial officials directed the creation of the new state. That early bombing also helped put in place a set of rules by which recalcitrant tribes were to be judged on whether they were sufficiently deviant to be subjected to bombing. Ultimately, the bombing of Barkat and Sufran draws attention to the combination of state vision and new technology that determined the direction of the new state institutions.

Political and technical reasons made the Samawah *qadha* in southern Iraq the ideal choice for the debut of air power. Until the bombing at the end of November 1923, this small area was portrayed as the epitome of all the problems the new state faced in establishing its authority. Military action in the area from 1914 onwards also highlighted the fitful nature of the control that British forces, at their strongest—at the end of the war and after the suppression of the 1920 rebellion—actually had over Iraq. For the whole of the war and up to the autumn of 1920, British troops had not entered the area. When Glubb was preparing to survey the *qadha* in October 1923 he complained that the civil authorities had no data on it at all.[77] When he traveled through Samawah he was surprised to find that "very few" of the shaikhs he met "had ever seen a British officer."[78]

For those planning air action the area had been "untouched and intolerant of Government" under the Turks and had remained so for the British.[79] The Barkat's and the al Sufran's constant defiance of government had ranged from refusing to pay the rifle fines levied on them in the aftermath of the rebellion, to the kidnapping and beating of the *Mudir* of Roumeith and the chasing of both the Iraqi Levies and the Police from the area when they attempted to make arrests. [80] Their proximity to the Baghdad-Basra railway meant that their rebelliousness threatened national communications, while their frequent raiding of major roads and towns in the area highlighted the continued weakness of government.[81]

This instability was blamed on the sub-standard nature of the al Sufran's and the Barkat's tribal solidarity. Their coherence as tribes had deteriorated under Turkish influence contributing to high levels of intratribal violence.[82] Glubb on his second reconnaissance of the area noted that the disintegration of tribal structures had led to the rise of a plethora of smaller shaikhs with the power to make mischief. These "petty chiefs" living in a state of anarchy were well armed and situated in over 44 forts in 40 square miles.[83] They built unauthorized dams that cut off other people from water supplies and also engaged in constant fighting.

The Samawah *qadha* exemplified social instability for the British. Its tribal structures had begun to deteriorate so that its internal logic and order were failing. It had escaped all governmental discipline and was ripe to be taught an exemplary lesson. There were good technical reasons too for choosing this particularly troublesome area. Part of the justification of air policing was to distinguish it from the traditional uses of ground troops. Samawah was the perfect place to demonstrate this alternative. The failure of troops, both British and Iraqi, to enter the area could be blamed for its instability. The area's rebelliousness could be explained primarily by its geography: the *qadha* was criss-crossed by numerous water channels, making the passage of pack animals or motor vehicles almost impossible. Hence the number of troops needed to dominate it would be "out of all proportion" to the possible results of any operation.[84] A suc-

cessful attempt to bring the area under control, carried out before reducing the British garrison to two battalions, would also boost confidence in
air policing and the ability of the remaining forces to control the country.[85] It was also claimed that this was exactly the type of area where the
intervention of ground troops would inflame the situation, uniting the
disparate sections of the tribe, allowing "the tribesmen to descend like a
swarm of bees on the troops."

The geographic and strategic inaccessibility of Samawah meant that it
had to be thoroughly mapped before any coercive action could be taken.
Both the Administrative Inspector in the *liwa* and the Air Officer Commanding stressed that the operations map drawn up in advance of the
bombing made it "possible and even simple."[86]

Glubb mapped the area during two trips in November 1923. Social
cognition was clearly supported and was in turn reinforced by the deployment of air power. Glubb saw his task as "pin-pointing the shaikhs for
subsequent bombing purposes." To this end he visited as many tribal
leaders as possible to establish which were important enough to warrant
bombing. The operations map that resulted was divided into two categories: the general positioning of the tribes; and "the location of the villages belonging to the Shaikhs and Headmen whose influence amongst
the tribes rendered them particularly suitable for attack."[87]

The society of Samawah had been "heroically simplified" by Glubb
using the discourse the British staff employed to create the state. First, the
area to be bombed was divided into the two sections of one tribe, the
Beni Huchaim, thought to dominate the district. Glubb then ranked the
shaikhs and headmen of each section in order of influence and size. The
point was to identify the "nominal shaikh" of each section. A complex
and "fuzzy" society was thus transformed, rationalized into discreet
objects of cognition and control. By deploying the collective social vision
through which they understood Iraqi rural society, the British ordered
Samawah in a way that they could understand. This ordering was seen
not as an imposition but as the delineation of authentic social structures.

The trigger for the bombing to start would be the issuing of a general
ultimatum. The "nominal shaikhs" identified by Glubb would be told to
surrender to the government in Samawah town within twenty-four
hours. They were to be informed of their long-standing delinquent
behavior, told they must deposit monetary security against their future

good behavior, guarantee the safety of all government officials entering the area and, finally, pay the arrears of their *koda* tax.[88] The weight of government-imposed order was to fall upon the shaikhs identified by Glubb. For Glubb and his commanders these shaikhs represented their communities. They were responsible for their tribe's obeying these orders.

The possibility of a mismatch between British perceptions of the position of the "nominal shaikh" and their actual role became apparent before the bombing started. Khashan al Jazi, the nominal shaikh of the Barkat, and Azzarah al Ma'jun, the nominal shaikh of the al Sufran, both duly arrived at *qadha* headquarters. Khashan and Azzarah were informed of their duties and sent back to "their" tribes with a government official to collect the bond for future good behavior. Much to the chagrin of the Administrative Inspector, not only did Azzarah return the next day empty-handed but he refused to accept responsibility for his section and even requested police support to enable him to maintain his own village. Khashan al Jazi delivered the same response the following day.[89] Far from being able to meet government demands, they had "made no real effort to comply with the terms imposed" and were "merely attempting to evade them." So "as they refused to come in, their area was severely bombed" for two days and nights.[90]

The effects of this sustained bombing raid surprised the tribesmen it targeted. It also induced awe of bombing's destructive powers in those who had ordered the attack. The novel deployment of night bombing caught villagers returning home after hiding from daytime raids. It also, according to RAF reports, did "away with the idea that they [the targets] will ever have any period of peace once an attack has begun."[91] Night bombing heightened the audiovisual spectacle of air power, making it apparent to tribes in a wide area, imposing upon them an understanding of the new might and reach of the state. A further technological innovation increased the planes' destructive power: incendiary bombs. With the huts of southern Iraq being constructed from reeds, the effect of night bombing was to spread fires throughout the target villages.[92]

The costs for these targeted villages were heavy. Flight Lieutenant Bowen, who was sent into the area to assess the damage, conservatively estimated that approximately 100 men, women and children had been killed, and six villages destroyed, along with six horses, 71 cows and 530 sheep.[93] This first foray into sustained aerial assault on the population of Iraq considerably undermined the ideological promotion of air policing as being humane. Indeed, the mismatch between the propaganda for air policing and its effects is strikingly borne out in Glubb's memoirs. Influenced by considerable British public disquiet about its use, he claimed that the whole two-day operation cost only one Iraqi life.[94]

If the damage to the population of Samawah had to be hidden from the British public, the impression that air power was having on its targets exceeded all expectations. The combination of night bombing and incendiary devices helped foster the apparent belief amongst tribes of the neighborhood that airplanes could seek them out wherever they fled. The shaikhs across the area surrounding the bombed villages all reported to government officials the next day despite not having been sent for. Overall it was felt that the "moral" effects of the operation on Samawah would be long-lasting. The tribes had formed "a most exaggerated idea of the capabilities of aircraft," which should be guarded for as long as possible.[95]

The order this new tool of modern social discipline could deliver when employed as part of the awesome arsenal of the liberal state turned out not to be as robust as the planners in Baghdad had hoped. The terms demanded for an end to the bombing were issued. Specific tasks were delivered in person to the nominal shaikhs. General demands were delivered all at once to all the shaikhs and *sarkals* gathered at a *majlis*. The meeting was addressed by the Minister of the Interior, Ali Jaudat Beg, and his adviser, Colonel Cornwallis, both of whom had flown down from Baghdad.[96]

The specific requirement delivered to the nominal shaikhs had three components. Each section had to deliver a rifle fine of 300 weapons, demolish its forts, pay one year's back taxes immediately and arrange terms for the phased payment of all other arrears. The latter two demands were agreed to and fulfilled without much trouble. The "guilty consciences" of the tribes meant that "many minor Shaikhs and sarkals have been scraping together money, in order to bring in at least a portion of their overdue taxes and make peace with Government."[97] However, the personal nature of the tax liability imposed was highlighted by the spread of indebtedness, with shaikhs and *sarkals* paying 60 per cent per half-yearly interest to urban money lenders to meet government demands.[98]

The raising of the rifle fines proved much more difficult and pointed to the limited authority of the shaikhs amongst the Sufran and the Barkat. When the demands were set before the Sufran after the bombing, the destruction of forts and the payment of taxes were readily agreed to, but the payment of 300 rifles within ten days was rejected as impossible. It was only after further consultation and a threat to resume bombing that the shaikhs reluctantly agreed to pay the fine.[99] Although these nominal shaikhs agreed to the rifle fine it soon became clear that the tribesmen themselves would not give up their weapons. [100] The two shaikhs managed to collect only 38 rifles each.

Since the tribespeople of the two sections were refusing to obey government instructions, both were subjected to another two days of bombing. But, by the time of the second bombing raids, Azzarah and Khashan had been recognized as the official shaikhs of their respective sections. It was also accepted that their efforts to collect rifles from their tribesmen had been genuine and their villages were exempt from bombing in an attempt to increase their prestige.[101]

The second deployment of extensive bombing on the Barkat and the Sufran had unforeseen results. Instead of delivering 600 rifles and unconditional loyalty to the government, the population dispersed. Leaving their villages and land, the people moved out of the area and took up residence amongst other tribes not targeted by the bombing.[102] Pursuing them amongst these dispersed groupings was discussed, but finally rejected because it would "entail serious slaughter" and was therefore deemed not feasible.[103]

The contradictory and confusing results of this air policing in Samawah were to become general and familiar themes in the deployment of air power under the Mandate regime. While the operation was called a success, the failure to extract the rifles and the loss of a large part of the population understandably made for a rather uninspiring finale. The weapons had worked well, with night bombing and the use of incendiary and heavier munitions delivering greater than expected destruction of houses and livestock. "Morally" the bombing had had a profound effect on those targeted and the surrounding population. People were terrified that this new technology could apparently target them night and day, dropping high explosives into the middle of their villages from an unassailable height. But the mixed utility of this awesome new power—good for raising tax; bad for extracting rifles—puzzled those in Air HQ, the Ministry of Interior and the Residency. On the face of it, the rifle fine had not been harsh, amounting to one rifle per nine or ten men.[104] The puzzle was that people would rather emigrate from the area than pay it. The conclusion arrived at was that they had fled in fear and not defiance. Air policing could not co-opt tribes but could only punish them.[105]

Despite the conundrums raised by the concluding stages of the Samawah operation the exercise allowed for the development of a standard template for justifying, deploying, and celebrating uses of air power. Its comparatively low cost, in terms of protecting the lives of government forces and lowering financial expenditure, meant that its role was secure. From 1922, the use of airplanes grew rapidly and became essential for asserting and defending the sovereignty of the state, internally and externally. Their deployment in 1923, then, marked the institutionalization of air power as the state's main weapon of coercion. The RAF was also credited with stopping a major threat to the sovereignty of Iraq by turning the tide against the *Ikhwan* raiders who caused havoc along the Saudi-Iraqi border in 1924 to 1925 and again in 1928 to 1929.[106] Again, it was the RAF that limited the political ramifications of the 1931 general strike by flying repeated missions over the Euphrates to highlight the consequences of a tribal revolt in support of the strike.[107] As the Mandate itself drew to a close, the RAF was central to the expansion of order into the periphery of Iraqi Kurdistan. Airplanes unleashed the full force of state-deployed violence against Shaikh Ahmad of Barzan from 1931 to 1932.[108] In the diverse geographical conditions of both northern and southern Iraq, the airplane's versatility against those fermenting revolt was unrivalled. The social imagination of domination that accompanied air power was reinforced amongst British staff in Iraq and eventually encouraged across the Empire.[109] When Shaikh Mahmud finally surrendered in 1931, after many years of revolt against the centralizing Iraqi state, he pointed to the winged insignia on an RAF officer present and said "You are the people who have broken my spirit."[110]

The deployment of air power was clearly a blunt weapon; bombs dropped from above 200 feet were wholesale in their effect. The power deployed was authoritative but ultimately despotic. Air power could not explain, it could not negotiate, and it could not distribute largesse. For air power to have any infrastructural effect on the population, the state needed a certain type of mediator. In theory, the office of shaikh would take the place of extended state institutions and would sharpen the blunt instrument of bombing. However, the figure of the shaikh did not deliver the mediated access to society that the British had hoped for; his position within society was secured only by the use of the state's coercive power.

Conclusion

Iraq's Past And Possible Iraqi Futures

If we think there is a fast solution to changing the governance of Iraq, then we don't understand history, the nature of the country, the divisions, or the underneath suppressed passions that could rise up. God help us if we think this transition will occur easily. The attempts I've seen to install democracy in short periods of time where there is no history and no roots have failed. Take it back to Somalia.[1] —*Marine General Anthony Zinni (retired) Head of U.S. Central Command from 1997 to 2000, 10 October 2002*

U.S. forces in Iraq today face the problem of how to deal with a country whose civil society was largely wiped out during the Baathist dictatorship. Politics in modern liberal democratic states are based on formal and semiformal legal rational links between the governed and the governing, transparently relaying information and resources, mutually constraining the behavior of both state and society. After thirty-five years of Baathist rule, the last twelve of which were spent under a sanctions regime explicitly designed to cripple state institutions, these intermediary institutions in Iraq do not exist.

U.S. forces can look elsewhere for models of state building and reform and seek out the best practices developed since the Cold War. Interventions into failed and rogue states for humanitarian or political proposes have become increasingly common since 1989.[2] But the most important question at the heart of such interventions—can states be rebuilt and, if so, how?—remains largely unanswered.[3] The evidence from post–Cold War interventions is hardly inspiring. The Cambodia mission, the first large-scale UN attempt at root-and-branch political reform, failed to deliver meaningful change.[4] Intervention in Somalia resulted in the ignominious exit of U.S. troops and the collapse of the UN mission. Direct U.S. military intervention in Haiti to facilitate regime change did little in the long term to alter the underlying political dynamics of the country. In the cases of Bosnia, Kosovo, and Afghanistan, the ongoing and very mixed results of intervention mean that it is probably too early to draw any long-term conclusions. This suggests that for U.S. forces currently involved in attempting to reform Iraq's political structures, the libraries are full of books that provide no guidance.

After surveying the rather disheartening examples of recent interventions L. Paul Bremer III, the former diplomat in charge of U.S. attempts to reform the Iraqi state, could turn to the first attempt at state building in the country, that of the British from 1914 to 1932. He would find in the example of the Iraqi Mandate a genuine but confused exercise in state formation, constrained by the international system of the time, domestic British politics, but also by the demands of Iraqis, keen to take their independence from the foreign state builders as quickly as they could. The Iraqis of the 1920s were deeply suspicious of British motives. Through violence and political mobilization, they forced the colonial power to leave much sooner than they had anticipated. Ultimately, however, it was the way the British understood Iraqi society that came to undermine their attempt to build a stable state. British colonial administrators, aware of the short time they would be in Iraq, set about devolving power to indigenous Iraqis they believed had social influence. Resources were channeled through these individuals in the hope that they could guarantee social order at the lowest possible cost. The resulting state was built on extremely shallow social foundations. The governments that inherited the state after independence had, like the British before them, to resort to high levels of violence and patronage to keep the population from rising up and unseating them.

Another lesson for Bremer to learn from the British experience stems from the ramifications of imposing order on an increasingly resentful population. The way a modern state attempts to impose order shapes both the society it seeks to repress and also the nature of the government itself. The technology that a state has at its disposal mediates the nature and extent of these attempts. Crucial to the dialectic of state-society relations is how soldiers and civil servants understand the way that society is structured. The British in Iraq in the 1920s, because of a lack of finance and soldiers, came to rely heavily on the coercive power of airplanes. Governance was delivered from two hundred feet, in the shape of regular bombing and machine-gun fire. This meant that state institutions never managed to fully penetrate society, mobilize resources, or ultimately engender legitimacy.

The two most important and urgent tasks facing Bremer are the reestablishment of order and government services. Faced with congressional worries about expenditure and the public's concerns about casualties, the strong temptation would be to cut corners, to search for local intermediaries to work through while depending on brute force to impose law and order. If Paul Bremer does succumb to this temptation, then he will not have learnt from the British experience but will run the distinct danger of repeating it.

Understanding Contemporary Iraqi Society

The country that the United States is struggling to pacify and reform is in many ways politically distinct, even among the states of the Middle East. Since seizing power in 1968, the Baath regime efficiently used extreme levels of violence and the powers of patronage delivered by oil wealth to co-opt or break any independent vestiges of civil society. Autonomous collective societal structures beyond the control of the state simply do not exist. In their place, society came to be dominated by aspects of the "shadow state,"[5] flexible networks of patronage and violence that were used to reshape Iraqi society in the image of Saddam Hussein and his regime.

The danger for U.S. administrators trying to make sense of a society they have little knowledge of is that they will grasp aspects of the shadow state as authentic representations of the Iraqi polity. In doing so they will be reproducing the very structures set up by Saddam Hussein to guarantee his own grip on power.

Another danger is that the United States, like the British in the 1920s, will succumb to "primordialization." This would involve them reimagining Iraqi society as dominated by the supposedly premodern structures of tribe and religious authority.[6] However, in doing this, U.S. administrators will not be discovering the "essence" of Iraq. They will again be picking up the structures of Baathist rule, aspects of society destroyed and then rebuilt by Saddam to perpetuate his presidency. There is strong evidence that in the early days of the occupation British and American forces did just that.

In the post–1974 era, the Baathist regime astutely used its newfound oil wealth to tie the population, on an individual basis, to the state. From 1958 to 1977, for example, the number of Iraqis employed by the state dramatically increased from 20,000 to more than 580,000, not including the estimated 430,000 in the armed and security services. The most recently available figures, produced in the aftermath of the 1990–91 Gulf War, estimated that the civilian arm of the state employed 21 percent of the working population, with 40 percent of Iraqi households directly depending on government payments.[7] This direct dependence on the state was exacerbated by the emasculation of trade unions. Workers were expected to petition the government, in the name of Saddam Hussein, on an individual basis, for improvements in their working conditions and wages.

The atomization of society and the dependence of individuals upon the state increased dramatically after the 1990–91 Gulf War. It was (and still is) the rationing system that provided food for the majority of the population in the south and center of the country. Under United Nations resolution 986, agreed to by Iraq in May 1996, Iraq was allowed to import and distribute humanitarian aid under UN supervision. The food is distributed through 53,000 neighborhood grocery shops and regulated through a government-controlled ration card. Applications to receive a ration card gave the government crucial information about every household under its control. The restrictions placed on ration cards meant individuals could not travel between different areas of the country and had to pick up their food within the same region each month. The rationing system became an additional way in which the regime secured loyalty from, and domination over, the population. Sixty percent of the population depends on these handouts for their day-to-day survival.[8]

Under the pressures of sanctions, the official institutions of the state, with the exception of the rationing system retreated from society during the 1990s, especially in the area of welfare and education.[9] The flexible, informal arms of the shadow state replaced them. The shadow state, with its structures of patronage and violence, underpinned Saddam Hussein's rule and guaranteed his survival throughout the 1990s. It is through the shadow state that Saddam Hussein, and before him Hasan al-Bakr, set about reshaping society so it could no longer pose a threat to the ruling elite.

At the heart of these distribution networks was Saddam Hussein's extended clan group, the al-Bu Nasir, based in Takrit, and the affiliated tribes in the northwest of Iraq above Baghdad. The al-Bu Nasir and the tribes linked to them provided the social cohesion needed to run this unofficial system of regime power. This group consisted of up to 50,000 people, including their families, in a population of 23 million. They are still spread throughout state institutions and dominate the official and unofficial economies. Members of these clans held the top positions in every state institution, they ran the command and control structures of the Iraqi army, dominating all major sections of the economy. Ultimately they realized their safety and survival depended on the rule of Saddam Hussein.[10]

For these networks to be effective, they had to spread out from the center of rule in Baghdad, through and beyond the al-Bu Nasir, to the rest of Iraq. They protected Saddam by penetrating all corners of society, Sunni, Shia and Kurd, rural and urban, north, central and south. The conscious and utilitarian targeting and co-opting of specific members of society profoundly changed the individual's relations with the wider population and the ruling elite in Baghdad. They became conduits for regime resources but in return had to guarantee the passivity of that section of society they had become responsible for. In that respect the "figures of social influence" that U.S. and UK forces are now using as intermediaries are almost certainly the very same individuals picked by Saddam Hussein to act as his eyes and ears. The UK and U.S. in selecting them did so for the very same reason that Saddam would have. They would act as channels for resources from the central government, thus generating good will but also power for the chosen individuals. In return they are expected to provide intelligence about society and guarantee its passivity. However, as Saddam fully understood (unlike the Coalition Provisional Authority), these informal and highly personalized networks undermine the creation of a legal-rational bureaucracy and have a flexibility and tenacity that make them very difficult to root out. Coalition forces run the danger of unconsciously bolstering the networks of the shadow state created by the regime they ousted.

A good example of this process is the Baathist regime's relations with Iraqi "tribes" and its attitude to "tribalism." In the late nineteenth century, the introduction of a market economy in land and agriculture and the slow increase in the strength of the state transformed the nature of rural life in what was to become Iraq. Tribal life and the role of the shaikh were caught up in this transformation.[11] On taking power, the Baathists sought to exacerbate what they saw as the disintegration of "premodern" tribalism, linked as it was in their minds to collaboration with British Imperialism, backwardness and state weakness. This process was driven forward by experiments in the collectivization of land ownership in 1970 and nationalization of land in 1971.[12]

However, with the rise in dominance of the Tikritis within the ruling elite and the increased personalization of power around Hasan al-Bakr and Saddam Hussein, the stability of Baath Party rule came to depend for its coherence on the al-Bu Nasir tribe, and within it the Beijat clan group and Majid extended family. So as the Baath sought to extend their total-itarian and patrimonial grip on society, they tried to either co-opt tribal groupings, where they would be useful for the stability of the ruling elite's power, or break them where they were perceived as a threat.[13] This process reached its peak in the 1991 Gulf War and the uprisings that swept across the north and south of the country in its aftermath.[14] The ruling elite where shocked at the hatred shown to senior Baath Party officials in the conurbations in the south of the country. However, one of the main rea-sons the rebellions in the south in 1991 did not succeed was that the rural population largely refused to take part. Instead, they chose to remain pas-sive until it was clear which side, the government or the rebels, would prevail. This allowed the Iraqi army to move through the largely passive countryside of southern Iraq dealing with one rebellious urban center after another.

After 1991, as sanctions began to take effect, there was a rapid decline in all the official institutions of the state. Baghdad was forced to cut back on the resources they could devote to the armed forces and security serv-ices. In the aftermath of the 1991 revolt, Saddam also marginalized the Baath Party's role as a vehicle for societal mobilization. The quiescence of the rural population during the 1991 revolt allowed Saddam Hussein to develop a further network of patronage. In effect he decentered respon-sibility for the provision of order to reinvigorated and recreated tribal net-works and tribal shaikhs. By appointing "recognized shaikhs" across Iraq, Saddam Hussein targeted another group of people to receive state resources in return for loyalty to him. He created yet another informal channel of power to run alongside the others that served him so well over the twenty or so years of his rule. It is these very same "recognized shaikhs" that the British and American forces have begun to look to for the cost-effective provision of order in the post-Saddam era. It is no great surprise that the reappointment of these figure has not been greeted with universal warmth by the rest of Iraqi society.

Washington's Approach to the Reform of Postwar Iraq: The Coalition Provisional Authority

Although it can be argued that the neoconservatives spent most of the 1990s plotting how they would remove Saddam Hussein once they returned to power, they appear to have put very little effort into planning what the United States would actually do with Iraq once Saddam was gone. There are two explanations for this apparent oversight. The first is the ideological vision of Iraq and its state-society relations that dominated key decision makers' perceptions. Advisers to the government anticipated that at the advent of the air war or in the immediate aftermath of the invasion, an uprising or coup would remove Saddam Hussein while leaving the rest of his governing structures in place.[15] The U.S. president himself, in a speech in the run-up to war, actively encouraged the Iraqi armed forces to move against their leaders.[16] In addition to this, the long and close association between one of the exiled opposition parties, the Iraqi National Congress, and the neoconservatives meant that excessively optimistic predictions about the welcome U.S. troops would receive once they reached Iraq where taken at face value.[17] Under this rubric, the need for large numbers of grounds troops or detailed planning was negated. Upon liberation, it was assumed that U.S. troops would find state structures largely in place and operating coherently. Civil servants, more than happy to serve their liberators, would staff them.

The reality of the war and its aftermath were quite different. Sections of the mainstream army fought more tenaciously than most people expected. The level of Iraqi resistance in the south, especially in Umm Qasr and Nassiriyah, surprised U.S. Central Command, Iraqi analysts, and possibly even the government in Baghdad itself. There were two possible reasons why the regular army in the south fought much harder than expected. The first was that the Iraqi command and control had been decentralized from Baghdad down to the level of each town. This means that although Baghdad had effectively been cut off from its troops outside the city early in the war, the troops continued to fight on because (unlike in 1991) the local commanders had been given executive power to run the battle in the best way they could. Many of these commanders were trusted high-ranking military figures, men like Ali Hasan Majid. The second reason for the tenacity of troops fighting in the south was, however, even more problematic: Iraqi nationalism. There is no doubt that ordinary conscript soldiers, the majority of whom were Shia, hated Saddam Hussein. But there exists in Iraq today a militant and aggressive Iraqi nationalism, born of three wars and over a decade of sanctions. This was rallied during the war to motivate troops fighting against U.S. forces and has now come to dog the CPA.

Once the initial military opposition had been overcome and Baghdad seized, plans to take state institutions more or less intact and use them to rule Iraq also proved to be misguided. After twelve years of sanctions, the fabric of Iraqi government had been stretched very thin. In 2003, the Iraqi state institutions faced their third war since 1980. This, combined with the three weeks of looting and the general lawlessness that greeted liberation, meant that large numbers of civil servants simply went home and stayed there. The CPA, instead of finding a coherent state, found a governmental shell that it will have to spend many years and a great deal of money to reconstitute.

The second reason for the lack of substantive planning in the run-up to the war has more to do with the internecine ideological battles that have come to be a hallmark of the Bush presidency. Initially, the State Department set up a series of committees, largely staffed by Iraqi exiles, to plan for the future of Iraq. In January 2003, the President signed a secret National Security Policy Directive authorizing the coordination of Iraq policy.[18] After much interdepartmental infighting, the Office for Post-War Planning at the Pentagon was given overall responsibility for Iraq. Given the long-running dispute between the State Department and the Pentagon, it was no surprise that the initial work done by the State Department on the future of Iraq was largely unused. It was Douglas Feith, the Under Secretary of State for Defense Planning, who gained overall responsibility for the project's management. The fact that Feith is a noted unilateralist signaled U.S. determination to thwart international coordination and United Nations involvement in the reform of the Iraqi state.

A former General, Jay Garner, headed the team of mostly retired diplomats, senior military figures and former CIA staffers who were first charged with rebuilding the Iraqi state in the immediate aftermath of the liberation of Baghdad.[19] The vast majority of the officials appointed did not speak Arabic. They were assisted by what Garner termed "the Michigan bunch," a group of exiled Iraqis on short-term contracts hired to act as translators. Below General Garner, three regional coordinators for the south, center, and north of the country were appointed. The division of the country into three governing sectors was presented as an arrangement designed to efficiently manage the huge task of administering Iraq. But the measure immediately gave rise to fears that it was intended to establish the basis for a permanent, decentralized federal structure, long promoted by neoconservative think tanks in Washington. Under the guise of "consociationalism," this policy recommendation had been put forward by the Office of the Vice President.

As the size of the administrative task began to dawn on U.S. officials, such long-term grand designs had to be shelved. General Garner appears to have been made to pay the price for lack of prewar planning and postwar progress. His replacement to head the Coalition Provisional Authority, Paul Bremer, was chosen in an attempt to bridge the battle lines between the neoconservatives in charge of postwar construction and their colleagues at the State Department. Politically close to the neoconservatives in the Pentagon, Bremer was trained as a foreign service officer in the State Department. With the president's ear and with his authority, the administration hoped that Bremer could weld together the CPA's disparate factions and provide the U.S. effort in Iraq with unified strategic leadership.

One of Bremer's first decisions upon arriving in Baghdad was to delay delegating power to a leadership council composed of the exiled parties. Movement toward creating a democratic body had been both hasty and ramshackle. The first two meetings, at Ur near Nassariyah on 15 March and then in Baghdad, on 28 April, were designed to draw together Iraqis into some form of representative assembly. In Ur the divisions between the State Department and the Pentagon and their proxies in the Iraqi opposition, immediately made themselves evident in petty bickering.[20] The meeting was even more notable for those who chose not to attend. The large demonstration against the meeting outside highlighted the small number of delegates (eighty) and the truth of the accusations that the delegates represented little more than themselves. With three hundred in attendance, the turnout in Baghdad was larger, but it did not reach the two to three thousand predicted in advance. The American organizers refused to reveal how many had been invited but did concede that the meeting was "not sufficiently representative to establish an interim authority".[21] The fact that over half the attendees were recently returned exiles indicates a larger problem of confidence in the U.S. occupation. Many Iraqis, aware of the unpopularity of the U.S. presence in their country and believing it to be temporary, are still simply sitting on their hands. Iraqis are shunning involvement in government institutions, political and administrative, until the situation becomes clearer and the risks of political involvement fewer.

Aside from the unpopularity of their presence, the small numbers of troops available for the commanders to deploy has plagued the U.S. effort at reconstruction of postwar Iraq. Lack of an adequate number of soldiers has determined both the nature and quality of the law and order American troops have been able to enforce. In the run-up to war, Army Chief of Staff Eric Shinseki in a senate hearing called for "hundreds of thousands" of troops to guarantee order. Michael O'Hanlon, of the Brookings Institute, based on his experience in the Balkans, took the figure of 150,000 as a minimum with at least 100,000 staying in the country for several years.[22] In July of 2003, there were only 21,000 U.S. troops attempting to impose order on Baghdad. One hundred and forty-five thousand troops were in Iraq overall.[23]

Interaction with Iraqi Society

The Coalition Provisional Authority, in the early going, was internally incoherent and politically divided. Externally its interaction with Iraqi society was, at best, intermittent. With very few Arabic speakers on their staff, the coalition assumed the Iraqi exiles it was bringing back would provide its eyes and ears. These intermediaries proved much less effective than was hoped. Despite setting up numerous offices around Baghdad, publishing party newspapers, and spending large sums of money, the two main exile groups, the Iraqi National Congress and Iraqi National Accord have not put down roots in society. They have instead elicited hostility and anger on the part of many Iraqi citizens. I spoke with one Baghdadi who, under Saddam's rule, had worked secretly for one of the exile groups. He had been arrested and sentenced to death. After nine months on death row in the notorious Abu Ghraib prison he survived only because the regime collapsed. When I asked about the party for which he had nearly lost his life, he replied, "I would have done anything to see the back of Saddam. But since the exiles have returned I have been disappointed; I do not trust them."

Given the lack of troops and intelligence available to U.S. administrators—and the "ad-hoc" nature of postwar planning—it is not surprising that U.S. and UK troops have been searching for "figures of local influence." Such individuals are needed to interpret Iraqi society, to guarantee order, and ultimately to reform and rebuild governing institutions. But the troops operating in chaotic circumstances on the ground have had little alternative but to take those individuals who have presented themselves at face value. In lieu of a coherent understanding of the society they are charged with ruling, they, like the British in the 1920s, are forced to rely upon what they think Iraq should look like rather than upon empirical knowledge supplied by experts with a deep knowledge of the social forces at work.

In Basra, for example, there has been the speedy return of the shadow state, both in its "tribal" and commercial guises. On 8 April 2003, a British colonel, Chris Vernon, announced that coalition administrators had appointed "a tribal leader, a shaikh" to form the civilian leadership within Basra province. Although the colonel was reluctant to name the shaikh, he assured journalists at the news conference—hastily convened to announce this breakthrough in civilian government—that they had ascertained that the individual was "worthwhile and credible and has authority in the local area, particularly with the tribal chiefs."[24] This individual turned out not to be the authentic representation of tribal society in and around Basra that Vernon had hoped, but Muzahim Mustafa Kanan Tameemi, a former brigadier in the Iraqi army and a member of the Baath Party. Tameemi's appointment caused a near riot outside his house. Demonstrators demanded that they not be represented either by a tribal figure or a member of the Baath Party.

In the aftermath of this embarrassing mistake, Tameemi was unceremoniously dropped. He was replaced by Ghalib Kubba, described as "the wealthiest businessman" in the city. Besides mistaking the nature of tribal representation in Iraq, the British army also misunderstood the nature of entrepreneurial activity under Saddam Hussein. "He's a partner of Uday Hussein. It's well known," asserted Abbas Mohammed Musa, forty-seven, a fertilizer merchant. "All commercial people from the first-class in Iraq, all of them are partners of Saddam Hussein. We want somebody who is representative of Iraqi people."[25]

American and British commanders on the ground in Iraq are hamstrung by a shortage of battlefield troops and have little accurate information about the country. In this situation they are forced to accept without verification or local knowledge Iraqis who present themselves at the barracks' gate claiming to be able to represent the needs and wants of the wider population. What appears "authentic" to these commanders is revealing. British forces, faced with the ongoing crisis in law and order across the south of Iraq, turned to their own history of state building in Iraq. According to reports, they are "dusting down the system of law used during the 38-year British mandate in Iraq in an urgent effort to reach a workable interim criminal and civil code before a new constitution and legal system is agreed."[26] The law being exhumed is the Tribal, Criminal, and Civil Disputes Regulations, drawn up by British occupying forces in February 1916 and introduced into Iraqi law by Royal *Iradah* in 1924. It fundamentally misconceived the nature of Iraqi society. By dividing Iraqi people into rural and urban communities, it entrusted the rural population to the authority of tribal shaikhs who had, even by the 1920s, lost any ability to influence the so-called tribal groups to whom they were meant to dispense justice. It was this misconception that underlay the social unrest that led to the bloody coup of 1958, resulting in the murder of the British-installed monarchy and opening a new, even more oppressive chapter in Iraqi political instability.[27]

Evidence from Umm Qasr suggests a different and more sustainable approach to rebuilding Iraq's governing structures. The experiment there has been acknowledged by American forces to be a potential model for the rest of Iraq.[28] This time, instead of grand figures of social influence, the Iraqis who presented themselves to British troops were modest, midlevel civil servants—teachers. They were self-selected and approached British soldiers asking when the schools could be reopened. The U.S. Agency for International Development moved quickly to capitalize on this development, giving the council formed by these men $41,000 for offices and computers. This experiment in "micromanagement" implies the value of a "root and branch" approach to the reform of Iraq's governing dynamics. If carried to its logical conclusion, such a policy would involve a sustained attempt not only to change the visible institutions of the state and their interaction with society, but also to transform the dynamics of the shadow state by creating the basis for social trust. This would be an extremely ambitious undertaking, whose ultimate aim would be to transform the values that have underpinned the last thirty-five years of Iraqi public life.[29] By choosing low-level technocrats in Umm Qasr over the remnants of the shadow state, a start has been made along this ambitious road. It remains to be seen if UK and U.S. forces have the local knowledge, resources, and staying power to sustain this immense and truly transformative task.

Conclusion

Iraqi politics, from the creation of the state in the aftermath of the First World War until the removal of Saddam Hussein, have been dominated by four interlinked structural problems. These are: first, the deployment of extreme levels of organized violence by the state to dominate and shape society; second, the use of state resources—jobs, development aid, and patronage—to buy the loyalty of sections of society; third, the use of oil revenue by the state to increase its autonomy from society; and, finally, the exacerbation and re-creation by the state of communal and ethnic divisions as a strategy of rule. These interlinked problems have fuelled the state's domestic illegitimacy, its tendency to embark on military adventurism beyond its own borders, and even the Baathist regime's drive to acquire weapons of mass destruction. Seen in this perspective, Saddam Hussein must be understood less as the cause of Iraq's violent political culture—or even of Iraq's role as a source of regional instability—and more as the symptom, albeit an extremely consequential one, of deeper, long-term dynamics within Iraq's political sociology. The degree to which these dynamics can be overcome—with what expenditure of resources— is the crucial question facing U.S. and UK administrators.

U.S. policy makers and their allies will have to decide if they can commit the time (up to ten years), resources, and personnel to tackle the underlying structural problems dominating Iraqi politics. Will they instead choose simply to change the personnel at the head of government and allow them to govern in a way very similar to that of the old regime? This minimalist approach may very well come to dominate policy. Now that the war has been won, the altruistic investment for U.S. involvement in Iraq will have to compete with a U.S. economy in recession and a U.S. public politically sensitive to increasing casualties. The long-term, costly, and ambitious reform of Iraq may well be sacrificed to the short-term electoral politics of the U.S.

Any serious postwar attempt to reform the state will have to take into account the members of the shadow state. They are still in their positions of influence across the country. They still run state institutions and still guarantee order. The temptation for U.S. administrators, short of resources and time because of American domestic pressures, will be to use these individuals to provide oppressive and violent stability at the lowest possible cost. As in post-Taliban Afghanistan, the military victors would, in effect, be choosing to use existing sociopolitical formations to restore the old ruling formula, foreclosing any real attempt at effective reform.

If this becomes the path chosen by the U.S. and its allies, resources are likely to be distributed both through the new or reformed state institutions set up by U.S. forces and through the remaining networks of the shadow state. As U.S. troops are withdrawn and U.S. public opinion loses interest in Iraq, the shadow state with new masters will once again come to dominate. A new governing structure will not have been built. Instead, a veneer of legal-rational bureaucracy will have been placed on top of the shadow state with its tried and tested use of violence, patronage, and favoritism. The shadow state will slowly come to dominate as international oversight diminishes. In the medium-term, Iraq will be prone to insecurity—mitigated only by the degree of ruthlessness and efficiency exhibited by the new rulers in Baghdad. The long-term result can be expected, at best, to resemble Egypt, with a population demobilized and resentful. The state will dominate society through the use of high levels of organized violence. The governing elite will colonize all aspects of the economy and corruption will be the major source of the regime's longevity.

Preface: Iraq and the Ordering of the Postcolonial World

1. See Hedley Bull, *The Anarchical Society: A Study in World Politics* (London: MacMillan, 1995), p. 13.

2. See Robert H. Jackson, *Quasi-States: Sovereignty, International Relations, and the Third World* (Cambridge: Cambridge University Press, 1993), pp. 29–38, 61.

3. See Hedley Bull, "The Revolt Against the West," in *The Expansion of International Society*, ed. Hedley Bull and Adam Watson (Oxford: Clarendon Press, 1989), p. 220.

4. Quoted in Robert H. Jackson, "The Weight of Ideas in Decolonization: Normative Change in International Relations," in *Ideas and Foreign Policy*, ed. Judith Goldstein and Robert Keohane (Ithaca, N.Y.: Cornell University Press, 1993), p. 124.

5. On the power of this norm for diplomatic practice, see Douglas Hurd Foreword to *Regime Change: It's Been Done Before*, ed. Roger Gough (London: policyexchange, 2003), p. 12.

6. Michael Mastanduno, "Models, Markets, and Power: Political Economy and the Asia-Pacific, 1989-1999," *Review of International Studies* 26, No. 4 (October 2000): 499.

7. David Williams, "Aid and Sovereignty: Quasi-States and the International Financial Institutions," *Review of International Studies* 26, No. 4 (October 2000): 568.

8. See Robert H. Jackson, "The Weight of Ideas in Decolonization:." Jackson first made this argument in *Quasi-States*, originally published in 1990.

9. See Bruce W. Jentleson, *Coercive Prevention: Normative, Political, and Policy Dilemmas* (Washington, D.C.: U.S. Institute of Peace, 2000), p. 27. The fact that Jentleson was a foreign policy advisor to former Vice President Al Gore and the Gore-Lieberman presidential campaign shows that the intellectual heritage of the Bush doctrine in the United States is largely bipartisan.

10. Quoted by Nicholas Leman, "After Iraq: The Plan to Remake the Middle East," *The New Yorker*, 17 February 2003.

11. See "U.S. Strategy Plan Calls for Insuring No Rivals Develop," *The New York Times*, 8 March 1992; Nicholas Leman, "The Next World Order: The Bush Administration May Have a Brand-New Doctrine of Power," *The New*

Yorker, 1 March 2002; and "Front Line Special: The War Behind Closed Doors," http://www.pbs.org/wgbh/ pages/frontline/shows/iraq/themes.

12. Richard N. Haass (director, State Department Policy Planning Staff), "The 2002 Arthur Ross Lecture: Remarks to Foreign Policy Association," New York, 22 April 2002.

13. See Leman, "The Next World Order."

14. Toby Dodge and Steven Simon, Introduction to *Iraq at the Crossroads: State and Society in the Shadow of Regime Change* (London and Oxford: International Institute for Strategic Studies and Oxford University Press, 2003), p. 11.

15. See Bob Woodward's description of the National Security Council meeting on 12 September 2001 in *Bush at War* (New York: Simon and Schuster, 2002), pp. 43, 48.

16. See "The President's State of the Union Address," the United States Capitol, Washington, D.C., 29 January 2002.

17. See Robert S. Litwak, "The New Calculus of Preemption," *Survival* 44, no. 4 (winter 2002–2003); and *The National Security Strategy of the United States of America*, September 2002, http://www.whitehouse.gov/nsc/ nss.html. This was made even more explicit in the President's 2003 State of the Union address: "Today, the gravest danger in the war on terror, the gravest danger facing America and the world, is outlaw regimes that seek and possess nuclear, chemical, and biological weapons. These regimes could use such weapons for blackmail, terror, and mass murder. They could also give or sell those weapons to terrorist allies, who would use them without the least hesitation."

18. See remarks by the President at 2002 Graduation Exercise of the United States Military Academy West Point, New York, 1 June 2002; *The National Security Strategy of the United States of America*, September 2002, http://www.whitehouse.gov/nsc/ nss.html, pp. 1, 2; Richard N. Haass, "The 2002 Arthur Ross Lecture"; and G. John Ikenberry, "America's Imperial Ambition," *Foreign Affairs* (September/October 2002): 52.

19. For a comparable view of the dangers facing the hegemon, see Stephen E. Ambrose and Douglas G. Brinklet, *The Rise to Globalism: American Foreign Policy Since 1938* (Harmsworth: Penguin Books, 1997).

20. See Michael Hirsh, "Bush and the World," *Foreign Affairs* (September/October 2002): 24.

21. See, for example, Bob Woodward, *Bush at War*, pp. 192, 229.

22. See, for example, Edward Rhodes, "The Imperial Logic of Bush's Liberal Agenda," *Survival* 45, no. 1 (spring 2003): 131–54.

23. For evidence of what might be hoped from this success, see David Frum, *The Right Man: The Surprise Presidency of George W. Bush* (New York: Random House, 2003), p. 232.

24. President Discusses the Future of Iraq at the American Enterprise Institute, Washington Hilton Hotel, Washington, D.C., 26 February 2003.

1. Understanding the Mandate in Iraq

1. John Glubb, reporting a conversation with the dying Fahad ibn Hadhdhal, Shaikh of the Amart division of the Anaizd, once "one of the most important Bedouin shaikhs in Arabia." In Glubb, *Arabian Adventures: Ten Years of Joyful Service* London: Cassell, 1978), pp. 97–98.

2. In British society of the 1920s the ideology of rational individualism was clearly dominant. But this position of dominance existed in an uneasy relationship with older forms of ideational ordering, specifically a more collective conception of social structures associated with the landed aristocracy and previous epochs of economic organisation. See Antonio Gramsci, *Selections from the Prison Notebooks*, edited and translated by Quintin Hoare and Geoffrey Nowell Smith (London: Lawrence and Wishart, 1998), p. 18. For effects of this process on social perception see Martin J. Wiener, *English Culture and the Decline of the Industrial Spirit, 1850–1980* (Harmondsworth: Penguin, 1992). For its effects on the economics see P. J. Cain and A. G. Hopkins, *British Imperialism: Innovation and Expansion, 1688–1914* (London: Longman, 1993).

3. Ideational constructions of social reality, from high social theory through political ideology to common sense, are dominated by the structure-agency dichotomy. This ideational dichotomy focuses on the causal weight to be given to individual agency and/or societal organization. The explanatory weight in dominant discourses placed on one to the exclusion of the other is dependent upon the construction of an organic ideology. This dichotomy runs through all modern European discourses, intellectual and popular. It would be present and influential in the common sense of colonial staff and its rationalization in colonial policy. See Roy Bhaskar, *Reclaiming Reality: A Critical Introduction to Contemporary Philosophy* (London: Verso, 1993), p. 74, W. H. Greenleaf, *The Ideological Heritage*, vol. 2 of The British Political Tradition (London: Methuen, 1983), p. 15, and Antonio Gramsci, *Selections from the Prison Notebooks*, pp. 327–330.

4. Two competing conceptions of society spring from the structure-agency, society-individual dichotomy. The first would be centered on the explanatory unit of the sovereign rational individual. Based upon the idea of societal voluntarism, society is ultimately reducible to the sum of its parts, individuals. Facts are person-centric, limited to what the individual can know through sen-

sory perception. The second approach views society itself as the ultimate unit of analysis. Within this approach therefore, individuals are created wthin the social structure they are born into; they are brought together and conditioned by their interaction with society. This division is well represented by differing conceptions of Iraqi society amongst the staff during the Mandate. Arguments focusing on how the Iraqi population was to be ideationally and materially ordered centered on which unit of analysis, tribal society or the rational individual, best described Iraq. Crucially, the outcomes of such debates directly shaped the institutions of the Iraqi state and how they interacted with Iraqi society.

5. "Industrial production, which had been growing at an annual rate of about 4% in the period 1820 to 1840 and about 3% between 1840 and 1870, became more sluggish; between 1875 and 1894 it grew at just over 1.5% annually, far less than that of the country's chief rivals . . . in 1870 the United Kingdom still contained 32% of the world's manufacturing capacity, this was down to 15% by 1910; and while its share of world trade was 25% in 1870, by 1913 this had shrunk to 14%." Paul Kennedy, *The Realities Behind Diplomacy: Background Influences on British External Policy, 1865–1980* (London: Fontana, 1985), pp. 22–23.

6. See Kennedy, *The Realities Behind Diplomacy*, p. 148; and Giovanni Arrighi, "The Three Hegemonies of Historical Capitalism," in *Gramsci, Historical Materialism and International Relations*, ed. Steven Gill (Cambridge: Cambridge University Press, 1993), p. 175.

7. See Paul Kennedy, *The Rise and Fall of the Great Powers: Economic Change and Military Conflict from 1500 to 2000* (London: Fontana, 1989), p. 363; and Karl Polanyi, *The Great Transformation: The Political and Economic Origins of Our Time* (Boston: Beacon Press, 1957), p. 20.

8. See Arrighi, "The Three Hegemonies of Historical Capitalism," p. 180; and Geoffrey Barraclough, "From the European Balance of Power to the Age of World Politics: The Changing Environment of International Relations," in *An Introduction to Contemporary History*, by Geoffrey Barraclough (Harmondsworth: Penguin, 1990).

9. See E. H. Carr, *The Twenty Years' Crisis, 1919–1939* (Basingstoke: Macmillan, 1978).

10. See for example John Stevenson, *History of Britain: British Society, 1914–1945* (Harmondsworth: Penguin, 1984); A. J. P. Taylor, *English History, 1914–1945* (Oxford: Oxford University Press, 1990); and Greenleaf, *The Ideological Heritage*.

11. See Kennedy, *The Realities behind Diplomacy*, p. 25.

2. The Mandate System, the End of Imperialism, and the Birth of the Iraqi State

1. Gareth Stedman Jones, "The History of U.S. Imperialism," in *Ideology in Social Science: Readings in Critical Social Theory*, ed. Robin Blackburn (London: Fontana/Collins, 1979), pp. 227–28.

2. See Geoffrey Barraclough, *An Introduction to Contemporary History* (Harmondsworth: Penguin, 1990), p. 118.

3. See Baraclough, *An Introduction to Contemporary History*, p. 93. E. H. Carr is a partial exception to the general view that the international system of the period was fundamentally adrift; he was aware of the fundamental difference in international relations in the post-war era but did not focus on the specific outcomes. See Friedrich V. Kratochwil, "Politics, Norms, and Peaceful Change," *The Review of International Studies* 24 (December 1998): 194, special edition: "The Eighty Years' Crisis, 1919–1999," ed. Tim Dunne, Michael Cox, and Ken Booth.

4. "[W]hen we turn our attention to President Wilson . . . we are struck first of all by his amateurishness, by the vagueness and incoherence of his ideas, and by his lack of contact with European or world affairs." Richard W. Van Alstyne, "Woodrow Wilson and the Idea of the Nation State," *International Affairs* 37, no. 3, p. 305.

5. Philip J. Baram, *The Department of State in the Middle East, 1919–1945* (State College, Penn.: University of Pennsylvania Press, 1978), p. 4.

6. John A. DeNovo, "On the Sidelines: The United States and the Middle East Between the Wars, 1919–1939," in *The Great Powers in the Middle East, 1919–1939*, ed. Uriel Dann (New York: Dayan Centre for Middle Eastern and African Studies, Holmes & Meier, 1988), pp. 230–33.

7. William Stivers, *Supremacy and Oil: Iraq, Turkey and the Anglo-American World Order, 1918–1930* (Ithaca, N.Y.: Cornell University Press, 1982), pp. 67–68.

8. Friedrich V. Kratochwil, "Politics, Norms and Peaceful Change," p. 204.

9. Paul Kennedy, *The Realities behind Diplomacy*, pp. 161, 211.

10. Briton Cooper Busch, *Britain, India, and the Arabs, 1914–1921* (Berkeley: University of California Press, 1971), p. 481.

11. Even after the power of a hegemon that set up an international institution has declined, the institution itself can still function efficiently. See Robert O. Keohane, *After Hegemony: Cooperation and Discord in the World Political Economy* (Princeton, N.J.: Princeton University Press, 1984).

12. See Cooper-Busch, *Britain, India, and the Arabs*, p. 481.

13. Cooper-Busch, *Britain, India, and the Arabs*, p. 477.

14. Peter Sluglett, *Britain in Iraq*, 1914–1932, (London: Ithaca Press, published for the Middle East Centre, St. Antony's College, Oxford University, 1976), p. 18.

15. T. E. Lawrence's letter to *The Times*, 22 July 1920, quoted in Sluglett, *Britain in Iraq*, p. 61.

16. Public Records Office (PRO), Foreign Office (FO) 371/5227, paper E6509.

17. See Stephen Longrigg, *Iraq, 1900 to 1950: A Political, Social, and Economic History* (Oxford: Oxford University Press, 1953), pp. 122-126; and David E. Omissi, *Air Power and Colonial Control: The Royal Air Force, 1919–1939* (Manchester: Manchester University Press, 1990), p. 22.

18. See A. T. Wilson, *Loyalties, Mesopotamia*, vol. 1, *1914–1917: A Personal and Historical Record* (London: Oxford University Press, 1930), pp. 140, 261.

19. See Sluglett, *Britain in Iraq*, p. 26.

20. See Robert Jackson, *Quasi-States: Sovereignty, International Relations and the Third World* (Cambridge: Cambridge University Press), 1993.

21. Major Sir Hubert Young, *The Independent Arab* (London: John Murray, 1933), p. 40. Young served in Basra with the expeditionary force.

22. See Sir Ronald Evelyn Wingate, "Mesopotamia and South-Eastern Arabia During and Just After the War," a talk given to the Middle East Centre, Oxford, on 2 March 1965, p. 8, Box 132/9/1, the Sudan Archive, University of Durham. Also see Philip Willard Ireland, *Iraq: A Study in Political Development* (London: Jonathan Cape, 1937), p. 81.

23. See Ireland, *Iraq*, pp. 148–49; and Longrigg, *Iraq, 1900 to 1950*, p. 119.

24. India Office Library (IOL), L/P&S/18 B281, "The Future of Mesopotamia," Note by Political Dept., India Office, on points for discussion with Sir Percy Cox, p. 1; also see Sluglett, *Britain in Iraq*, p. 18; and Ireland, *Iraq*, p. 108.

25. See David Gilmour, *Curzon* (London: Papermac, 1994), p. 474.

26. A. T. Wilson, *Loyalties, Mesopotamia*, vol. 1, pp. 103, 110.

27. Quoted in Gilmour, *Curzon*, p. 485.

28. Wilson, *Loyalties, Mesopotamia*, vol. 1, p. xi.

29. Gertrude Bell, *From Her Personal Papers*, vol. 2, *1914–1926*, ed. Elizabeth Burgoyne (London: Ernest Benn Limited, 1961), p. 104. Also, "Throughout the country there is very little belief in an Arab Government. Basra frankly dislikes it, the tribesmen scoff at it." Copies of letters from Gertrude Bell to Sir Valentine Chirol, 1916–1923, 29 November 1920, Box 303/4/245, Sudan Archive, Durham University.

30. See PRO, Colonial Office (CO) 730/34, p. 782; and Sluglett, *Britain in Iraq*, p. 18 n. 35.

31. See Stivers, *Supremacy and Oil*, p. 42.

32. On the negative effect of Wilson's rhetoric in 1918 see Mejcher, *Imperial Quest for Oil: Iraq, 1910–1928* (London: Ithaca Press, published for the Middle East Center St. Antony's College, Oxford University, 1976), p. 55.

33. Woodrow Wilson, "Address Delivered to the Senate, 22 Jan. 1917," in *Readings in World Politics*, vol. 2 (Chicago: American Foundation for Political Education, 1957), p. 113.

34. Colonel House, Wilson's chief troubleshooter in Europe, was charged by the President to set up an inquiry team to look into the potential problems facing America in the post-war world. G.L. Beer was a member of this committee. See Sluglett, *Britain in Iraq*, p. 18 n. 35; and George Louis Beer, "The Future of Mesopotamia," written for the inquiry team, finished 1 Jan. 1918, in *African Questions at the Paris Peace Conference, with papers on Egypt, Mesopotamia and the Colonial Settlement*, edited with introduction, annexes and additional notes by Louis Herbert Gray (London: Dawsons of Pall Mall, 1968), pp. 413–27.

35. Beer, "The Future of Mesopotamia," p. 424.

36. Beer, "The Future of Mesopotamia," p. 425.

37. Point three centered on the right to equality of trade conditions for all states. Point five stated, "A free, open-minded, and absolutely impartial adjustment of all colonial claims, based upon a strict observance of the principle that in determining all such questions of sovereignty the interests of the populations concerned must have equal weight with the equitable claims if the government whose title is to be determined." Point twelve stated that non-Turkish nationalities in the Ottoman Empire "should be assured an undoubted security of life and an absolutely unmolested opportunity of autonomous development." Woodrow Wilson, "A Speech Before a Joint Session of Congress, 8 Jan. 1918," *Readings in World Politics*, vol. 2 (Chicago: American Foundation for Political Education, 1957), pp. 23–25.

38. Mark Sykes, "Our Position in Mesopotamia in Relation to the Sprit of the Age," FO 800/22, reproduced in full as appendix 1 in Mejcher, *Imperial Quest for Oil*.

39. IOL, L/P&S/18/B281, "Future of Mesopotamia," Note by the Political Dept., India Office, on points for discussion with Sir Percy Cox, 3 April 1918, p. 2. "The main new factors in the situation may be classified broadly under two heads, viz. : (i) the general trend of the war in Europe; and (ii) the general change in outlook in regard to questions of imperial policy which the war has brought about, and, in particular, the spread of the doctrine of 'self-determi-

nation' under the powerful advocacy of the President of the United States" (L/P&S/18/B281, p. 2). " 'Autonomy' and 'separate national conditions' do not seem compatible with annexation (as was contemplated by His Majesty's Government in the case of Basra) in any form; while it is not easy to reconcile them even with British suzerainty or a British Protectorate, unless the people concerned, or the local chiefs or leaders on their behalf, can be induced to accept our assistance and supervision of their own accord" (L/P&S/18/B281, p. 3).

40. IOL L/P&S/18 B284 Eastern Committee, The Future of Mesopotamia, E.C. 173, Note by Sir Percy Cox, p. 2.

41. See H. Duncan Hall, "The British Commonwealth and the Founding of the League Mandate System," in *Studies in International History: Essays Presented to W. Norton Medlicott, Stevenson Professor of International History in the University of London*, ed. K. Bourne and D.C. Watt (London: Longman, 1967), p. 346.

42. H. Duncan Hall, "The British Commonwealth and the Founding of the League Mandate System," p. 354; and H. Duncan Hall, *Mandates, Dependencies, and Trusteeship* (New York: Klaus Reprint Company, 1972), p. 352.

43. Thus the former German colonies that the countries of the British Empire delegation wanted to have annexed were allocated to them, placed in the C category and were in a very different situation to those in the Middle East. Independence was to come, but in the distant future. See Duncan Hall, *Mandates, Dependencies, and Trusteeship*, p. 93.

44. "The whole idea of the international supervision of dependent territories was revolutionary. The normal assumption was that European Powers had a natural right to rule 'natives.' " F. S. Northedge, *The League of Nations: Its Life and Times, 1920–1946* (Leicester: Leicester University Press, 1986), pp. 201–2.

45. Wilson quoted in Hall, "The British Commonwealth and the Founding of the League Mandate System," p. 354.

46. Sluglett, *Britain in Iraq*, p. 14.

47. PRO, FO 371/5227, paper E6830. Also see telegram no. 344436/75/19, Office of the Civil Commissioner, Baghdad, 15 November 1919, P.8253/19, Dispatch from the Civil Commissioner, Mesopotamia, to Secretary of State for India, Sudan Archives, Durham, Box 303/1/67 and ST48/12 (2), Baghdad, 15 November 1919, from Wilson to the Secretary of State for India; accompanying note by G. Bell, "Syria in 1919," the British Library Official Publications.

48. See Cooper-Busch, *Britain, India, and the Arabs*, p. 279.

49. See IOL, L/P&S/18, B317, Mesopotamia: Future Constitution, letter from A. T. Wilson, Baghdad, 6 April 1919.

50. See A. T. Wilson, *Loyalties, Mesopotamia*, vol. 2, *1917–920: A Personal and Historical Record* (London: Oxford University Press, 1931), pp. 99, 140, 240, 261 and PRO FO 371/5227, File 2719, E6509, 16 June 1920 and E6830, 21 June 1920, Inter-Dept.al Conference on Middle Eastern Affairs.

51. PRO, FO 371/5227, File 2719, E6830, 21 June 1920, p. 54.

52. See Thomas Lyell, *The Ins and Outs of Mesopotamia* (Cambridge: Allborough Publishing, 1991), p. 168.

53. In August of 1920 the draft instructions to be given to Cox as High Commissioner were placed before the cabinet in London. These stated that Faisal was to be king, with a government that "must be as completely Arab as possible. That is to say, that it must be composed, as far as, or as soon as, practicable, of Arab ministers for each Dept. of State, responsible to the Arab Ruler, each assisted by a British expert as Secretary, such experts to be considered employees of the Arab Government." Britain would be responsible for Foreign Affairs and would oversee finances as long as the Exchequer was wholly or partly financing the Iraqi state. IOL, L/P&S/18, B.347, Appointment of Sir Percy Cox as High Commissioner: Instructions of His Majesty's Government, Draft Instructions submitted to the cabinet, 5 August 1920.

54. "Finance not merely the governing but the only factor in the eyes of the British public." H. W. Young to Shuckburgh, Baghdad 23 October 1921, CO 55863, Affairs in Iraq, CO 730/18, p. 504. Also see Sluglett, *Britain in Iraq*, pp. 47–8.

55. See CO 730/34, Note prepared by the Middle East Dept., Colonial Office, printed for the cabinet, Dec. 1922, Secret I.R.Q.3., p. 783.

56. See Sir Percy Cox, "Historical Summaries," in *The Letters of Gertrude Bell,* by Gertrude Bell, vol. 2, selected and edited by Lady Bell (Harmondsworth: Penguin, 1939), p. 541.

57. "Broadly speaking, the root principle is that official control as such should be exercised by no one but the High Commissioner. In order to enable him to decide at what points his intervention is necessary, he must be kept fully informed, at every stage, of action which the Iraq Government propose to take." Minute by H. W. Young, CO 16522, 7 April 1922, "The Finances of Iraq," CO 730/33, p. 309.

58. The Council of Ministers met for the first time on 2 November 1920. IOL, L/P&S/18/ B365, Establishment of Council of State for Iraq, no. S.D./170A, dated 30 November 1920, issued by P.Z. Cox, High Commissioner for Mesopotamia, to all officers of the Civil Administration in Mesopotamia, signed by C. C. Garbett, Secretary to the High Commissioner.

59. Longrigg, *Iraq*, p. 129. Under the British Civil Administration the country had been divided into fourteen divisions. The Council of Ministers divided the country into ten *liwas*, thirty-five *qadhas*, and eighty-five *nahiyahs* on December 12 1920. See Ireland, *Iraq*, pp. 294–96.

60. Indian National Archive, Baghdad High Commision Files (BHCF) BHCF File no. 23/2, Proceeding of Council of State, from November 1920 to April 1921, Draft Instructions for the Council of State, p. 4; and IOL L/P&S/18/ B365, Note on the proceedings of Cox since arriving in Basra, p. 4.

61. "The question of ultimate responsibility, as between the British and Arab Governments, is perturbing alike the king, the ministers and the public. At the meetings of the Council it is the subject of frequent informal discussions and the ministers, including Sasun Effendi, are all of opinion that an explicit definition of their powers and position cannot be delayed." Intelligence Report no. 26, Baghdad 1 December, 1921, BHCF, File no. 19/1, vol. 2, Intelligence Reports.

62. CO 730/16, CO 5618 10 NOV 21, British Staff in Iraq, extracts from Major Young's letter of the 23 October 1921 from Baghdad, p. 205.

63. See, for examples of this approach, BHCF, File no. 19/1, vol. 2, Intelligence Reports, Intelligence Report no. 25, Baghdad, 15 November 1921, Proceedings of the Council of Ministers, File no. 19/1, vol. 4 (4), Intelligence Report no. 14 Baghdad, 15 July 1922, Intelligence Report no. 23, Baghdad, 1 December 1922.

64. In 1920 there were 2,035 officials of the Government of India in Iraq, by 1923 this number had fallen to 1,270. In 1920 there were 364 British gazetted officers in Iraq, by 1923 there were 181. See Ireland, *Iraq*, p. 367.

65. In October 1921 H. W. Young described the role of the adviser thus, "it will be sufficient if the second-in-command of the Arab minister, whether you call him an Under-Secretary or Inspector-General or a Director, is an Englishman." CO 730/16, CO 5618 10 NOV 21, British Staff in Iraq, Extracts from Major Young's letter of the 23 Oct. 1921 from Baghdad, p. 205. L/P&S/18/, B365, Note on the proceedings of Cox since arriving in Basra, p. 4. CO 5618 10 NOV 21, British Staff in Iraq, Extracts from Major Young's letter of the 23 October 1921 from Baghdad, CO 730/16, p. 205.

66. The problem of having such an informal understanding between the adviser and the High Commissioner's staff was recognized by the Colonial Office in 1921 but not acted upon: "we know by experience that British officials appointed to posts in the service of a foreign Government rapidly lose their British political status and become more native than the native himself." CO 730/18, CO 63592 24 DEC 21, Affairs of Iraq, to Shuckburgh from Young, Baghdad, 8 December 1921, p. 595.

67. See IOL, L/P&S/18, B.347, Appointment of Sir Percy Cox as High Commissioner: Instructions of His Majesty's Government, Draft Instructions submitted to the cabinet 5 August 1920.

68. Terence Ranger argues that in colonial Africa the notion of kingship provided a structure of ideational and material order for Imperial rule. See "The Invention of Tradition in Colonial Africa," in *The Invention of Tradition*, ed. Eric Hobsbawn and Terence Ranger (Cambridge: Cambridge University Press, 1993), p. 211. At the Cairo Conference in March 1921 T. E. Lawrence

argued that the scattered and backward peoples of Iraq needed the unifying figure of a king. See Mejcher, *Imperial Quest for Oil*, p. 77.

69 For the role Faisal was to play in the Iraqi state see, Note on the Organic Law, CO 63592 24 DEC 21, Affairs of Iraq, CO 730/18, p. 609.

70. For Bell, Sassun Effendi summed up the situation well when he argued that "no local man would be acceptable as head of state because every other local man would be jealous of him"; Gertrude Bell, *The Letters of Gertrude Bell*, vol. 2, p. 489. The naqib of Baghdad, Abd al-Rahman al-Gailani, was discounted because he was both too old and too closely associated with the Sunni population. Saiyid Talib, the naqib of Basra, was considered to be too closely associated with the regional interests of Basra, an area which had a long-expressed wish not to be included in an Iraqi state. He had also had a violent reputation under the Ottoman administration. He was unceremoniously bundled out of the country and sent into exile when his presence was seen as destabilizing. See Sluglett, *Britain in Iraq*, pp. 36–45.

71. See Sluglett, Britain in Iraq, pp. 44–46. For a wider discussion of this approach, with reference to Transjordan, see Toby Dodge, *An Arabian Prince: English Gentlemen and the Tribes East of the River Jordan. Abdullah and the Creation and Consolidation of the Transjordanian State*, (London: Centre of Near and Middle Eastern Studies Occasional paper 13, SOAS, 1993).

72. On 18 August 1921 the Interior Minister informed the Council of Ministers that 96 percent of those who voted in the referendum had voted for Faisal. Faisal became king on August 23. CO 730/4, CO 41616, Rulership of Iraq, Reports on conversations with Faisal regarding the difficult position in which he now finds himself & submits suggestions for a settlement, paraphrase telegram from the High Commissioner to Secretary of State for the Colonies, 17 August, 1921, p. 256. Faisal went so far as to refuse to be crowned if this proviso was not removed. See Sir J. Richmond, "G. L. Bell as a Political Influence," text of a talk given at the Ashmolean Museum, Oxford, 16 May 1977, Box 639/8/1, The Sudan Collection, University of Durham, p. 18. Also Sluglett, *Britain in Iraq*, p. 70.

73. CO 730/4, CO 41616, Rulership of Iraq, Reports on conversations with Faisal regarding the difficult position in which he now finds himself & submits suggestions for a settlement. paraphrase telegram from the High Commissioner to Secretary of State for Colonies, 17 August 1921, p. 256.

74. CO 730/4, CO 41616/21, paraphrase telegram from Secretary of State Colonies to High Commissioner, 20 August 1921, pp. 260–262.

75. Mr Churchill telegraphed to Sir P. Cox on the 20 April as follows: "The question which the king should now address himself to is the following. Does he desire us to quit Iraq forthwith?" "We could begin the evacuation immedi-

ately after the hot weather, and all British troops and civilians could be out of the country before the end of the Christian year. If this is the king's wish, he should say so, with the knowledge that the responsibility for what follows will rest with him." CO 730/34, CO 62086, cabinet committee on Iraq, p. 749.

76. "Six months ago we were paying his hotel bill in London, and now I am forced to read day after day 800-word messages on questions of his status and his relations with foreign powers." CO 730/16, 24 Nov. 1921, Note by Secretary of State, the Colonial Office, Downing Street, p. 387.

77. See Bell, *The Letters of Gertrude Bell*, vol. 2, pp. 279, 285; BHCF File no. 19/1 vol. 4 (4); Intelligence Report no. 17, Baghdad, 1 September 1922 and CO 730/34, CO 36475 26 JUL 22, Pan-Arab Activities, p. 91.

78. BHCF File no. 19/1, vol. 4 (4), Intelligence Report no. 17, Baghdad, 1 September 1922, Notes on Public Opinion and Affairs in Baghdad and News from Provinces, pp. 4–5. Also see Cox, "Historical Summaries," in Bell, *The Letters of Gertrude Bell*, vol. 2, p. 524.

79. BHCF File no. 19/1, vol. 4 (4), Intelligence Report no. 17, Baghdad, 1 September 1922, p. 5.

80. "I realise that the success or failure of Faisal as king of Iraq and of our policy involved therewith is a matter of much more than local import, and that collapse of project in pursuance of which we brought him here, besides being humiliating to us vis-à-vis France, would probably involve recasting of our Arabian policy as a whole." "I quite recognise that, having put up Faisal and Iraq having accepted him, it may not be possible for us or worth the candle to contemplate any change and that Faisal and Iraq must take their chance." Telegram from the High Commissioner for Iraq to the Secretary of State for Colonies, Secret and Personal, 24 August 1922, CO 730/34, pp. 263–264. Also see paraphrase telegram from Churchill, the Secretary of State for the Colonies, to Cox, 29 August 1922, CO 730/24, CO 43045 29 AUG 22, Political Situation, p. 209.

81. Telegram from the High Commissioner to the Secretary of State for the Colonies, no. 605, 26 August 1922, CO 730/34, p. 263.

82. See CO 44086, The Political Situation in Iraq, CO 730/24, p. 261.

83. CO 730/4, CO 41616; Rulership of Iraq; Reports on conversations with Faisal regarding the difficult position in which he now finds himself & submits suggestions for a settlement, p. 253. Sluglett suggests that this was apparent to Montagu, the Secretary of State for India, as early as the summer of 1920. See Sluglett, *Britain in Iraq*, p. 42.

84. Paraphrased telegram, from the High Commissioner to the Secretary of State for the Colonies, no. 163, dated 27 February 1922, pp. 323–324.

85. See Cox, "Historical Summaries," pp. 522–523; paraphrased telegram from the High Commissioner to the Secretary of State for the Colonies, no.

163, dated 27 February 1922; CO 730/20 (vol. 2), Iraq 1922, p. 323; Shuckburgh, CO 62086, cabinet committee on Iraq, further memorandum by the Middle East Dept., Colonial Office, 12 December 1922, CO 730/34, p. 798. Or, to quote Faisal's explanation, "the people have acquired a repugnance towards the term 'Mandate,' its terms, and interpretations, which is a result of what they have observed in the way of abuse by the [French] Mandatory of his Mandate and his employment of the authority vested in him under the said Mandate for the realisation of private aims and objectives." Translation of a letter from King Faisal to Sir Percy Cox, dated 23 February 1922, CO 1354 9 MAR 22, treaty With Faisal, CO 730/20 (vol. 2), Iraq 1922, pp. 319–320.

86. Paraphrase telegram from the High Commissioner to the Secretary for State for the Colonies, 17 August 1921, CO 730/4, p. 254.

87. CO 62086, cabinet committee on Iraq, 12 December 1922, CO 730/34, p. 797.

88. See telegram no. 163, from the High Commissioner to the Secretary of State for the Colonies, dated 27 February 1922, CO 730/20 (vol. 2), Iraq 1922, pp. 321–23.

89. A coffee-shop anecdote, expressing al-Wadha' al-Shadh [the perplexing predicament] of relations between Iraqi statesmen and the British advisers, reported by Gertrude Bell to her father, 16 February 1922, Bell's Letters, Newcastle Library.

90. See Gilmour, Curzon, p. 543.

91. See Barraclough, An Introduction to Contemporary History, p. 72; and A. P. Thornton, The Imperial Idea and its Enemies: A Study in British Power (London: Macmillan, 1959), p. 190.

92. See Thornton, The Imperial Idea and its Enemies, p. 185 and A. J. P. Taylor, English History, 1914-1945 (Oxford: Oxford University Press, 1990), p. 163.

93. Bonar Law's response to the Chanak Crisis in a letter to The Times, 7 October 1922, quoted in M. E. Yapp, The Near East Since the First World War: A History to 1995 (London: Longman, 1996), p. 380.

94. Law quoted in Paul Kennedy, The Realities Behind Diplomacy, p. 267.

95. On the role of Iraq in the election campaign see Ireland, Iraq, p. 377; and Elizabeth Monroe, Britain's Moment in the Middle East, 1914–1917 (London: Chatto and Windus, 1981), pp. 77–78.

96. Bonar Law and Ormsby Gore reflecting in the House of Commons on Law's election statements, quoted in The Times, 21 February and 2 March 1923.

97. See The Times, 21 February 1923; and Ireland, Iraq, p. 377.

98. The Times, 21 February 1923.

99. Law's election manifesto promised: "The nation's first need is, in every walk of life, to get on with its own work, with the minimum of interference at

home and of disturbance abroad." Quoted in A. J. P. Taylor, *English History*, p. 196. British taxes per head of population had risen six fold from 1914 to 1922. See Thornton, *The Imperial Idea and its Enemies*, p. 184.

100. See Ireland, *Iraq*, p. 377.

101. Cox's advice was deemed so important that it was printed and circulated to the whole of the cabinet. See I.R.Q. 30, Secret, copy no. 103, Reply to Questionnaire by Sir P. Cox, printed for the cabinet, February 1923, CO 6851 7 FEB 23, cabinet committee on Iraq, CO 730/53.

102. See CO 730/53, CO 6851 7 FEB 23, cabinet committee on Iraq; Sluglett, *Britain in Iraq*, p. 80; and Ernest Main, *Iraq From Mandate to Independence* (London: George Allen and Unwin, 1935), p. 84.

103. *The Times*, 21 March 1923.

104. Secret, to the High Commissioner Sir Percy Cox, from the Secretary of State for the Colonies, Duke of Devonshire, CO 19114 17 APR 23, Organic Law, CO 730/47, p. 430.

105. General instructions as to the manner the High Commissioner for Iraq discharges his duties, Iraq Confidential B, from Devonshire, the Secretary of State for Colonies, to Sir Henry Dobbs, the High Commissioner for Iraq, Downing Street, 20 September 1923, Sudan Collection, University of Durham Library, Box 472/13/141, pp. 1–14.

106. For example, "The aim of our policy in Iraq is, after all, to leave the Iraq Government strong enough to hold its own and friendly to us and it would be an absurd anti-climax if we simultaneously weakened and antagonised that Government by insisting on its always tamely accepting our views." "The first necessity of this situation was to convince the politically minded part of the Iraq people of the disinterested attitude of Great Britain and to disabuse them of the suspicion that she was aiming at the perpetual domination of Iraq. A suspicion which persisted in spite of the expressed reluctance of the newly elected Conservative Government of Great Britain to accept the Mandate for the country." From Sir Henry Dobbs, the Residency, Baghdad, 10 January 1924, to Devonshire, the Secretary of State for the Colonies, CO 730/57, Iraq 1924, vol. 1, Dispatches (January–February), pp. 282–83 and 276–77. Also see CO 8563 23 FEB 25, CO 730/73, Iraq 1925, Despatches (21 February–18 March).

107. See Secret from H. Dobbs, High Commissioner to the Duke of Devonshire, Secretary of State for the Colonies, 22 November 1923, CO 60034 10 DEC 23, cabinet crisis, CO 730/43, Iraq 1923, Dispatches (October–November).

108. From Sir Henry Dobbs, the Residency, Baghdad, to the Duke of Devonshire, Secretary of State for the Colonies, 10 January 1924, CO 730/57, Iraq 1924, vol. 1, Dispatches (Janu–February), p. 282.

109. See, for example, private letter from Dobbs to Shuckburgh, 7 February 1924, CO 8246 20 FEB 24, Relations between the High Commissioner and the Colonial Office on economic questions, CO 730/71, Iraq 1924, vol. 15, Individuals, p. 165.

110. See Minutes, no. c.f. 15656, Appointment of an additional Assistant Secretary to the High Commissioner, CO 730/107/67, Iraq 1926, and Minutes, C. 1845 29 SEP 1926, Meeting of the PMC, Nov. 1926, CO 730/95, Iraq 1926, vol. 4, Dispatches (August–September).

111. British Gazetted Officers in Iraq in 1923 numbered 181, by 1926 they numbered 148. British non-Gazetted Officers numbered 361 in 1923 but only 53 in 1926. Indian Officials numbered 1,270 in 1923 but only 250 in 1926. See Ireland, *Iraq*, p. 367. According to Dobbs, by December 1926 there were only 104 British officers holding senior appointments in Iraq and only 12 officers responsible for regional administration, compared to 473 and 91 in 1920. See Sir Henry Dobbs, oral statement on Iraq by the accredited representative, League of Nations Permanent Mandate Commission, tenth session, Provisional Minutes of the Seventh Meeting held on Monday, 8 November 1926, CO 730/96, Iraq 1926, vol. 5, Despatches (October–December), p. 714.

112. See Ireland, *Iraq*, p. 367.

113. To Shuckburgh from Young, Baghdad, 8 December 1921, CO 63592 24 DEC 21, Affairs of Iraq, CO 730/18, p. 595; and to Shuckburgh from Young, London, 20 February 1922, CO 6360 9 FEB 22, High Commission Staff, CO 730/19, vol. 1, Iraq 1922, p. 641.

114. Although his resignation was explained on health grounds, Slater's "attitude," taking the side of the Iraqi Government against both Dobbs and the Colonial Office in London was a strong contributing factor to his dismissal. See CO 55465 26 NOV 24, CO 730/71, Iraq 1924, vol. 15, Individuals, p. 302.

115. To Henry Dobbs from J. E. Shuckburgh, Private, NC/62556/23, Downing Street, 4 January 1924, CO 62556 21 DEC 23, Financial adviser to the Iraq Government, CO 730/44, Dispatches, December 1923, p. 322.

116. To Sir Henry Dobbs from S. H. Vernon, Baghdad, 21 September 1924, CO 59869 23 DEC 24, S.H. Slater, the late Financial Secretary to the Iraq Government, CO 730/71, Iraq 1924, vol. 15, Individuals, pp. 339–40.

117. Dobbs, quoted by Shuckburgh, to Dobbs from J. E. Shuckburgh, Private, NC/62556/23, Downing Street, 4 January 1924, CO 62556 21 DEC 23, Financial adviser to the Iraq Government, CO 730 /44, Dispatches, December 1923, p. 312.

118. Personal note prepared by Sir Hugh Trenchard in regard to his views on the situation that has arisen in Iraq, in answer to a request by Sir Samuel

Wilson, no. 40104, part 1, Defence Forces Reorganisation, Iraq, CO 730/114/4, p. 39.

119. It was viewed with suspicion at the Colonial Office which complained that Henry Dobbs, as acting High Commissioner, had not kept it informed in enough detail about the issues surrounding the legislation. See Young's minute dated 6 April 1923, Administrative Inspector Regulations, CO 13465 16 MAR 23, CO 730/38, 1923, p. 298. Cox wrote to the Council expressing his concern "that the very important change in practice which was proposed should be put into effect in such manner as not to deprive the High Commissioner of the opportunity of watching the development of the administration and its bearing on the interests of H.M.G., with special regard to the employment of Imperial forces." BHCF, File no. 19/1, vol. V (5), Internal Intelligence Reports, Intelligence Report no. 4, Baghdad, 14 Feb. 1923, p. 2.

120. See the Administrative Inspectorate Regulations, CO 13465 16 MAR 23, CO 730/38, 1923, p. 301. Both Cox and then Dobbs recognized that this effect was inherent in the legislation but by this time could not insist that this part of the legislation be dropped. See BHCF, File no. 19/1, vol. 5, Internal Intelligence Reports, Intelligence Report no. 4. Baghdad, 14 February 1923.

121. Confidential letter from P. Cox to Shuckburgh, 27 April 1923, CO 23128 9 MAY 23, Instructions for the High Commissioner, Iraq, CO 730/55, p. 48.

122. Confidential letter from P. Cox to Shuckburgh.

123. See Shuckburgh's Minute, CO 8563 23 FEB 25, CO 730/73, Iraq 1925, Dispatches (21 February–18 March).

124. For the growing power of the Permanent Mandate Commission see Northedge, *The League of Nations*, pp. 198–201.

125. See CO 730/169/7, 1931, no. 88379/1, part 1, Conditions Governing Termination of Mandatory Control, League of Nations, C.P.M. 1210 (1), Geneva, 26 June 1931, Permanent Mandates Commission, Twentieth Session, p. 2.

126. For a summary and the conclusions of the Commissions report, see CO 730/119/10, part I, 1927 Iraq, no. 40299, Admission of Iraq to League of Nations and Revision of the Anglo-Iraq treaty, pp. 166–70.

127. CO 730/119/10, part 1, 1927 Iraq, no. 40299, Admission of Iraq to League of Nations and Revision of the Anglo-Iraq treaty, pp. 167–68.

128. See Peter J. Beck, " 'A Tedious and Perilous Controversy': Britain and the Settlement of the Mosul Dispute, 1918–1926," *Middle East Studies* 17 (April 1981): 265.

129. CO 730/119/10, part 1, 1927 Iraq, no. 40299, Admission of Iraq to League of Nations and Revision of the Anglo-Iraq treaty, p. 169.

130. See Sluglett, *Britain in Iraq*, p. 125.

131. See DO no. SO 448, from Sir Henry Dobbs, the Residency, Baghdad,

24 February 1927, to Leopold Amery, the Secretary of State for the Colonies, CO 730/119/10, part I, 1927, p. 180. Also see Sluglett, *Britain in Iraq*, p. 130.

132. DO no. SO 448, from Sir Henry Dobbs, the Residency, Baghdad, 24 February 1927, to Leopold Amery, the Secretary of State for the Colonies, CO 730/119/10, part 1, 1927, pp. 187–88.

133. J. Hall, 26 June 1927, CO 730/119/10, part I, 1927 Iraq, no. 40299, Admission of Iraq to League of Nations and Revision of the Anglo-Iraq treaty, Minutes 1–35, p. 16.

134. See Sluglett, *Britain in Iraq*, pp. 156–67.

135. DO no. SO 1334, Secret and Personal, from Sir Henry Dobbs, The Residency, Baghdad, 14 June 1927, to Leopold Amery, Secretary for State for the Colonies, CO 730/114/4, 1927 Iraq, no. 40104, part 1. Although he said this after a state dinner when he was drunk, it was one of a number of such statements Nuri made during 1927. See DO/2c/9, from E. L. Ellington, Headquarters Iraq Levies, Mosul, 15 June 1927 to Trenchard, CO 730/120/1, part 2, no. 40299, Admission of Iraq to League of Nations and Revision of Anglo-Iraq treaty, p. 3.

136. See DO no. RO 213, Immediate and Secret, from Bourdillion, the Residency, Baghdad, to King Faisal, 22 July 1927, CO 730/120/1, part 2, no. 40299, Admission of Iraq to League of Nations and Revision of Anglo-Iraq treaty.

137. "If we go in 1928, the State will fall to pieces." Leo Amery describing the Iraqi state after a month's visit in 1925. CO 730/82, CO 22162 15 MAY 25, The Situation in Iraq, Memorandum by the Secretary of State for the Colonies dealing with his visit to Iraq, draft report, p. 17.

138. See Sluglett, *Britain in Iraq*, p. 156.

139. Document no. 40299A, Revision of the Anglo-Iraq treaty, Middle East Dept., Colonial Office, September 28, CO 730/120/2, p. 3.

140. Memorandum by the Secretary of State for the Colonies, dealing with his visit to Iraq, CO 22162 15 MAY 25, CO 730/82, Iraq 1925, vol. 11, Colonial Office (January–May), p. 18.

141. Memorandum by the Chancellor of the Dutchy of Lancaster, 17 June 1927, Paper C.P. 182 (27), SECRET O.P. 182 (27) cabinet, Entry of Iraq into the League of Nations, CO 730/119/10, part 1, 1927 Iraq, pp. 3–4.

142. See Thornton, *The Imperial Idea and its Enemies*, pp. 298–99. Also A. J. P. Taylor, *English History, 1914–1945*, pp. 51, 264–71.

143. See Sluglett, *Britain in Iraq*, p. 168.

144. Secret B, from Gilbert Clayton, the High Commission, the Residency, Baghdad, to Lord Passfield, the Secretary of State for the Colonies, 22 July 1929, CO 730/148/8, 1929 Iraq, part 1, pp. 145–59.

145. Draft Memorandum for the cabinet, Future Policy in Iraq, CO 730/148/8, 1929 Iraq, part 1, pp. 96–97.

146. See Wm. Roger Louis, *In the Name of God Go! Leo Amery and the British Empire in the Age of Churchill* (New York: W. W. Norton and Company, 1992).

147. Sir Henry Dobbs, in retirement, predicting the future of Iraq after the 1929 declaration in a letter to Shuckburgh at the Colonial Office, 28 December 1929, CO 730/150/12, 1929 Iraq, pp. 4–5.

148. See Taylor, *English History, 1914–1945*, p. 272.

149. Paul Kennedy, *The Realities Behind Diplomacy*, p. 243; and Taylor, *English History, 1914–1945*, pp. 272–98.

150. Kennedy, *The Realities Behind Diplomacy*, p. 244.

151. Article 22 quoted by Henry Dobbs; CO 730/119/10, part 1, 1927 Iraq, no. 40299, Admission of Iraq to League of Nations and Revision of the Anglo-Iraq treaty, pp. 172–73. The terms for ending a Mandate were further codified by the PMC in January 1931, see CO 730/166/8, League of Nations, Permanent Mandates Commission, Minutes of the Twentieth Session, Annex 3. Conditions to be fulfilled before the Mandate Regime can be brought to an end in respect of a country, pp. 195–210. Also see Wilbur Laurent Williams, *The State Of Iraq: A Mandate Attains Independence, Foreign Policy Reports, Foreign Policy Association*, vol. 8, no. 16 (12 October 1932), p. 186.

152. CO 730/166/8, League of Nations, Permanent Mandates Commission, Minutes of the Twentieth Session, Annex 3. Conditions to be fulfilled before the Mandate Regime can be brought to an end in respect of a country, p. 196.

153. DO no. SO 448, Secret Draft, from Sir Henry Dobbs, Baghdad, to the Secretary of State for the Colonies, London, 24 February 1927, CO 730/119/10, part 1, 1927 Iraq, no. 40299, Admission of Iraq to the League of Nations and Revision of the Anglo-Iraq treaty, 1927, p. 173.

154. Dobbs compares Iraq "to the Papal States between 1849 and 1870, with a French garrison maintained in Rome at the request of the sovereign Pope and somewhat similar to that of Haiti and Cuba, which are members of the League." DO no. SO 448, Secret Draft, from Sir Henry Dobbs, p. 173.

155. Dobbs, DO no. SO 448, Secret Draft, pp. 174–75.

156. Colonial Office, *Special Report by His Majesty's Government in the United Kingdom of Great Britain and Northern Ireland to the Council of the League of Nations on the Progress of Iraq During the Period 1920–1931* (London: His Majesty's Stationery Office, 1931), pp. 10–11.

157. Sir Francis Humphrys's opening statement to the sixteenth meeting of the twentieth session of the Permanent Mandates Commission, Provisional Minutes, Iraq: Examination of the Special Report for the period 1920–1931, CO 730/166/7, Iraq 1931, no. 88149, part 1, p. 38.

158. See Ireland, *Iraq: A Study in Political Development*, p. 148 and Sluglett, *Britain in Iraq*, p. 211.

3. *Corruption, Fragmentation, and Despotism:*
British Visions of Ottoman Iraq

1. See for examples of this A. T. Wilson, *Loyalties, Mesopotamia*, vol. 1, *1914–1917: A Personal and Historical Record* (London: Oxford University Press, 1930), p. 21; and Sir Ronald Evelyn Wingate, "Mesopotamia and South-Eastern Arabia during and just after the War," a talk given to the Middle East Center, Oxford, 2 March 1965. Text in the Durham University Sudan Collection, Box 132/9/1–34, Sir Ronald Evelyn Wingate (1889–1978).

2. See Stephen Hemsley Longrigg, *Iraq 1900 to 1950: A Political, Social and Economic History* (Oxford: Issued under the auspices of the Royal Institute of International Affairs by Oxford University Press, 1953), p. 85. Also see, Public Records Office (PRO), Colonial Office (CO) 696/1, Iraq Administration Reports, 1917–1918, p. 11.

3. PRO, CO 730/121/1, no. 40311, Report on Iraq by Ahmed Fahmi, Accountant-General, Baghdad.

4. See Nick Hostettler, "The Asiatic Mode of Production." Unpublished paper, Department of Political Studies, School of Oriental and African Studies, April 1993, p. 3.

5. The debacles at Kut and Gallipoli saw the supposedly inferior Ottoman troops inflict stunning defeats on allied forces. The Gallipoli campaign in the Turkish Dardanelles, started as an ill-fated attempt to break the stalemate on the Western front by marching on Constantinople. After a 259-day siege, Commonwealth and British troops retreated with each side suffering a quarter of a million casualties in bloody trench warfare. At Kut al-Amara, a small village on the Tigris, British troops suffered a grueling 146-day siege, only surrendering to Ottoman forces when their rations had run out. See David Fromkin, *A Peace to End All Peace: Creating the Modern Middle East, 1914-1922* (Harmondsworth: Penguin Books, 1991), pp. 128-66, 200–3.

6. See Bruce Westrate, *The Arab Bureau: British Policy in the Middle East, 1916–1920* (State College, Penn.: Pennsylvania State University Press, 1992), pp. 11, 58, 140.

7. See Graham Dawson, "The Blond Bedouin: Lawrence of Arabia, Imperial Adventure and the Imagining of English-British Masculinity," in *Manful Assertions, Masculinities in Britain since 1800*, ed. Michael Roper and John Tosh (London: Routledge, 1991), p. 123.

8. Bryan S. Turner, *Marx and the End of Orientalism* (London: George Allen and Unwin, 1978), p. 166.

9. See Haim Gerber, *The Social Origins of the Modern Middle East* (Boulder: Lynne Rienner Publishers, 1987), p. 4.

10. For the role of such a construct in colonial India see Bernard S. Cohn, "Representing Authority in Victorian India," in *The Invention of Tradition*, ed. Eric Hobsbawn and Terence Ranger (Cambridge: Canto, Cambridge University Press, 1993), pp. 166–167.

11. Public Records Office (PRO), Colonial Office (CO) 696/1, vol. 1, Reports of Administration for 1918 of Divisions and Districts of the Occupied Territories in Mesopotamia. Iraq Administration Reports, 1917–1918. Basra division. Administrative Reports for Basra Division for the year 1918, p. 240. This theme was more explicitly developed in Mosul in 1919, see CO696/2, Iraq Administration reports, 1919, Mosul Division Report by Lieutenant-Colonel L. S. Nalder, p. 13.

12 Longrigg, *Four Centuries of Modern Iraq* (Oxford: Oxford University Press, 1925), and *Iraq, 1900 to 1950*.

13. For details of S. H. Longrigg's career see Indian National Archive Baghdad High Commission Files (BHCF) File no. 6/3/104 I, Ministry of Finance, Major S. H. Longrigg.

14. Longrigg, *Four Centuries of Modern Iraq*, p. 321. We find a very similar attitude in A. T. Wilson's book, see 'Prologue' in *Loyalties Mesopotamia*, vol. 1.

15. Longrigg, *Four Centuries of Modern Iraq*.

16. For examples of the book's influence on policy see BHCF File no. 6/34/22, DO/9894, from Secretariat of the High Commissioner to Longrigg, 19 August 1926, pp. 74–5. Also Gertrude Bell had a copy of *Four Centuries of Modern Iraq* in her small library when she died. See BHCF File no. 35/143-I, The Estate of the late Miss G.L. Bell, CBE, p. 201.

17. See Asli Cirakman, "The Prejudice of Montesquieu: Intellectual Roots of Modern Eurocentrism," paper presented at the Middle East Studies Association, 32nd Annual Meeting, Chicago, Illinois, 3–6 December, 1998 p. 20.

18. See Asli Cirakman, p. 20; and Albertine Jwaideh, "Midhat Pasha and the Land System of Lower Iraq," *St Antony's Papers* 16 (Oxford, 1963), p. 112.

19. Eugene L. Rogan, *Frontiers of the State in the Late Ottoman Empire: Transjordan, 1850–1921* (Cambridge: Cambridge University Press, 1999), p. 13.

20. See, for example, Selim Deringil, *The Well Protected Domains: Ideology and Legitimation in the Ottoman Empire, 1876–1909* (London: I.B. Tauris, 1998).

21. Lady Anne Blout, *Bedouin Tribes of the Euphrates*, vol. 1 (London: Frank Cass, 1968) (first published in 1870), p. 109.

22. Longrigg, *Iraq*, p. 35.

23. Longrigg, *Iraq*, p. 36.

24. Minute signed by Young, CO 13377, 20 March 1924; The murder of Taufiq el Kh'alidi, CO 730/71, vol. 15, Individuals, p. 139.

25. See the Sudan Archive, University of Durham, Box 472/13/127, letter from Sir Henry Dobbs, High Commissioner, to Leopold Amery, Secretary of State for the Colonies, 4 December 1928, p. 4.

26. Glubb argued that Hameed Beg, the *qa'immaqam* of Ana, "was convinced that a European suit and a smattering of French placed him in a different world from the good people of Ana," John Glubb, *Arabian Adventures. Ten Years of Joyful Service* (London: Cassell, 1978), p. 73.

27. See Gokhan Cetinsaya, "Ottoman Administration of Iraq, 1890–1908," (Ph.D. diss., University of Manchester, 1994), pp. 43–57; and Sluglett, *Britain in Iraq*, p. 235.

28. Cetinsaya, "Ottoman Administration of Iraq," pp. 54–55. This role was not exclusive to the naqib of Baghdad. A similar position involving state society mediation and even Persian Gulf diplomacy was taken by the naqib of Basra in the 1880s and 1890s.

29. See Jwaideh, "Midhat Pasha and the Land System of Lower Iraq," p. 112.

30. Namik Pasha was removed from office in Baghdad in Oct. 1902. See Cetinsaya, "Ottoman Administration of Iraq," pp. 133–138.

31. Gertrude Bell, "The Basis of Government in Turkish Arabia," *Arab Bulletin* 24 (5 October 1916), p. 320.

32. Sir Edgar Bonham Carter, the man who wrote the judicial code for the nascent Iraqi state, in Gertrude Bell, *Mesopotamia: Review of Civil Administration*, E13898, FO 371/5081, 1920, p. 96.

33. See C. A. Hooper, Note on the extent to which Ottoman Law is in force in Iraq, 40641, CO 730/125/16, 28 December 1927, p. 4.

34. A. T. Wilson, *Loyalties, Mesopotamia*, vol. 1, p. 68.

35. CO 730/35, CO 15296, 31 March 1922, the Organic Law, p. 339.

36. Minute from Bullard to Shuckburgh, on the Organic Law, CO 15296, CO 730/35, p. 400.

37. See Longrigg *Iraq*, pp. 166, 201.

38. Preliminary Note II, On Settlement of Rights in pump areas, BHCF File no. 6/34/65, opened January 1931. Subject: Report by Sir Ernest Dowson—on land settlement in Iraq and allied subjects—p. 6. For other examples see Gertrude Bell's letters, Newcastle Library, 9 November 1921, Trip to Kurdistan, Administration Report of Diwaniyah district, CO 696/1, Iraq Administration reports 1917–1918, vol. 1, Reports of Administration for 1918 of Divisions and Districts of the Occupied Territories in Mesopotamia, p. 197.

39. See *The Times*, 22 July 1927, Imperial and Foreign News, "Irrigation in Iraq, Progress in recent years," by 'our own correspondent in Baghdad," and The Dujail Plain, Administrative Report, Samarra District, 1917, CO 696/1, Iraq Administration Reports 1917–1918, p. 9.

40. See Gertrude Bell, *Mesopotamia: Review of Civil Administration*, 1920, E13898, FO 371/5081, p. 22.

41. Lt. Col. E.B. Howell, Revenue Secretary to the Civil Commissioner, "Land revenue demand: Turkish theory and practice," Administration Report on the working of the Revenue Dept. for the year 1919, CO 696/2, Iraq Administration Reports, 1919.

42. Sir Ernest Dowson (Formerly Surveyor-General of Egypt, and later successively Under-Secretary of State for Finance, then Financial Adviser to the Egyptian Government), *Government of el Iraq: An Inquiry into Land Tenure and Related Questions with Proposals for the Initiation of Reform* (Letchworth, England: printed for the Iraqi Government by the Garden City Press, 1931); BHCF File no. 6/34/65. Subject: Report by Sir Ernest M. Dowson—on land settlement in Iraq and allied subjects—p. 20. Also see Thomas Lyell, *The Ins and Outs of Mesopotamia* (Cambridge: Allborough Publishing, 1991), p. 164.

43. S. H. Longrigg, Inspector-General Revenue and Acting Director, Annual Report on the Operations of the Revenue Dept. for the Financial Year 1927–1928, CO 696/6, Iraq Administration Reports, 1925–1928, p. 4; and A. T. Wilson, *Loyalties, Mesopotamia*, vol. 1, p. 77.

44. Jwaideh, "Midhat Pasha and the Land System of Lower Iraq," p. 106.

45. Jwaideh, "Midhat Pasha and the Land System of Lower Iraq," p. 108.

46. Note by the High Commissioner, Sir Henry Dobbs, 10 July 1926, BHCF File no. 6/34/22, heading Finance, sub-head Revenue. Subject: Mr S.H. Longrigg's note on Revenue Policy in Iraq, p. 2.

47. Longrigg, *Four Centuries of Modern Iraq*, p. 306.

48. Note by the High Commissioner, Sir Henry Dobbs, 10 July 1926, BHCF File no. 6/34/22, heading Finance, sub-head Revenue. Subject: Mr S. H. Longrigg's note on Revenue Policy in Iraq, p. 3.

49. Dobbs, Note by the High Commissioner, p. 15.

50. Dowson, *Government of el Iraq*.

51. S. H. Longrigg, Ministry of Finance, 25 June 1926, Note on Land and Revenue Policy, BHCF File no. 6/34/22, heading Finance, sub-head Revenue. Subject: Mr S. H. Longrigg's note on Revenue Policy in Iraq, p. 120.

52. Longrigg, *Iraq*, p. 37.

53. See Glubb, *The Changing Scenes of Life: An Autobiography* (London: Quartet Books, 1983), p. 75.

54. Note by the High Commissioner on pump irrigation on the rivers of Iraq and connected questions, CO 730/95, Iraq 1926, vol. 4, Despatches (August–September), C. 16338, 23 August 1926, Pump Irrigation, p. 9.

55. Glubb, *The Changing Scenes of Life*, p. 77.

56. Longrigg, *Four Centuries of Modern Iraq*, p. 307.

57. See Timothy Mitchell, *Rule of Experts* (Berkeley: University of California Press, 2002), p. 57.

58. See Sluglett, *Britain in Iraq*, p. 231; and Jwaideh, "Midhat Pasha and the Land System of Lower Iraq," p. 119.

59. See Charles Issawi, ed., *The Economic History of the Middle East, 1800–1914: A Book of Readings* (Chicago: University of Chicago Press, 1975), p. 166; Jwaideh, "Midhat Pasha and the Land System of Lower Iraq," p. 119; and Cetinsaya, "Ottoman Administration of Iraq," p. 31.

60. See Assistant Political Officer Mylles, IOL, L/P&S/10/621, p. 7; P6705, Notes on the Tribes and Shaikhs of Anah-Albu Kamal District, by Captain C.C. Mylles, APO, 1920. Ireland and Longrigg both describe 'primitive communities' still living untouched by civilised government and unable to visualise any alternative to their lives. Ireland, *Iraq*, p. 89; and Longrigg, *Four Centuries of Modern Iraq*, p. 289.

61. BHCF File no. 6/34/22, DO/8165, from R. S. M. Sturges, Secretariat to the High Commissioner, to S. H. Longrigg, Revenue Secretary, Ministry of Finance, 14 July 1926, p. 1. This perception also runs through pre-war travel writing on the Ottoman Empire, see Lady Anne Blunt, *Bedouin Tribes of the Euphrates* (London: Frank Cass, 1968), vol. 1.

62. Gertrude Bell, *Mesopotamia: Review of Civil Administration*, 9 November 1920, FO 371/5081, E13898, p. 94. Also see A. T. Wilson, *Loyalties, Mesopotamia*, vol. 1, p. 77; and Lyell, *The Ins and Outs of Mesopotamia*, p. 164.

63. Longrigg, *Iraq*, p. 25. For a similar attitude see also Administration Report of Suq-esh-Shuyukh and district for the year 1916–17, by H.P.P. Dickson, Assistant Political Officer, 9 May 1917, IOL, File no. 1736, L/P&S/10/618, p. 506.

64. BHCF File no. 6/34/22, DO/8165, from R. S. M. Sturges [for Henry Dobbs], Secretariat to the High Commissioner, to S. H. Longrigg, Revenue Secretary, Ministry of Finance, 14 July 1926, p. 56.

65. BHCF File no. 6/34/22, DO/8165, p. 5.

66. BHCF File no. 6/34/22, DO/8165, pp. 3–4.

67. See Cetinsaya, "Ottoman Administration of Iraq, 1890–1908," p. 198.

68. See Jwaideh, "Midhat Pasha and the Land System of Lower Iraq," pp.

130–131; and Cetinsaya, "Ottoman Administration of Iraq, 1890–1908," pp. 198–206.

69. See for example Martin J. Wiener, *English Culture and the Decline of the Industrial Spirit, 1850–1980* (Harmondsworth: Penguin, 1992); Gerard J. Degroot, *Blighty: British Society in the Era of the Great War* (London: Longman, 1996); and Mark Girouard, *The Return of Camelot: Chivalry and the English Gentleman* (New Haven, Conn.: Yale University Press, 1989).

70. Alexis de Tocqueville, *Democracy in America*, vol. 2 (New York: Vantage Books, 1990), pp. 221–22.

4. Rural and Urban: The Divided Social Imagination of Late Colonialism

1. Bernard S. Cohn, *Colonialism and its Forms of Knowledge: The British in India* (Princeton, N.J.: Princeton University Press, 1996), p. 5.

2. Gertrude Bell, Preface to *The Desert and the Sown* (1907; reprint, Boston: Beacon Press, 1985).

3. Public Records Office (PRO), Colonial Office (CO) 730/33, Letter, GHQ British Forces in Iraq, 27 March 1922, from Haldane, Head of British Forces, Iraq, to Winston Churchill.

4. Indian National Archive (INA), Baghdad High Commission Files (BHCF), File no. 19/1, vol. 4, Intelligence Report no. 22, Baghdad, 15 November 1922, paragraph 1097.

5. PRO, AIR 23/445, I/2106, part 8, Euphrates, Samawah to Fallujah, 1923, p 10. D/582 of 27 December 1923, to 'I' Branch Air Staff, from Special Service Officer (SSO) Nasiriyah.

6. CO 730/21, CO 21941 9 MAY 22, Situation in Iraq, from Cox to Shuckburgh, Baghdad 28 April 1922, p. 389.

7. CO 730/21, Cox, Situation in Iraq, p. 389. CO 730/24, CO 43361, from Cox, the Residency, Baghdad, 31 August 1922, p. 22.

8. CO 730/114/4, Secret and Personal, DO no. SO 1334, the Residency, Baghdad, 14 June 1927, from Dobbs to Amery, appendix 1, note dated 2 August 1923. The theme of sexual depravity found wider purchase in a report by the Adviser to the Ministry of Education who claimed that "fifteen hundred years ago Ammianus Marcellinas stated that the Arabs of both sexes were inordinately addicted to matrimonial pleasures' and it is today, I believe, the unanimous opinion of every European connected with education in Iraq, that a very large part of the adult Moslem population has been permanently dulled, mentally and morally, by premature and excessive indulgence in various sexual vices which induce a general moral degradation. The Christians are less open to reproach in this respect but the very precau-

tions which they take tend to produce a character lacking in strength and virility. The only remedy lies in some application of the English Public School and Boy Scout ideal." The results of such activity were seen "in the middle classes of the urban population of Iraq, where, after the age of puberty, an inveterate dignity allows to few the indulgence of more vigorous hobbies than tea drinking and gossip in public and in private certain unmentionable indoor sports. It is not from this soil that we can expect to grow such humble virtues as a sense of duty, self sacrifice and sober patriotism." See CO 730/14, to the High Commissioner from the Adviser to the Ministry of Education, "The Education Dept. in its Relations to the Mandate and the League of Nations," p. 103.

9. CO 730/120/1, part 2, Reference DO/2c/9, Headquarters Iraq Levies, Mosul, 15 June 1927, Very Secret, from E. L. Ellington to Trenchard.

10. CO 730/123/10, Secret, Note on the Political Situation to 27 September 1927, from C. J. Edmonds, p. 129.

11. BHCF, File no. 5/1/1, vol. 2, Correspondence with the Ministry of Education, 27 December 1929, Note on the Present State of Education in Iraq, C/165, from the Inspector General of Education, p. 44.

12. CO 730/22, Iraq Intelligence Report no. 10, dated 15 May 1922, paragraph 408, p. 148, by Major Yetts, Adviser to Mutasarrif of Nasiriyah.

13. CO 696/3, Iraq Administration Reports 1920–1921, Administrative Report of Kirkuk Division, 1 January 1920 to 31 December 1920, p. 7.

14. CO 730/59, Iraq 1924, Despatches (May), CO 27354 9 JUNE 1924, Intelligence Report, the Residency Baghdad, 29 May 1924, Intelligence Report no. 11, Iraq Internal Affairs, p. 434.

15. Haj, *The Making of Iraq*, p. 146; and Owen, "Class and Class Politics in Iraq Before 1958."

16. Foreign Office (FO) 371/5227, E8267, Copy of Sir H. Dobbs's memo on the Proposals of Sir E. Bonham-Carter's Committee, 14 July 1920, p. 2.

17. Stephen Hemsley Longrigg, *Four Centuries of Modern Iraq* (London: Oxford University Press, 1925), p. 322.

18. See, for example, Colonial Office, *Iraq: Report on Iraq Administration, April 1922-March 1923* (London: His Majesty's Stationery Office, 19240; Colonial no. 4., p. 5; and CO 696/1, vol. 1, Reports of Administration for 1918 of Divisions and Districts of the Occupied Territories in Mesopotamia, Shamiyah Division Annual Administration Report, 1 January to 31 Dece 1918, p. 67; Longrigg, *Iraq, 1900 to 1950: A Political, Social, and Economic History* (Oxford: Oxford University Press, 1953), p. 10.

19. Gertrude Bell, August 1920, *From Her Personal Papers, 1914–1926*, vol. 2, ed. Elizabeth Burgoyne (London: Ernest Benn Limited, 1961), p. 157. Bell to

her father, 3 October 1920, the Letters of Gertrude Bell, Newcastle Library. This points to the development of an Orientalist view of Islam as having its roots in an analysis of Britain's own normative march to modernity. The perceived negative effect of the Shia *Mujtahids* on the development of a strong and modern state is comparable to Rome's resistance to the independence and development of the modern British state.

20. Gertrude Bell letter to her mother, 14 March 1920, Bell's Letters, Newcastle Library. Sudan Archives, Durham, Box 303/1/82, Mesopotamia Lecture by Lieutenant-Colonel Sir Arnold Wilson, given after leaving Iraq, p. 5. AIR 23/382, I/130, Intelligence Reports on Internal Politics, Baghdad, 1930–1932, from Special Services Officer, Baghdad, to Air Staff Intelligence, Air Headquarters, Hinadi, I/Bd/39, 18 March 1931.

21. See CO 696/3, Iraq Administration Reports, 1920–1921, Administrative Report of the Muntafiq Division for the year 1920, p. 19. See BHCF File no. 19/1, vol. 4, Intelligence Report no. 17, 1 September 1922, p. 4; and BHCF File no. 19/1, vol. 5, Intelligence Report no. 9, 1 May 1923; and CO 730/57, vol. 1, CO 3273, 21 January 1924, Intelligence Report no. 1, p. 139. See BHCF File No. 7/44/2, Letter from the Adviser to the Ministry of Interior, Mr. Edmonds, to the High Commissioner, 12 October 1931.

22. Bell, Letter to her father, 3 October 1920, Bell's Letters, Newcastle Library. But strategic reasons would have had a greater part to play in official calculations on the inclusion or otherwise of Mosul; see Robert Olson, "The Battle for Kurdistan: The Churchill-Cox Correspondence Regarding the Creation of the State of Iraq, 1921–1923," *The International Journal of Turkish Studies* (1993); and Robert Olson, "The Second Time Around: British Policy towards the Kurds (1921–1922)," *Die Welt des Islams* 27 (1987).

23. Longrigg, *Iraq*, 1900 to 1950, p. 10.

24. CO 696/1, vol. 1, Reports of Administration for 1918 of Divisions and Districts of the Occupied Territories in Mesopotamia, Shamiyah Division Annual Administration Report, 1 January to 31 December 1918, p. 65. Also see AIR 23/382, I/130, Intelligence Reports on Internal Politics, Baghdad, 1930–1932, p. 26a.

25. See, for example, Martin J. Wiener, *English Culture and the Decline of the Industrial Spirit, 1850–1980* (Harmondsworth: Penguin, 1992), p. 6.

26. See, for example, the discussion of Sir Thomas Munro's early career in India in Eric Stokes, *The English Utilitarians and India* (Oxford: Oxford University Press, 1959), pp. 12–13; and P. J. Musgrave, "Social Power and Social Change in the United Provinces, 1860–1920," in *Economy and Society: Essays in Indian Economic and Social History*, ed. K. N. Chaudhuri and Clive J. Dewey (Delhi: Oxford University Press, 1979), p. 10.

27. See V. G. Kiernan, *The Lords of Human Kind: European Attitudes to the Outside World in the Imperial Age* (Harmondsworth: Penguin, 1972), p. 55.

28. See Lord Lugard, *The Dual Mandate in British Tropical Africa* (London: Frank Cass, 1965), p. 79.

29. See Tim Youngs, *Travellers in Africa: British Travelouges, 1850–1900* (Manchester: Manchester University Press, 1994), p. 89.

30. Henry Dobbs to L.C.E.S. Amery, Secretary of State for the Colonies, 4 December 1928, Box 427/13/127, Durham University Library, Sudan Collection, p. 4.

31. CO 730/40, CO 33280 4 JULY 1923, Local forces in Iraq, Minutes, by Meinertzhagen, 10 November 1923, p. 734.

32. CO 730/1, Iraq (Mesopotamia), vol. 1, Dispatch 9829, Mesopotamian Intelligence Report no. 4, 31 December 1920, Proceedings of the Council of Ministers.

33. Durham University Library, Sudan Archives, Box 303/1/67, P 8253/19, Dispatch from the Civil Commissioner, Mesopotamia, to Secretary of State for India, no. 344436/75/19, Office of the Civil Commissioner, Baghdad, 15 November 1919, p. 7.

34. Batatu, *The Old Social Classes and the Revolutionary Movements of Iraq*, p. 35.

35. Batatu, *The Old Social Classes and the Revolutionary Movements of Iraq*, p. 13. Batatu details this movement of people without drawing the wider analytical conclusion that tribal allegiances, although changed by modernity, can and do survive these transformative effects.

36. See Batatu, *The Old Social Classes and the Revolutionary Movements of Iraq*; Haj, *The Making of Iraq*, p. 146; and Owen, "Class and Class Politics in Iraq Before 1958," p. 158.

37. See, for example, CO 730/14, p. 189, *Report by His Britannic Majesty's Government on the Administration of Iraq for the Period April 1923–Dec. 1924* (London: His Majesty's Stationery Office, 1925), Colonial no. 13, section 28; *Report by His Britannic Majesty's Government to the Council of the League of Nations on the Administration of Iraq for the Year 1925*, (London: His Majesty's Stationery Office, 1926), Colonial no. 21, p. 138; CO 730/1, Iraq vol. 1, Despatch no. 9829; CO 730/40, CO 33280, 4 July 1923, letter from Dobbs to Devonshire, 20 June 1923, p. 739; CO 730/57, CO 3271, letter from Dobbs to Devonshire, 10 January 1924, to name but a few sources.

38. As described by an RAF Intelligence Officer in April 1924, quoted in Sluglett, *Britain in Iraq*, p. 267.

39. J. B. Glubb, *The Changing Scenes of Life: An Autobiography* (London: Quartet Books, 1983), p. 71.

40. Gertrude Bell, Mesopotamia: Review of Civil Administration, November 1920, Foreign Office (FO) 371/5081, E13898, p. 150. See also BHCF, File no. 19/1, VI Internal, Intelligence Report no. 4, Baghdad, 21 February 1924; and Longrigg, *Iraq, 1900 to 1950,* p. 114.

41. India Office Library (IOL), L/P&S/18, B284, Note by Sir Percy Cox to the Eastern Committee, The Future of Mesopotamia, E.C. 173, 22 April 1918, p. 5. IOL, L/P&S/18, B317, enclosure no. 9, in a letter from A.T. Wilson on the future of Iraq, dated 6 April 1919, by R.E. Wingate, Political Officer, Najaf, p. 8.

42. *Great Britain, Report on the Administration of Iraq, April 1923–December 1924,* p. 214, quoted in Batatu, *The Old Social Classes and the Revolutionary Movements of Iraq,* p. 93; and BHCF, File no. 7/20/19, Ministry of Interior, Personalities of Diwaniyah Division, "Muhammad al Haji Hassan," p. 2.

43. BHCF File no. 4/69I, Conscription Bill, no. SO/1715, from R. S. M Sturges, Political Secretary to the High Commissioner, to the Ministry of Defence, p. 2; and no. C/1670, from Cornwallis, Adviser to the Ministry of Interior, to the High Commissioner, 1 July 1926, p. 27.

44. CO 730/5, CO 489631, Mesopotamian Intelligence Report, no. 20, 1 September 1921, p. 125.

45. See Bell's Letters, Newcastle Library; to her father, 16 February 1922.

46. Summed up by the Special Services Officer, Baghdad, I/Bd/39, 19 May 1931, PRO, AIR 23/282, p. 32a. See Glubb, *Changing Scenes of Life,* p. 81.

47. CO 730/5, CO 50265 10 OCT. 1921, Report of Divisional Adviser, Dulaim, 15 August to 31 August, p. 245.

48. BHCF, File no. 19/1, vol. 4, Intelligence Report no. 16, Baghdad, 15 August 1922.

49. BHCF, File no. 6/34/55, heading Finance, sub-head Revenue, DO/816, from the Secretariat to the High Commissioner, to S. H. Longrigg, 14 July 1926, p. 57.

50. Sir Ronald Evelyn Wingate, "Mesopotamia and South-Eastern Arabia During and Just After the War," a talk given to the Middle East Centre, Oxford, 2 March 1965. Text in the Durham University Sudan Collection, Box 132/9/1–34, Sir Ronald Evelyn Wingate (1889–1978). He entered the Indian Civil Service in 1912 and served in Mesopotamia from 1917 to 1919.

51. Sudipta Kaviraj, "On the Construction of Colonial Power: Structure, Discourse, and Hegemony," in *Contesting Colonial Hegemony, State and Society in Africa and India,* ed. Dagmar Engles and Shula Marxs (London: British Academic Press, 1994), p. 43.

52. Timothy Mitchell, *Colonizing Egypt* (Berkeley, Calif.: University of California Press, 1991), p. x.

53. Owen, "Class and Class Politics in Iraq Before 1958," p. 158.

54. A. T. Wilson, *Loyalties, Mesopotamia*, vol. 1, *1914–1917: A Personal and Historical Record* (London: Oxford University Press, 1930), p. 21.

55. See Longrigg, *Iraq 1900 to 1950*, p. 85. Also see CO 696/1, Iraq Administration Reports, 1917–1918, p. 11.

56. Both Owen, "Class and Class Politics in Iraq Before 1958," and Tarbush, *The Role of the Military in Politics*, mention British attempts to carry out a census but Ahmed Fahmi, the Accountant-General of Iraq in 1927, states "it is quite impossible to give the exact census of the inhabitants who live within the rice area, as no general census has as yet been carried out in the country." CO 730 /12 /1, no. 40311, Report on Iraq by Ahmed Fahmi.

57. Longrigg states that "no civilised country" is without a cadastral survey: BHCF File no. 6/34/22. Subject: Mr S. H. Longrigg's note on Revenue Policy in Iraq, p. 16.

58. CO 696/1, Iraq Administration Reports 1917–1918, Administrative Report, Samarra District, 191, p. 10.

59. For example, Secret, Office of Special Services Officer (SSO), Basra, 23 January 1926, Visit to Amara, "I proceeded by River to Amara on 15 Jan., arriving on the 17th, visiting many of the Shaikhs on the way up to obtain corrections for the tribal lists, which are now being copied out and will be forwarded when completed'. AIR 23/101, 1/5/3, part 1, Intelligence Report, Lower Tigris, from October 1924 to September 1926, p. 22.

60. See for examples of these lists BHCF, File no. 24/44, Gazette and Publications, Mesopotamian Tribal Lists.

61. Longrigg, *Iraq, 1900 to 1950*, p. 8; and A. T. Wilson, *Loyalties, Mesopotamia*, vol. 2, *1917–1920: A Personal and Historical Record* (London: Oxford University Press, 1931), p. 78.

62. P 8253/19, Dispatch from the Civil Commissioner, Mesopotamia, to the Secretary of State for India, 15 November 1919, Box 3030/1/67, Durham University Library. CO 730/95, Iraq 1926, vol. 4, Despatches August to September, Secret, from Dobbs to Amery, September 1926.

63. IOL, L/P&S/10/619, p. 304, Land Revenue Report on Kirkuk, Baghdad, 12 March 1919, sub-heading the British Administrative System.

64. See, for example, CO 696/1, Iraqi Administration Reports, 1917–1918, p. 10.

65. Longrigg, *Iraq, 1900 to 1950*, p. 23.

66. Wilson, *Loyalties, Mesopotamia*, vol. 2, p. 71.

67. For a wonderful example of this see John Glubb, *Arabian Adventures: Ten Years of Joyful Service* (London: Cassell, 1978), p. 97.

68. Air 23/447, 1/2106, part 10, Euphrates-Samawah to Fallujah, 1924, Con-

siderations of the Abdul Wahid Land Case, by the Special Services Officer Hillah [Glubb], 19 July 1924, pp. 76–77.

69. IOL, L/P&S /1/621, P6705, Notes on the Tribes and Shaikhs of Anah-Albu Kamal District, by Captain C.C. Mylles, Assistant Political Officer (APO), 1920, p. 7. See also Administrative Report by Major C.F. MacPherson, Political Officer, Hillah District, 1917, CO 696/1, Iraq Administration Reports, 1917–1918, p. 106. Also see Glubb, *Arabian Adventures*, p. 65.

70. See, for example, CO 696/1, Iraq Administration Reports, 1917–1918, p. 119, Hillah Division, Review of District Administration Reports, 1 January to 31 Dece 1918.

71. D. G. Hogarth, *Arab Bulletin: Bulletin of the Arab Bureau in Cairo, 1916–1919*, with introduction by Dr Robin Bidwell (Archive Editions, 1986), no. 32, 26 November 1916, vol. 1, p. 489.

72. Dispatch no. 10/223, the Office of the High Commissioner, Baghdad, 1 July 1920. Further correspondence on the future of Baghdad, note by Mr. H. R. C. Dobbs, C.S.I, C.I.E, I.C.S, Proposals for a Constitution on Mesopotamia, The British Library.

73. Gertrude Bell, Mesopotamia: Review of Civil Administration, November 1920, Foreign Office (FO) 371/5081, E13898, pp. 150, 197.

74. IOL, L/P&S/10/761, P. 2581, Memo no. 7442, dated 5 December 1920, from the Political Officer, Nasiriyah Division.

75. PRO, CO 696/4, Iraq Administration Reports, 1921–1922, Report by His Majesty's High Commissioner on the Finances, Administration and Condition of the Iraq for the period from October 1, 1920 to 31 March 1922, Administrative report on the Muntafiq Division for the year 1921, written by A. H. Ditchburn, Divisional Adviser, Muntafiq Division, Nasiriyah, p. 4.

76. PRO AIR 23/18, part 1, from December 1924 to June 1925, Memorandum on the Relations between Hamud as Suwait and Lizzam aba Dhrahi of the Dhafir, signed by Glubb and date stamped by Air Staff Intelligence 20 April 1925.

77. See Sluglett, *Britain in Iraq*, p. 240. For further examples see BHCF, File no. 6/34/22, heading Finance. Subject: Mr. S. H. Longrigg's note on Revenue Policy in Iraq. Note by the High Commissioner, 10 July 1926, pp. 43–44.

78. See, for example, Bell's letter to Sir Valentine Chirol, 29 January 1918, Box 303/4/189, Durham University, Sudan Archive.

79. For a more detailed account of his continual rebellion see Sluglett, *Britain in Iraq*.

80. PRO CO 730/163/6, 1931, Iraq no. 88069, part II, Shaikh Mahmud, Report by the Air Officer Commanding Iraq on the operations in Southern Kurdistan against Shaikh Mahmud from October 1930–May 1931, Note by Captain V. Holt on Shaikh Mahmud, pp. 44–77.

5. Using the Shaikhs: The Rational Imposition of a Romantic Figure

1. See Hanna Batatu, *The Old Social Classes and the Revolutionary Movements of Iraq: A Study of Iraq's Old Landed and Commercial Classes and of its Communists, Ba'athists, and Free Officers* (Princeton, N.J.: Princeton University Press, 1989), pp. 77, 99, 110.

2. Indian National Archive (INA), Baghdad High Commission Files (BHCF), File no. 6/34/22, Finance, sub-head revenue. Subject: Mr S. H. Longrigg's note on Revenue Policy in Iraq, Note by the High Commissioner, 10 July 1926, p. 33.

3. BHCF, File no. 19/1, vol. 6, Intelligence Report no. 23, 1 December 1923, p. 6.

4. BHCF, File no. 19/1, vol. 6, Intelligence Report no. 23, 1 December 1923, p. 6.

5. See Sudipta Kaviraj, "On the Construction of Colonial Power: Structure, Discourse, Hegemony," in *Contesting Colonial Hegemony: State and Society in Africa and India*, ed. Dagmar Engles and Shula Marxs (London: British Academic Press, 1994), pp. 21–32.

6. BHCF, File no. 19/1, vol. 5, Intelligence Report no. 12, 7 June 1923, p.1.

7. Public Records Office (PRO), Foreign Office (FO) 371/5072, p. 75.

8. BHCF, File no. 19/1, vol. 5, Intelligence Report no. 11, Baghdad 1 June 1923, p. 4. Also see PRO, Air Ministry Files (AIR) 23/546, dated 4 June 1923, Operations in Basrah, Amarah and Nasiriyah, part 2.

9. See India Office Library (IOL), L/P&S/18 B. 342, Mesopotamian Constitution, Memorandum by Mr. H. R. C. Dobbs, C.S.I., Foreign Secretary to the Government of India, on the proposals of the Bonham-Carter Committee, 26 May 1920, p. 3. Here Dobbs is intimating that these residue of tribes are an unimportant minority, not representative of the wider social order.

10. BHCF, File no. 7/22/15I, heading Ministry of Interior, sub-head Dulaim Liwa. Subject: Shaikh Ali al Sulaiman, Chief of the Dulaim tribes, DO no. 203, from: L. M. Yetts, Office of the Divisional Adviser to Cornwallis, 30 January 1922, pp. 11–12.

11. From L. M. Yetts, Office of the Divisional Adviser, to Cornwallis, 30 January 1922, pp. 11–12.

12. BHCF, File no. 7/22/15I, heading Ministry of Interior, sub-head Dulaim Liwa. Subject: Shaikh Ali al Sulaiman, Chief of the Dulaim tribes, extract from Revenue Report of the Administrative Inspector Dulaim Division for the period 27 August to 13th November 1924, pp. 89–90.

13. BHCF, File no. 7/22/15I, heading Ministry of Interior, sub-head Dulaim Liwa. Subject: Shaikh Ali al Sulaiman, Chief of the Dulaim tribes, no. C/2779,

to Secretary to the High Commissioner, from Adviser to Interior, Cornwallis, 9 December 1924, p. 92.

14. BHCF, File no. 7/22/15I, heading Ministry of Interior, sub-head Dulaim Liwa. Subject: Shaikh Ali al Sulaiman, Chief of the Dulaim tribes, from H. Dobbs to Cornwallis, Adviser, Interior, 17 October 1925, pp. 103–5.

15. See BHCF, File no. 19/1, vol. 5, Intelligence Report no. 9, 1 May 1923, p. 2.

16. BHCF, File no. 7/22/15I, heading Ministry of Interior, sub-head Dulaim Liwa. Subject: Shaikh Ali al Sulaiman, Chief of the Dulaim tribes, DO no. C/3079, from Cornwallis, to Dobbs, 21 October 1925, pp. 108–109.

17. Sir Percy Cox, quoted in Peter Sluglett, *Britain in Iraq, 1914–1932* (London: Ithaca Press, published for the Middle East Centre, St Antony's College, Oxford University, 1976), p. 42.

18. The Bonham-Carter Committee which drew up proposals for the constitution of Iraq also included E. B. Howell, Revenue Secretary; H. F. M. Tyler, Political Officer Hillah; F. C. C. Balfour, Military Governor and Political Officer for Baghdad; and R. W. Bullard, Deputy Revenue Secretary. See British Library, S.T. 48/12 (1), no. S/138, Office of the Civil Commissioner, Baghdad, 30 April 1920, IOL, L/P&S/18, B.342, Mesopotamian Constitution, PRO FO 371/5227, E8267, pp. 193–197.

19. Official Publications Library, British Library, 48/12 (1), no. S/138, Office of the Civil Commissioner, Baghdad, 30 April, Reference Committee on proposals for a constitution for Iraq, Appendix C. Method of election to Legislative Assembly, p. 10.

20. He was then Foreign Minister to the Government of India, having left Iraq after his first term of service there. See IOL L/P&S/18, B. 342, Mesopotamian Constitution, Memorandum by Mr. H. R. C. Dobbs, 26 May 1920.

21. IOL, L/P&S/10/759, P. 7367, 1920, Note on Proposals for the Electoral Law for Mesopotamia, written by E. L. Norton, I.C.S, Secretary to the Committee of ex-Turkish Deputies on Electoral Law, 20 August 1920.

22. IOL, L/P&S/10/759, Minute Paper, P. 7366, Mesopotamia, Proposals for an Electoral Law, written by R. Marrs, 12 November 1920.

23. See PRO, CO 730/1, Mesopotamian Intelligence Report no. 4, 31 December 1920, Proceedings of the Council of Ministers; also Stephen Longrigg, *Iraq, 1900 to 1950: A Political, Social, and Economic History* (Oxford: Oxford University Press, issued under the auspices of the Royal Institute of International Affairs, 1953), p. 128; and Gertrude Bell, *From Her Personal Papers*, vol. 2, *1914–1926*, ed. Elizabeth Burgoyne (London: Ernest Benn Limited, 1961), p. 190.

24. See Batatu, *The Old Social Classes and the Revolutionary Movements of Iraq*, p. 95; and Mohammad Tarbush, *The Role of the Military in Politics: A Case Study of Iraq to 1941* (London: Routledge Kegan Paul, 1985), p. 27. The registering of a large numbers of tribesmen as primary voters in the run up to the elections for the 1924 Consultative Assembly meant that the British were happy to see the provision of 20 percent of the seats for tribal shaikhs set aside thereafter; see CO 730/61, p. 187 and CO 730/76, p. 198.

25. Longrigg's term, used in *Iraq, 1900 to 1950*, p. 150.

26. PRO CO 730/22, Iraq Intelligence Report no. 10, 15 May 1922, p. 147.

27. Gertrude Bell, *From Her Personal Papers*, vol. 2, p. 302, November 1 1922.

28. Mamdani sees similar divisions in African colonialism as having been consciously created or exacerbated whereas both with the case of Lugard in Africa and the Mandate official in Iraq, policy was driven by far more subconsciously structured perceptions than consciously enacted agency. Mahmood Mamdani, *Citizen and Subject: Contemporary Africa and the Legacy of Late Colonialism* (Princeton, N.J.: Princeton University Press, 1996), p. 23. Also see Batatu, *The Old Social Classes and the Revolutionary Movements of Iraq*, p. 24; and Roger Owen, "Class and Class Politics in Iraq before 1958: The 'Colonial and Post-Colonial State,' " in *The Iraqi Revolution of 1958: The Old Social Classes Revisited*, ed. Robert A. Fernea and Wm. Roger Louis (London: I. B. Tauris, 1991).

29. See PRO CO 730/74, CO 15898. Also see Philip Willard Ireland, *Iraq: A Study in Political Development* (London: Jonathan Cape, 1937), p. 85; and A. T. Wilson, *Loyalties, Mesopotamia*, vol. 2, *1917–1920: A Personal and Historical Record* (London: Oxford University Press, 1931), p. 85.

30. See A. T. Wilson, *Loyalties, Mesopotamia*, vol. 1, p. 68; and *Report by His Britannic Majesty's Government to the Council of the League of Nations on the Administration of Iraq for the Year 1927* (London: His Majesty's Stationery Office, 1928), p. 122.

31. See IOL, L/P&S/10 /618, File no. 1854, 1918, Tribal Disputes Regulation, p. 461.

32. Gertrude Bell, writing in *The Arab Bulletin: Bulletin of the Arab Bureau in Cairo, 1916–1919* (Slough: Archive Editions, 1986), no. 24, 5 October 1916, p. 318. Also see PRO, CO 696/1, Iraq Administration Reports, 1917–1918, Administration Report, Amarah Division, 1918, p. 253.

33. CO 730/168/8, no. 88271/31 Iraq, J. B. Glubb, An Annual Report on the Administration of the Shamiya Desert & the Defence of the Iraq Frontiers lying therein 1 May 1929–15 May 1930, part 3, Administration of the TCCD. Regulations.

34. CO 730/103, Iraq, 1926, Individuals, (A–D), no. 1301, from the Resi-

dency, Baghdad, 18 October 1923 to E. M. Drower, Esqr., C.B.E. Adviser to the Ministry of Justice, Baghdad, Proposed Amendments to the Tribal Disputes Law, p. 284.

35. PRO CO 730/96, Iraq 1926, vol. 5, Despatches (October–December), League of Nations, C.P.M./10 Session/P.V.8, Permanent Mandates Commission, Tenth session, Provisional Minutes, Eighth Meeting, held Monday, 8 November 1926, p. 735.

36. Bell further develops this example by comparing Iraq with Britain: "In our own history, from the Moot Court through Magna Charta, to the Imperial Parliament was the work of centuries, yet the first contained the germ of all that came after. The tribes of the Iraq have advanced but little beyond the Moot Court, and should the shaping of their destinies become our care in the future, we shall be wise to eschew any experiments tending to rush them into highly specialised institutions a policy which could commend itself only to those who are never wearied by words that signify nothing." *The Arab Bulletin* 24, p. 322.

37. CO 730/103, Iraq 1926, vol. 12, Individuals (A–D), no. 1301, from the Residency, Baghdad, 18 October 1923, to E. M. Drower, Adviser to the Ministry of Justice, Baghdad, p. 280.

38. BHCF File no. 8/4, vol. 1, DOSO no. 2140, 28 September 1924, Dobbs to Pulley (Interior); quoted in Sluglett, *Britain in Iraq*, p. 242.

39. See PRO CO 696/1 and 2; and David E. Omissi, *Air Power and Colonial Control: The Royal Air Force, 1919–1939* (Manchester: Manchester University Press, 1990), p. 168, for an explanation of this policy and its problems.

40. See *Report by His Britannic Majesty's Government on the Administration of Iraq for the period April 1923–December 1924* (London: His Majesty's Stationery Office, 1925), p. 59; and CO 730/6, CO 52858 24 OCT 21, Administration of Justice in the Tribal Areas, Confidential Memorandum no. S. 679, July 1921, from the Judicial Adviser, Baghdad, to the High Commissioner, Baghdad, p. 148. Also see CO 730/74, Iraq 1925, Despatches, March 30–April 1925, CO 15898, Tribal Criminal and Civil Disputes Regulations.

41. Tribal Disputes Regulations, Appendix, pp. 144–156, Tribal Criminal and Civil Disputes Regulation (Revised), Iraq Occupied Territories. Definitions in *Report by His Britannic Majesty's Government to the Council of the League of Nations on the Administration of Iraq for the Year 1925* (London: His Majesty's Stationery Office, 1926).

42. See CO 730/168/8, no. 88271/31, Iraq, J. B. Glubb, An Annual Report on the Administration of the Shamiya Desert & the Defence of the Iraq Frontiers lying therein 1 May 1929–15 May 1930, part 3, Administration of the TCCD Regulations and BHCF File no. 7/32/57. Subject: Proposed Conven-

tion between Syria and Iraq for the regulation of the affairs of nomadic tribes, to the Acting High Commissioner, Beyrout, pp. 64—63a.

43. See Intelligence Report no. 1, 1 January 1922, BHCF, File 19/1, vol. 2, Internal Intelligence Reports, p. 4; and BHCF, File no. 7/22/15I, heading Ministry of Interior, sub-head Dulaim Liwa. Subject: Shaikh Ali al Sulaiman, Chief of the Dulaim tribes, from H. Dobbs to Cornwallis, Adviser, Interior, 17 October 1925, p. 105.

44. CO 696/2, Iraq Administration Reports, 1919, Mesopotamian Judicial Dept., Report on the Administration of Justice for the Year 1919, p. 6; and CO 730/6, Memorandum no. A. 12/1571, 12 April 1921, from the Judicial Adviser to the Adviser to the Ministry of Interior, Baghdad, p. 154.

45. CO 730/6, pp. 154–155.

46. CO 730/6, p. 153.

47. CO 730/103, Iraq 1926, vol. 12, Individuals (A–D), p. 286, copy, DO no. S/142, Ministry of Justice, Baghdad, 21 October 1923, to Sir Henry Dobbs from E. M. Drower.

48. E. M. Drower, Ministry of Justice, Baghdad, p. 287.

49. Al Sha'ab, no. 6, 17 April 1924, CO 730/59, Iraq, Despatches (May), CO 22547 12 MAY 1924, Intelligence Reports, no. 9, Baghdad, 1 May 1924, Press Supplement.

50. Al Iraq, no. 1198, 18 April 1924, CO 730/59.

51. 'Ali Mahmud Al Mahami writing in Al Istiqlal, no. 491, 9 November 1924, CO 730/63, Iraq 1924 Dispatches (November–December), CO 55054 24 NOV 24, Intelligence Reports, no. 23, Baghdad, 13th November 1924, press supplement, p. 165.

52. See CO 730/6, p. 151.

53. CO 730/103, Iraq 1926, vol. 12, Individuals (A–D), pp. 263—88.

54. CO 730/103, Iraq 1926, vol. 1, Individuals (A–D), Confidential, the Residency, Baghdad, 9 June 1926, DO no. SO 1177, from Dobbs to Cornwallis, p. 277.

55. BHCF, File no. 6/34/65. Subject: Report by Sir Ernest Dowson—on land settlement in Iraq and allied subjects, p. 20.

56. This view springs from the same philosophical heritage as James Mills's conception of India; that the progress of any country can be judged by the level of encouragement of rational thought and individual action. For similar examples see Shamiyah Division, Annual Administration Report, 1 January–31 December 1918, vol. 1, Reports of Administration for 1918 of Divisions and Districts of the Occupied Territories in Mesopotamia, CO 696/1, Iraq Administration Reports 1917–1918, p. 72. Also Administration Report of the Suq al Shuyukh for the year 1921, by G.C. Kitching, Assistant Divisional Adviser, CO 696/4 Iraq Administration Reports 1921–1922, p. 56.

57. See, for example, J. B. Glubb, *The Story of the Arab Legion* (London: Hodder and Stoughton, 1948), p. 8; and Glubb, *Arabian Adventures: Ten Years of Joyful Service* (London: Cassell, 1978), p. 65. That the tribal system was killed by the effects of modernity, the advance of "civilization" and urbanization was the dominant view. See, for example, *Iraq: Report on Iraq Administration, October 1920–March 1921* (London: His Majesty's Stationery Office, 1922), p. 19; and IOL, L/PS/10/619, File no. P433, 2 December 1918, The Future of the Tribal System by the Assistant Political Officer, Hillah, p. 526.

58. Glubb, *Arabian Adventures*, p. 65.

59. Diary entry for April 1923, quoted in Glubb, *Arabian Adventures*, p. 73.

6. The Social Meaning of Land: State, Shaikh, and Peasant

1. A. T. Wilson speaking about land policy in 1918; see his *Loyalties, Mesopotamia, vol. II, 1917–1920: A Personal and Historical Record* (London: Oxford University Press, June 1931), pp. 76–77.

2. For a more detailed discussion of this, see chapter 3.

3. See A. T. Wilson, speaking of Dobbs's role in organizing revenue, finance, and education in 1915 and 1916 in *Loyalties, Mesopotamia, vol. I, 1914–1917: A Personal and Historical Record* (London: Oxford University Press, 1930), pp. 70–72.

4. James C. Scott, *Seeing Like a State: How Certain Schemes to Improve the Human Condition Have Failed* (New Haven: Yale University Press, 1998), p. 22.

5. For the transformative effects of "military Keynesianism," see Michael Mann, *A History of Power from the Beginning to A.D. 1760*, vol. 1 of *The Sources of Social Power* (Cambridge: Cambridge University Press, 1986), pp. 146–55. For the application of this concept to Trans-Jordan under the Mandates, see Vartan Amadouny, "Infrastructural Development under the British Mandate," in *Village, Steppe, and State: The Social Origins of Modern Jordan*, ed. Eugene L. Rogan and Tariq Tell (London: British Academic Press, 1994), pp. 129–31.

6. See Scott, *Seeing Like a State*, p. 4; and Sudipta Kaviraj, "On the Construction of Colonial Power, Structure, Discourse, Hegemony," in *Contesting Colonial Hegemony, State, and Society in Africa and India*, ed. Dagmar Engles and Shula Marxs (London: British Academic Press, 1994), p. 21.

7. Scott, *Seeing Like a State*, pp. 2–3.

8. See Kaviraj, "On the Construction of Colonial Power," p. 32.

9. See Scott, *Seeing Like a State*, p. 80.

10. See Anislie T. Embree, "Landholding in India and British Institutions," in Eric Frykenberg, ed., *Land Control and Social Structure in Indian History* (Madison: University of Wisconsin Press, 1969), pp. 37–39.

11. See Scott, *Seeing Like a State*, p. 83; also pp. 33–49, 80–82.

12. See Saree Makdisi, *Romantic Imperialism: Universal Empire and the Culture of Modernity* (Cambridge: Cambridge University Press, 1998), p. 15; and P. J. Cain and A. G. Hopkins, *British Imperialism: Innovation and Expansion, 1688–1914* (London: Longman, 1993), p. 84.

13. See Jan P. Nederveen Pieterse, *Empire and Emancipation: Power and Liberation on a World Scale* (London: Pluto Press, 1990), pp. 30–31.

14. See Mahmood Mamdani, *Citizen and Subject: Contemporary Africa and the Legacy of Late Colonialism* (Princeton, N.J.: Princeton University Press, 1996), p. 139.

15. See Nicholas B. Dirks, "From Little King to Landlord: Colonial Discourse and Colonial Rule," in Nicholas B. Dirks, ed., *Colonialism and Culture* (Ann Arbor: University of Michigan Press, 1995), p. 177.

16. See Michael Richard Fischbach, "State, Society, and Land in 'Ajlun (Northern Transjordan), 1850–1950," 2vols., Ph.D. diss., Georgetown University, 1992, pp. 244–245; and Matthew H. Edney, *Mapping Empire: The Geographical Construction of British India, 1765–1843* (Chicago: University of Chicago Press, 1997), p. 334.

17. See Scott, *Seeing Like a State*, p. 6.

18. See Kaviraj, "On the Construction of Colonial Power," p. 29.

19. See, for example, Fischbach, "State, Society, and Land in 'Ajlun," p. 246–47; and Dirks, "From Little King to Landlord," pp. 176–84.

20. See Scott, *Seeing Like a State*, p. 36.

21. See Nader Saiedi, *The Birth of Social Theory: Social Thought in the Enlightenment and Romanticism* (Lanham, Md.: University Press of America, 1993); and Charles Taylor, *Philosophy and the Human Sciences*, Philosophical Papers 2, (Cambridge: Cambridge University Press, 1995), p. 160.

22. See chapter 2.

23. See E. Hilton Young and R. V. Vernon, *Iraq: Report of the Financial Mission Appointed by the Secretary of State for the Colonies to Enquire Into the Financial Position and Prospects of the Government of Iraq* (Baghdad, 1925). The aim of dramatically raising taxes was never realized. In 1911 under the Ottoman Empire, taxes from land accounted for 42 percent of national income. By 1933 this had actually fallen to 14 percent. See Peter Sluglett, *Britain in Iraq, 1914–1932* (London: Ithaca Press, for the Middle East Centre, St Antony's College, Oxford University, 1976), p. 232.

24. See, for example, Gertrude Bell, 14 February 1920, *The Letters of Gertrude Bell*, vol. 2 (Harmondsworth, U.K.: Penguin, 1939), p. 468. In 1926 the settlement of land tenure was listed as the second most important policy aim after the creation of an effective army. See Intelligence Report no. 10,

Baghdad, 29 April 1926, Baghdad High Commission Files, Indian National Archives, New Delhi (BHCF), File no. 19/1, vol. 10, p. 4. Also see *Report by His Britannic Majesty's Government to the Council of the League of Nations on the Administration of Iraq for the Year 1928* London: His Majesty's Stationery Office, 1929), p. 47.

25. "There is at the moment in this Ministry no recorded agreement on any matter of Land or Revenue policy at all: no authoritative reply can be given to any question on such matters of fact: and it must be admitted (as I have pointed out to the Adviser) that we seem to be rather further from, than nearer to, a considered policy than we were in 1919." DO 3317, Ministry of Finance, 30 June 1926, to R. S. M. Sturges, Political Secretary to the High Commissioner, from Longrigg, BHCF, File no. 6/34/22, heading Finance, subhead Revenue. Subject: Mr. S.H. Longrigg's note on Revenue Policy in Iraq. Also see Ernest Dowson, Preliminary Note 5, BHCF, File no. 6/34/65. Subject: Report by Sir Ernest Dowson on land settlement in Iraq and allied subjects, p. 52. Samira Haj, *The Making of Iraq, 1900–1963: Capital, Power, and Ideology* (New York: State University of New York Press, 1997), pp. 28–32.

26. See Albertine Jwaideh, "Aspects of Land Tenure and Social Change in Lower Iraq During Late Ottoman Times," in *Land Tenure and Social Transformation in the Middle East*, ed. Tarif Khalidi (Beirut: American University of Beirut, 1984), pp. 349–50.

27. Report of the subcommittee appointed under paragraph 17 of the Minutes of 21 March 1917, 27 March 1917, Mesopotamian Administration Committee, India Office Library (IOL), L/P&S/18/B254. This was reconfirmed in 1926. Mr. S. H. Longrigg's Note on Revenue Policy in Iraq, BHCF, File no. 6/34/22, p. 7. Also see Sluglett, *Britain in Iraq*, p. 239. Added to this desire to perpetuate the status quo was an international legal requirement. The Turkish legal code had to be used until a state of war had officially ceased. This did not happen until the signing of the treaty of Lausanne, 23 July 1923. For the effects of this on revenue policy see Bertram Thomas, *Alarms and Excursions in Arabia* (London: George Allen & Unwin, 1931), p. 80.

28. See Ahmed Fahmi, Accountant-General, Baghdad, Public Records Office (PRO), Colonial Office (CO) 730/121/1, no. 40311, Report on Iraq.

29. See E. Hilton Young and R. V. Vernon, *Iraq: Report of the Financial Mission*, p. 14.

30. Ahmed Fahmi, Accountant-General, Report on Iraq, p. 10.

31. The British government began to consult Sir Ernest Dowson in 1926 as the debate about Iraqi land became urgent. However, until they employed him, Colonial Office officials appeared content to let Dobbs and Longrigg develop a policy for land tenure; this was despite their being well aware of the long-

running dispute the two men had had over the matter. See J. Hall's minute, 28 August 1926, and H. W. Young's minute to Shuckburgh, 4 October 1926, C. 15136, 2 August 1926, Revenue Notes, CO 730/94, Iraq 1926, vol. 3, Dispatches.

32. A note by the High Commissioner on pump irrigation on the rivers of Iraq and connected questions, C. 16338, 23 August 1926, CO 730/95, Iraq 1926, vol. 4, Dispatches (August–September), pp. 1–2.

33. A note by the High Commissioner on pump irrigation on the rivers of Iraq and connected questions.

34. BHCF, File no. 6/34/22, heading Finance, subheading Revenue. Subject: Mr. S. H. Longrigg's Note on Revenue Policy in Iraq, Note by the High Commissioner, 10 July 1926, p. 33.

35. See the conclusion of chapter 3 for a more complete exposition of this argument.

36. See L/P&S/10/618, no. 74, 19769, 20 Sept. 1918, Revenue Notes on Qizil Rabat, Kadhimain, Diwaniyah, Musaiyib, Samawah, Shamiyah and Ramadi, by C. C. Garbett, First Revenue Officer, p. 125.

37. L/P&S/10/618, no. 74, 19769, p. 125.

38. *Iraq: Report on Iraq Administration, April 1922–March 1923* (London: His Majesty's Stationery Office, 1923), pp. 67–68. The ideational and material centrality of the Amarah shaikhs as representative of tribal society for the British administrators remained to the end of the Mandate in 1932. See Secret from Flight-Lieutenant Howes, Special Services Officer Basra, to Air Staff Intelligence, Air HQ, Hinaidi, 17 March 1932, PRO Air Ministry File (Air) 23/102 1/5/3, part 2, p. 5.

39. See Haj, *The Making of Iraq*, p. 29.

40. See extract from summary of outstanding events in the Dulaim Liwa for the year 1931, Intelligence Reports Upper Euphrates from 1927 to 1932, AIR 23/119, 1/5/6, part 7, p. 64a.

41. See extract from Revenue Report of the Administrative Inspector Dulaim Division for the period 27 August to 13 November 1924, BHCF, File no. 7/22/15I, p. 89.

42. See Extract from Revenue Report of the Administrative Inspector Dulaim Division, p. 67.

43. See Notes on Provincial Affairs, Mesopotamian Intelligence Report no. 5, 15 January 1921, CO 730/1, vol. 1, p. 94.

44. See Notes on Provincial Affairs, Intelligence Report no. 24, Baghdad, 1 November 1921, BHCF, File no. 19/1, vol. II, Internal Intelligence Reports, p. 5.

45. See BHCF, File no. 19/1, vol. 5, Internal Intelligence Reports, Intelligence Report no. 4, 14 February 1923, p. 8.

46. See Thomas, *Alarms and Excursions in Arabia*, pp. 76–77.

47. See Revenue Notes on Qizil Rabat, Kadhimain, Diwaniyah, Musaiyib, Samawah, Shamiyah, Ramadi, by C. C. Garbett, First Revenue Officer, Administration report of Suq-esh-Shuyukh and District, 1916–17, for Suq tribal affairs and the situation generally, L/P&S/10/618, no. 74, 19769, 20 September 1918, p. 506.

48. CO 696/2, Iraq Administration Reports 1919, Administration Report of the Muntafiq Division for the year ending 31 December 1919, by Captain A. H. Ditchburn, Officiating Political Officer, Muntafiq Division, Nasiriyah, p. 3.

49. See chapter 3.

50. See BHCF File no. 19/1, vol. 5, Internal Intelligence Reports, Intelligence Report no. 4, 14 February 1923, p. 7; and a report on the Accountant-General's tour in Shamiyah, printed at the Government Press, 1926, CO 730/121/1, no. 40311, p. 25.

51. BHCF, File no. 19/1, vol. 4, Intelligence Report no. 16, Baghdad the 15 August 1922, p. 10.

52. Rauf Kubaisias was appointed as *Mutasarrif* in November 1921. In August 1922 it was reported that he had travelled to Muntafiq with a personal injunction from the king to "bring the shaikhs to heel. Upon his arrival he immediately surrendered to the extremists." See Intelligence Report no. 16, Baghdad, 15 August 1922, p. 10.

53. See Notes on Provincial Affairs, Iraq Intelligence Report no. 2, 15 Jan. 1923, CO 730/38, p. 120.

54. See CO 730/23, CO 43319 30 August 22, Activities of the tribes of Nasiriyah District, CO 528, from Percy Cox, to the Secretary of State for the Colonies, London 17 August 1922, p. 699; and BHCF, File no. 19/1, vol. 4, Intelligence Report no. 16, Baghdad, 15 August 1922, p. 10.

55. See appendix A, Sa'dun history and activities leading up to the present state of affairs between the landlord and tenant, 1/Bd/39, secret from the office of the Special Service Officer Baghdad to Air Staff Intelligence, Air 23/105, I/5/4, part 3, Lower Euphrates, p. 7f.

56. See, for example, Intelligence Report no. 2, 15 January 1923, CO 730/38; and appendix A 1/Bd/39, Air 23/105 I/5/4, part 3, p. 7f.

57. Administration report from the Amarah Division for the year 1920–1921, written by the Official Adviser, 'Amarah Division, to the Revenue Secretary, Baghdad, 11 November 1920, CO 969/3, Iraq Administration Reports 1920–21, p. 25.

58. Administration report from the Amarah Division for 1920–21, p. 26.

59. See Secret no. D/2(a), from the Office of Special Service Officer, Baghdad to Air Staff Intelligence, October 26 1924, AIR 23/113, I/5/6, part 1, Upper Euphrates from October 1924 until March 1925.

60. Extract from Revenue Report of the Administrative Inspector Dulaim Division 27 August to 13 November 1924, BHCF, File no. 7/22/15I, p. 90.

61. See Intelligence Report no. 12, 15 October 1925, CO 730/79, p. 3.

62. No. C/1771, from Cornwallis to the Political Secretary to the High Commissioner, 4 July 1926, BHCF, File no. 7/18/36, p. 147.

63. See BHCF, File no. 7/22/15I, p. 86.

64. No. M.I./2567, 24 February 1926, from Cornwallis, the Adviser to the Ministry of Interior, to the Administrative Inspector Ramadi, Memorandum, BHCF, File no. 7/22/15I.

65. See Intelligence Report no. 20, 1 October 1925, CO 730/78, vol. 7, Dispatches (September), CO 46166 13 OCT 25, Intelligence Reports, p. 693.

66. Intelligence Report no. 20, CO 730/78, p. 693.

67. S. H. Longrigg, Note on Land and Revenue Policy, 25 June 1926, BHCF, File no. 6/34/22, p. 14.

68. Longrigg, Note on Land and Revenue Policy, p. 13.

69. See Do/8165, from the Secretariat of the High Commissioner for Iraq, 14 July 1926, pp. 55–59; and Do/9894, from the Secretariat of the High Commissioner, 19 August 1926, pp. 74–76, BHCF, File no. 6/34/22.

70. Captain A. H. Ditchburn, Officiating Political Officer, Muntafiq Division, Nasiriyah, Administration Report of the Muntafiq Division for the year ending 31 December 1919, CO 696/2, Iraq Administration Reports, 1919, p. 4.

71. Administration Report of the 'Amarah Division, CO 696/2, Iraq Administration Reports, 1919, p. 26.

72. See Ahmed Fahmi, Accountant-General, Report on Iraq, p. 26.

73. See Revenue derived from properties, no. I/n/25, Nasiriyah, 19 March, 1927, Air Staff, AIR 23/105, I/5/4, part 3, lower Euphrates, January 1927 to November 1927.

74. Colonial administrators in India at the peak of utilitarian influence drew similar conclusions. See Clive Dewey, *Anglo-Indian Attitudes: The Mind of the Indian Civil Service* (London: Hambledon Press, 1993), p. 16.

75. AIR 23/119, 1/5/6, part 7, Intelligence Reports, upper Euphrates, from 1927 to 1932, p. 68a.

76. See Philip Ireland, *Iraq: A Study in Political Development* (London: Jonathan Cape, 1937), p. 149.

77. See, for example, IOL L/P&S/10/618, A. L. Gordon Walker, Revenue Officer, Basrah, 31 May 1918, p. 122.

78. Bernard S. Cohn, "Representing Authority in India," in *The Invention of Tradition*, ed. Eric Hobsbawn and Terence Ranger (Cambridge: Cambridge University Press, 1993), p. 166.

79. Charles Townsend, "Civilisation and Frightfulness in Air Control in the Middle East Between the Wars," in *Warfare Diplomacy and Politics: Essays in Honour of A. J. P. Taylor*, ed. Chris Wrigley (London: Hamish Hamilton, 1986), p. 143.

80. Dobbs served on the North West Frontier as Judicial Commissioner and was from 1909 to 1911 Revenue and Judicial Commissioner, Baluchistan. Humphrys was personal assistant to Chief Commissioner, North Western Frontier Province in April 1905. See CO 730/148/9, no. 68444, part 2, p. 105; and CO 730/149/9, no. 68509.

81. See Thomas Henry Thornton, *Colonel Sir Robert Sandeman: His Life and Work on Our Indian Frontier. A Memoir, with Selections from His Correspondence and Official Writings* (London: John Murray, 1895).

82. "I am a fervent admirer of the Sandeman policy . . . in Iraq . . . I introduced the same system for the management of the tribes": Dobbs commenting on Colonel C. E. Bruce's lecture, "The Sandeman Policy as Applied to Tribal Problems of Today," both reproduced in *The Journal of Royal Central Asian Society* 19 (1932): 45–67. For the wider influence of Sandeman in the Middle East see, Riccardo Bocco and Tariq Tell, "Pax Britannica in the Steppe: British Policy and the Transjordanian Bedouin, 1923–39," in *Village, Steppe, and State: The Social Origins of Modern Jordan*, ed. Eugene L. Rogan and Tariq Tell (London: British Academic Press, 1994), p. 241.

83. For example, PRO, CO 730/103, Iraq 1926, vol. 12, Individuals (A–D), C. 12513, Tribal Disputes Regulation, p. 280, no. 1301, from Dobbs, 18 October 1923, to E. M. Drower, Adviser to the Ministry of Justice, Baghdad. Also see Sluglett, *Britain in Iraq*, p. 242.

84. Thornton, *Colonel Sir Robert Sandeman*, p. 304.

85. Philip Woodruff, *The Guardians*, vol. 2 of *The Men Who Ruled India* (London: Jonathan Cape, 1954), p. 146.

86. Edward Said, *Orientalism: Western Conceptions of the Orient* (Harmondsworth, U.K.: Penguin, 1991), p. 36.

87. See T. E. Lawrence, *Observer*, 8 August 1920, quoted in Wilson, *Loyalties, Mesopotamia, vol. II*, p. 110.

88. Earl of Cromer, *Political and Literary Essays, 1908–1913* (London: Macmillan, 1913), p. 50.

89. Cromer, *Political and Literary Essays*, p. 254.

90. BHCF, File no. 6/34/65. Subject: Report by Sir Ernest Dowson—on land settlement in Iraq and allied subjects, to His Excellency the High Commissioner, Baghdad, from Ernest Dowson, p. 128–29.

91. See Fischbach, *State, Society, and Land in 'Ajlun*, p. 257.

92. BHCF, File no. 6/34/65, Reply to Longrigg's Note on Land and Revenue Policy, H. Dobbs, 10 July 1926, pp. 38, 42.

93. BHCF, File no. 6/34/22, note by H. Dobbs, 10 July 1926, p. 36.

94. C. 16338, 23 August 1926, note by the High Commissioner on pump irrigation on the rivers of Iraq and connected questions, CO 730/95, Iraq, 1926, vol. 4, Dispatches (August–September), p. 22.

95. BHCF, File no. 6/34/22, H. Dobbs, 10 July 1926, pp. 43–44.

96. BHCF, File no. 6/34/22, DO 3826, from Longrigg to Sturges, Secretary to the High Commissioner, 22 July 1926, p. 2.

97. S. H. Longrigg, Annual Report on the operations of the Revenue Dept. for the financial year 1927–1928, 1 July 1928, Iraq Administration Reports, 1925–26 to 1927–28, CO 696/6, p. 5.

98. Provisional Note on Land Reform, no. 4, 27 February 1931, BHCF, File no. 6/34/4 II, Alienation of Government Land, p. 4.

99. Note by Dobbs, the High Commissioner, on pump irrigation on the rivers of Iraq and connected questions, C. 16338, 23 August 1926, CO 730/95, Iraq 1926, vol. 4, Dispatches (August–September), p. 9.

100. Letter to the Prime Minister, Abdul Munshin Beg al Sa'dun, from B. H. Bourdillon, Secretariat to the High Commissioner, DO no. P.O. 215, 27 August 1925, BHCF, File no. 8/10/7-I.

101. See Letter to Leopold Amery, Secretary of State for the Colonies, from Sir Henry Dobbs, Baghdad, 4 December 1928, Box 472/13/127, Durham University Library.

102. See telegram no. C.O./1375, from Dobbs, to Amery, 22 October 1926, CO 730/96, Iraq 1926, vol. 5, Dispatches (October–December), p. 345.

103. See BHCF, File no. 6/34/22, Note by the High Commissioner, H. Dobbs, 10 July 1926, p. 41.

104. BHCF, File no. 6/34/22, p. 38.

105. BHCF, File no. 6/34/22, p. 45 also see pp. 40 and 44.

106. To the High Commissioner, from Ernest Dowson, BHCF, File no. 6/34/65, pp. 119–128.

107. Dowson, BHCF, File no. 6/34/65, p. 19; and Dowson, *Government of el Iraq: An Inquiry Into Land Tenure and Related Questions with Proposals for the Initiation of Reform* (Letchworth, U.K.: Garden City Press Limited, 1931), p. 26.

108. Dowson, *Government of el Iraq*, p. 26. Jwaideh argues that Dowson's understanding was based on a historical fallacy, that tribal rights were allotted a status inferior to Ottoman law. See her "Aspects of Land Tenure and Social Change in Lower Iraq during Late Ottoman Times," p. 335.

109. Dowson, *Government of el Iraq*, p. 20.

110. Longrigg, 25 June 1926, BHCF, File no. 6/34/22, pp. 11–16.

111. Longrigg, Note on Land and Revenue Policy, pp. 5, 14.

112. Longrigg, Note on Land and Revenue Policy, p. 14.

113. Longrigg, Note on Land and Revenue Policy, pp. 14–15.

114. For the "fluidity in the meaning and the contestation over the title 'shaykh' among the tribes of southern Iraq," before the arrival of the British, see Haj, *The Making of Iraq*, p. 3.

7. The Imposition of Order: Social Perception and The "Despotic" Power of Airplanes

1. Leopold Amery, Secretary of State for the Colonies, summing up the situation in Iraq after returning from a month-long tour of inspection in 1925. Public Records Office (PRO), Colonial Office (CO) 730/82, Iraq 1925, vol. 2, p. 12.

2. A tribesman speaking to G. A. Moore, the Special Services Officer (SSO), Hillah *Liwa*, 7 January 1924, PRO, Air Ministry Files (AIR) 23/445, I/2106, part 8, p. 50.

3. See John Gallagher, "The Decline, Revival, and Fall of the British Empire," in *The Decline, Revival, and Fall of the British Empire: The Ford Lectures and Other Essays*, ed. Anil Seal (Cambridge: Cambridge University Press, 1982), p. 94. Also see Keith Jeffery, *The British Army and the Crisis of Empire, 1918–1922* (Manchester: Manchester University Press, 1984).

4. Antony Giddens, *The Nation-State and Violence*, vol. 2 of *A Contemporary Critique of Historical Materialism* (Cambridge: Polity Press, 1985), p. 10.

5. See Michel Foucault, *Discipline and Punish: The Birth of the Prison*, trans. Alan Sheridan (Harmondsworth: Penguin, 1991), p. 137.

6. See Michael Mann, "The Autonomous Power of the State: Its Origins, Mechanisms, and Results," in *States, War, and Capitalism: Studies in Political Sociology*, ed. Michael Mann (Oxford: Blackwell, 1988), p. 4.

7. Giddens, *The Nation-State and Violence*, p. 7.

8. See Mann, "The Autonomous Power of the State," pp. 5–7.

9. Mann, "The Autonomous Power of the State," p. 5.

10. See Sir Philip Sasson (Under-Secretary of State for Air), Anniversary Lecture, "Air Power in the Middle East," *Journal of the Royal Asian Society* 20 (1933): 399. Also see Michael Howard, "The Military Factor in the European Expansion," in *The Expansion of International Society*, ed. Hedley Bull and Adam Watson (Oxford: Clarendon Press, 1989).

11. See Foucault, *Discipline and Punish*, p. 9.

12. See John Darwin, *Britain, Egypt, and the Middle East: Imperial Policy in the Aftermath of War, 1918–1922* (London: Macmillan, 1981), p. 205.

13. See Paul Kennedy, *The Realities Behind Diplomacy: Background Influ-*

ences on *British External Policy, 1865–1980* (London: Fontana, 1985), p. 226; and Gallagher, "The Decline, Revival and Fall of the British Empire," p. 95.

14. See Darwin, *Britain, Egypt, and the Middle East*, p. 168.

15. Quoted in Gallagher, "The Decline, Revival and Fall of the British Empire," p. 96.

16. See Darwin, *Britain, Egypt, and the Middle East*, p. 30.

17. See John Glubb, *Arabian Adventures: Ten Years of Joyful Service* (London: Cassell, 1978), pp. 28–29.

18. See David E. Omissi, *Air Power and Colonial Control: The Royal Air Force, 1919–1939* (Manchester: Manchester University Press, 1990), pp. 22, 123.

19. See Darwin, *Britain, Egypt, and the Middle East*, pp. 197–202.

20. See Jafana L. Cox, "A Splendid Training Ground: The Importance to the Royal Air Force of its Role in Iraq, 1919–1932," *The Journal of Imperial and Commonwealth History* 8, no. 2 (January 1985): 161.

21. For descriptions of the Cairo Conference see Omissi, *Air Power and Colonial Control*, p. 25; William Stivers, *Supremacy and Oil: Iraq, Turkey, and the Anglo-American World Order, 1918–1930* (Ithaca, N.Y.: Cornell University Press, 1982), pp. 76–78; and Mohammad A. Tarbush, *The Role of the Military in Politics: A Case Study of Iraq to 1941* (London: Routledge Kegan Paul, 1985), p. 78.

22. Churchill summed up these conclusions thus: "I wish to make it perfectly clear that I have from the outset contemplated holding Mesopotamia not by sheer force, but by the acquiescence of the people of Mesopotamia as a whole in a Government and Ruler whom they have freely accepted, and who will be supported by the Air Force, and by British organised levies, and by four Imperial battalions. At a later stage I contemplate still further reductions, and look forward eventually to the country being in the condition of an Independent Native State friendly to Great Britain, favourable to her commercial interests, and costing hardly any burden upon the Exchequer." Quoted in Stivers, *Supremacy and Oil*, p. 78.

23. Note prepared by the Middle East Dept., Colonial Office, by the instruction of the Committee to implement the skeleton statement; circulated as I.R.Q.2, Secret I.R.Q.3, cabinet Committee on Iraq, December 1922, CO 730/34, CO 61243 11 December 1922, p. 778.

24. See Dobbs's letter of appointment, 20 September 1923, University of Durham Library, Sudan Collection, Box 472/13/141, p. 4.

25. Situation in Iraq, Memorandum by the Secretary of State for the Colonies dealing with his visit to Iraq, CO 730/82, Iraq 1925, vol. 2, p. 12.

26. See Omissi, *AirPower and Colonial Control*, p. 37.

27. These were the officers, about 300 in all, who had deserted the Ottoman

army to fight with the Hashemites during the Arab Revolt. See Hanna Batatu, *The Old Social Classes and the Revolutionary Movements of Iraq: A Study of Iraq's Old Landed and Commercial Classes and its Communists, Ba'thists, and Free Officers* (Princeton, N.J.: Princeton University Press, 1989), p. 319.

28. Ja'far and Nuri personified the Hashemite circle around Faisal. They were both of urban middle- or lower-class origin (one the son of a brigadier the other the son of an auditor), linked to each other by marriage and alienated from the tribal, religious, merchant, and landowning elites who saw them as upstart adventurers. See Batatu, *The Old Social Classes and the Revolutionary Movements of Iraq*, pp. 115–17, 319–33.

29. See Batatu, *The Old Social Classes and the Revolutionary Movements of Iraq*, p. 333.

30. Batatu, *The Old Social Classes and the Revolutionary Movements of Iraq*, p. 321.

31. For examples of this drive for military expansion at other times during the mandate period see: Defence of Iraq, CO 19004 27 APR 25, Memorandum of discussions, CO 730/74, p. 5; and CO 16563 11 APR 25, Re-organisation of Iraq Army, CO 730/90, p. 6.

32. See Proceedings of the Council of Ministers, Intelligence Report no. 14, 1 July 1921, CO 730/3, p. 294.

33. See Proceedings of the Council of Ministers, Intelligence Report no. 14, 1 July 1921, CO 730/3, p. 295.

34. See BHCF File no. 19/1, vol. 3, Internal Intelligence Reports, Intelligence Report no. 7, Baghdad, 1 April 1922, p. 5.

35. The High Commissioner's Secret Intelligence Report no. 13, dated 1 July 1922, CO 730/32, pp. 670–71.

36. See Notes of conversation with the Prime Minister and King Faisal on 2 April 1925, CO 730/82, Iraq 1925, vol. 11.

37. View of Ja'far Pasha al Askari regarding the formation of an Army for the Arab State, signed by him, 12 November 1920, AIR 23/439, p. 17.

38. See view of Ja'far Pasha al Askari, and also notes from a conversation with Ja'far Pasha, Confidential GSOI, initialled W.J.B, AIR 23/439.

39. See no. 58047, Defence Forces Re-organisation, Personal letter from Nuri Said, Minister of Defence, to Henry Dobbs, dated 27 October 1928, CO 730/128/1, p. 5.

40. Secret paraphrase telegram no. 423, from the High Commissioner to the Secretary of State for the Colonies, 17 August 1928, CO 730/134/12, p. 65.

41. Dobbs, when faced with complaints about the inefficiency of the Iraqi army, complained that "the Iraq Government has persisted in the face of the most discouraging changes of policy on the part of the British Government in

pressing for the rapid expansion, better training and better equipment for the Iraq Army. They have been ordered to cut it down; the best of their British officers have been taken away; their Training College has been abolished; there have been inordinate delays in the provision of material by the Crown Agents; they have not received the inspection and attention from British officers which they had hoped to receive." Confidential memorandum by the High Commissioner reviewing the policy of HMG as to the progress made by the army and difficulties encountered by it, 1 April 1925, CO 730/82, vol. 11, pp. 12–13.

42. See Intelligence Report no. 10, Baghdad, 29 April 1926, BHCF File no. 19/1, vol. 10, Internal Intelligence Reports, p. 4.

43. See C.18358, 28 September 1926, the organisation of the Defence Forces, secret, from the High Commissioner to the Secretary of State for the Colonies, 16 September 1926, CO 730/95, pp. 5–6.

44. Even this plan would stretch Iraqi government finances to the limit. See personal and secret letter to Leopold Amery from Henry Dobbs, 23 June 1926, CO 730/103, p. 304.

45. See for example V. G. Kiernan, *The Lords of Human Kind: European Attitudes to the Outside World in the Imperial Age* (Harmondsworth: Penguin, 1972), pp. 55–56.

46. See *Iraq: Report on Iraq Administration, April 1922–March 1923* (London: His Majesty's Stationery Office, 1924), p. 112; and secret letter from Dobbs to Devonshire, Secretary of State for the Colonies, 20 June 1923, CO 33280 4 JUL 23, Local forces in Iraq, CO 730/40, pp. 742–43.

47. The military college was opened as early as 1921 but then closed as part of the financially motivated cutbacks on the growth of the military. It opened again in 1924. See Mark Heller, "Politics and the Military in Iraq and Jordan, 1920–1958: The British influence," *Armed Forces and Society* 4, no. 1 (November 1977): 83–84. See Regulations for the Admission of Tribal Cadets into the Iraq Royal Military College in September 1929, no. C.R.I.A./423 (A) 2, 34/2, Iraq Army H.Q., 23 June 1929, BHCF File no. 4/75 I, p. 13.

48. See Tarbush, *The Role of the Military in Politics*, p. 78; *Iraq: Report on Iraq Administration, April 1922–March 1923*, p. 112; *Report by His Britannic Majesty's Government to the Council of the League of Nations on the Administration of Iraq for the Year 1925* (London: His Majesty's Stationery Office, 1926), p. 105; and *Report by His Britannic Majesty's Government to the Council of the League of Nations on the Administration of Iraq for the Year 1928* (London: His Majesty's Stationery Office, 1929), p. 110.

49. Memorandum of Discussion between the High Commissioner, the Air Officer Commanding and General Daly, 23 June 1926, BHCF File no. 4/69I, Conscription Bill.

50. No. SO/510, from the Secretariat of the High Commissioner, 10 July 1926, BHCF File no. 4/69I, Conscription Bill, p. 45.

51. See Secret, C. 17572 14 SEP 1926, Conscription for Iraq, from Henry Dobbs, to Leopold Amery, Secretary of State for the Colonies, 1 September 1926, CO 730/95.

52. See no. C/1670, from Cornwallis, to Henry Dobbs, 1 July 1926, p. 26; and no. C/2341 8/3 from Cornwallis to Dobbs, 22 August 1926, p. 64, BHCF File no. 4/69I, Conscription Bill.

53. See no. SO/1715, from the Secretariat of the High Commissioner for Iraq to the Ministry of Defence, 13 July 1925; BHCF File no. 4/69I, Conscription Bill, p. 2.

54. For a justification of this policy see, secret letter from Sir Henry Dobbs, to Leopold Amery, Secretary of State for the Colonies, 4 December 1928, University of Durham Library, Sudan Collection, Box no. 427/13/127, pp. 11–12.

55. See secret from the Secretariat of the High Commissioner to Air HQ, Baghdad, 26 May 1923, CO 730/40, p. 748.

56. See paraphrase telegram from Sir Percy Cox, High Commissioner to the Secretary of State for the Colonies, 7 December 1923, CO 730/44, p. 36.

57. See telegram from the High Commissioner to the Secretary of State, 10 January 1924, CO 730/57, p. 153; Organisation of the Defence Forces, Secret, from the High Commissioner to the Secretary of State for the Colonies, Baghdad, 16 September 1926, CO 730/95, p. 2; and C. 19845 22 OCT 1926, Training of Iraqi Air Officers, CO 730/95, p. 253; Formation of Iraqi Air Force, C. 15845 14 AUG 1926, CO 730/103, p. 298.

58. Charles Townsend, " 'Civilisation' and 'Frightfulness' in Air Control in the Middle East between the Wars," in *Warfare, Diplomacy, and Politics: Essays in Honour of A. J. P. Taylor*, ed. Chris Wrigley (London: Hamish Hamilton, 1986), p. 143.

59. See Omissi, *Air Power and Colonial Control*, p. 18.

60. See Townsend, " 'Civilisation' and 'Frightfulness,' " p. 144.

61. See Memorandum by the Air Staff on the effects likely to be produced by intensive aerial bombing of semi-civilised people, CO 58212 22 NOV 21, CO 730/18, pp. 39, 40, 96. Interestingly the deployment of another and widely reviled technology, gas, was defended in exactly the same way during the First World War. See Paul Fussell, *The Great War and Modern Memory* (London: Oxford University Press, 1975), p. 10.

62. BHCF, File no. 26/2/65, vol. 1, Confidential, Air Staff Memorandum no. 14. Some Points on the Administration of Air Control in Underdeveloped Countries, 1 September 1929, p. 98.

63. See Statement by Air Marshal Sir J. M. Salmond of his views on the

principles governing the use of air power in Iraq, CO 62797 29 DEC 23, CO 730/46, p. 209; and BHCF, File no. 26/2/65, vol. 1, Confidential, Air Staff Memorandum no. 14, p. 98.

64. See Statement by J. M. Salmond, CO 730/46, pp. 209–10.

65. Confidential, Air Staff Memorandum no. 14, Notes by the Air Staff on the regulation of air control in undeveloped countries, BHCF File no. 26/2/65, vol. 1, p. 98.

66. See A. T. Wilson, cited in Note on use of air force in Mesopotamia in its political aspects and as to its utility actual & potential in support of the civil government of the country, CO 730/13, p. 449; and Report by Sir A. Haldane, C. in C. Mesopotamia E.F. on the work of the RAF in O/184/106, d/25.11.20, CO 58212 22 NOV 21, CO 730/18, p. 401.

67. See CO 730/18, p. 32.

68. On the Power of the Air Force and the Application of this Power to Hold and Police Mesopotamia, Air Staff, March 1920, IOL, L/P&S/10/762, p. 2.

69. *Iraq: Report on Iraq Administration, April 1922–March 1923*, p. 66.

70. *Report by His Britannic Majesty's Government on the Administration of Iraq for the Period April 1923–December 1924* (London: His Majesty's Stationery Office, 1925), p. 27.

71. Statement by Air Marshal Sir J. M. Salmond, CO 62797 29 DEC 23, CO 730/46, p. 209.

72. See Omissi, *Air Power and Colonial Control*, p. 38.

73. See for example, note on the use and effect of aircraft during the Rania disturbances, 14 to 22 August 1921, by Major H.A. Goldsmith, P. 2036/7/4, CO 58013 22 NOV 21, CO 730/7, p. 120; and Intelligence Report no. 19, 15 August 1921, BHCF, File no. 19/1, vol. 2, Internal Intelligence Reports, p. 10.

74. See, for example, "Air raids on recalcitrant tribes," a paraphrase telegram from the High Commissioner to the Secretary of State for the Colonies, 8 December 1922, CO 61179 11 DEC 22, CO 730/26, p. 414. He lists nine operations along the Euphrates. In every case a shaikh was explicitly targeted, bombed and told to supply guarantees of future good behavior.

75. Quoted in Peter Sluglett, *Britain in Iraq, 1914–1932* (London: Ithaca Press, for the Middle East Centre, St. Antony's College, Oxford University, 1976), p. 262.

76. Jafana Cox, "A Splendid Training Ground," p. 167.

77. Glubb, *Arabian Adventures*, p. 106.

78. Report on a second reconnaissance of the Beni Huchaim area, D/ 495, 18 November 1923, to 'I' Branch Air Staff, Air 23/443, part 6, I/2106, Euphrates Samawah to Fallujah (Beni Huchaim Operations) 1923, p. 14.

79. See statement by Air Marshal Sir J. M. Salmond of his views upon the

principles governing the use of air power in Iraq, CO 62797 29 DEC 23, CO 730/46, p. 207.

80. See Memorandum from the Ministry of Interior to the Secretary to the High Commissioner, 3 October 1923, AIR/505/B, part 1, operations against the Beni Huchaim tribe, Samawah district, AIR 23/548, p. 414; and Report on the possibilities of operations on the Beni Huchaim, by Special Service Officer, Nasiriyah, AIR 23/443, part 6, I/2106, p. 1.

81. See AIR 23/548, p. 415.

82. See Glubb, *Arabian Adventures*, p. 107.

83. See telegram from the High Commissioner to the Secretary of State for the Colonies, no. 67, 2 February 1924, AIR 23/549.

84. See letter from L. N. Reed, Administrative Inspector Diwaniyah Liwa, to the Adviser to the Ministry of Interior, 12 October 1923, AIR 23/548, p. 417.

85. See telegram from the High Commissioner to the Secretary of State for the Colonies, no. 67, reviewing the reasons for the operation, 2 February 1924, AIR 23/549.

86. AIR/505/B/23, letter from Sir J. M. Salmond, to the Secretary Air Ministry, 12 December 1923, AIR 23/548, p. 41.

87. Letter from Sir J. M. Salmond, AIR/505/B/23, p. 41.

88. The tax demand was placed at the bottom of the list because of British press and parliamentary disquiet about bombing tribes into paying tax. See secret memorandum no. C/2667, from K. Cornwallis, the Ministry of Interior, to the Administrative Inspector, Diwaniyah, 19 November 1923, p. 403.

89. See Secret no. 20, from Reed, Administrative Inspector, Diwaniyah, to the Ministry of Interior, 3 December 1923, AIR 23/444, I/2106, part 8, p. 9; and BHCF File no. 19/1, vol. 6, Internal, Intelligence Report no. 24, 15 December 1923, p. 4.

90. CO 5682 5 FEB 24, telegram from the High Commissioner describing the operation to the Secretary of State for the Colonies, 2 February 1924, CO 730/57, p. 570.

91. Report of the bombing from the Special Services Officer, Hillah, 7 December 1923, AIR 23/443, part 6, I/2106.

92. Report on operations against the Barkat and Sufran, 30 November to 1 December 1923, from the Special Services Officer (SSO), Hillah, AIR 23/443, part 6, I/2106, p. 122.

93. See estimated casualties inflicted on Barkat and Sufran, Air 23/443, p. 128. The Iraqi police estimated a higher toll on human life as did Internal Intelligence Report no. 25, 27 December 1923, which was the official record of the Mandate authorities, BHCF, File no. 19/1, vol. 6, Internal.

94. Glubb, *Arabian Adventures*, p. 119.

95. See report on operations against the Barkat and Sufran, Air 23/443, part 6, I/2106, p. 124. The fear induced by airplanes was prolonged by the refusal of flights to tribesmen so that they would not know that the planes did not communicate with each other or that visibility from them was not as great as those on the ground believed.

96. Seventy shaikhs and headmen of the Beni Huchaim tribes were assembled on December 10 to meet the minister and his adviser. It was arranged for a flight of Snipe airplanes to fly over the tent as the meeting began. It had the desired effect of imposing a sombre atmosphere: "The shaikhs thought their last moment had come." Gertrude Bell, *From Her Personal Papers*, vol. 2, *1914–1926*, ed. Elizabeth Burgoyne (London: Ernest Benn Limited, 1961), p. 322; also see AIR 23/445, p. 15; and AIR 23/548, pp. 48, 65–66.

97. See telegram no. C/21, from G. N. Moore, SSO Diwaniyah, to Air Staff Intelligence AHQ, 21 December 1923, AIR 23/444, p. 113.

98. See telegram C/2, from SSO Hillah, to Air Staff Intelligence HQ, 2 January 1924, AIR 23/445, p. 33.

99. See report on operations against the Barkat and Sufran 30 November and 1 December 1923, from SSO, Hillah, AIR 23/443, p. 119.

100. The distinction between the shaikh and "his" tribespeople began to be made in explanations of why the rifle fine had not been paid. But it was never explicitly investigated. The dynamic of the supposedly consensual relationship between the two was never raised as a subject.

101. See AIR/505/B, part 2, second operation against Beni Huchaim tribe, Samawah, AIR 23/549, p. 43.

102. See report on the operations against the Barkat and Sufran, second phase, AIR 23/445, I/2106, part 8, pp. 16–18.

103. Air Commodore Chief Staff Officer, note for file Air/505/B, 21 December 1923, AIR 23/548, p. 214.

104. Or, if the bedouin section of each tribe was excluded, one rifle to every five cultivators. AIR 23/445, p. 19.

105. Report on operations against the Barkat and Sufran, from the SSO, Hillah, 7 December 1923, AIR 23/443, part 6, p. 124.

106. See Omissi, *Air Power and Colonial Control*, p. 37.

107. See Ministry of Interior, Baghdad, 12 October 1931, to the High Commissioner, copy of a further note by Edmonds, the Adviser, Ministry of Interior, 12 October 1931, C/3/32, BHCF, File no. 7/44/2, p. 18.

108. See CO 730/174 /11, no. 96393, part 1, Activities of Shaikh Ahmad of Barazan.

109. Omissi's investigation of colonial air power in India and Aden clearly indicates a comparative perception of society being deployed. Shaikhs or other

tribal leaders were made to take collective responsibility for their tribes. See Omissi, *Air Power and Colonial Control*, pp. 166–67.

110. Quoted in Cox, "A Splendid Training Ground," p. 171.

Conclusion: Iraq's Past And Possible Iraqi Futures

1. Speech by retired Marine General Antony Zinni, head of the U.S. Central Command from 1997 to 2000, the Middle East Institute, Washington D.C., October 10th 2002.

2. Of the fifty-four peace-keeping operations the United Nations has mounted since its formation, 80 percent have started since 1989. See *America's Record on Nation Building*, RAND, forthcoming.

3. The two definitive reports on intervention, "Report of the Panel on United Nations Peace Operations," UN document A/55/305 S/2000/809, chaired by Lakhdar Brahimi, and "The Responsibility to Protect," Report of the International Commission on Intervention and State Sovereignty, IDRC, 2001, between them take many hundreds of pages to say how intervention and reform should be carried out with greater technocratic efficiency but do not go into any detail about how institutions can be built, reformed, or gain acceptance amongst the population.

4. See Steve Heder "Cambodia, 1990–98: The Regime Didn't Change," in *Regime Change, It's Been Done Before*, ed. Roger Gough (London: policyexchange, 2003).

5. See Charles Tripp, "After Saddam," *Survival* 44, no. 4 (winter 2002–2003): 26; and "What Lurks in the Shadows?" *The Times Higher*, 18 October 2002, p. 17.

6. See Isam al Khafaji, "A Few Days After: State and Society in a post-Saddam Iraq," in *Iraq at the Crossroads: State and Society in the Shadow of Regime Change*, ed. Toby Dodge and Steven Simon (London and Oxford: International Institute for Strategic Studies and Oxford University Press, 2003).

7. See Isam al-Khafaji, "The Myth of Iraqi Exceptionalism," *Middle East Policy* no. 4 (October 2000): 65.

8. Federick D. Barton and Bathsheba Crocker, "Winning the Peace in Iraq," *The Washington Quarterly* 26, no. 2 (spring 2003): 10.

9. A visit to any government institution during this decade was a sobering event. In the middle of May 2001, I secured an interview with a provincial governor in the south of the country. On entering the building I had to step over a pool of raw sewage to reach his office door. Clearly the power of the state was no residing in this building.

10. See Toby Dodge, "Cake Walk, Coup, or Urban Warfare: The Battle for Iraq," in *Iraq at the Crossroads: State and Society in the Shadow of Regime Change*, ed. Toby Dodge and Steven Simon (London and Oxford: International Institute for Strategic Studies and Oxford University Press, 2003); and Amatzia Baram, "Building Towards Crisis: Saddam Husayn's Strategy for Survival," Policy Paper No. 47, The Washington Institute for Near East policy, 1998, pp. 7–31.

11. See Hanna Batatu, *The Old Social Classes and the Revolutionary Movements of Iraq: A Study of Iraq's Old Landed and Commercial Classes and Its Communists, Ba'thists, and Free Officers* (Princeton, N.J.: Princeton University Press, 1989), p. 22; and Peter Sluglett, *Britain in Iraq, 1914-1932* (London: Ithaca Press, 1976), p. 239.

12. Charles Tripp, *A History of Iraq* (Cambridge: Cambridge University Press), 2000, pp. 205–6.

13. Faleh A. Jabar, "Sheikhs and Ideologues: Deconstruction and Reconstruction of Tribes under Patrimonial Totalitarianism in Iraq, 1968–1998," in *Tribes and Power: Nationalism and Ethnicity in the Middle East*, ed. Faleh A. Jabar and Hosham Dawod (London: Saqi, 2003), pp. 69–101.

14. See Amatzia Baram, "Neo-tribalism in Iraq: Saddam Hussein's Tribal Policies, 1991–99," *International Journal of Middle Eastern Studies* 29 (1997): 1–31.

15. "British government sources admitted yesterday that there had been a general expectation' on both sides of the Atlantic that 'the Iraqi people would revolt against Saddam as they had in 1991' or at least that there might be a coup 'with in the higher echelons' of the regime." See R. Beeston and T. Baldwin, "Washington Hawks Under Fire for Ignoring Advice," *The Times*, 28 March 2003, p. 5.

16. "It is not too late for the Iraq military to act with honor and protect your country." George W. Bush's address to the American People, 17 March 2003.

17. "When Makiya and two other Iraqis were invited to the Oval Office in January [2003], he told President Bush that invading American troops would be greeted with 'sweets and flowers.' " See George Packer, "Kanan Makiya, Dreaming of Democracy," *New York Times Magazine*, 2 March 2003. Some Middle East experts were also prone to over confident analysis, see Fouad Ajami, "Iraq and the Thief of Baghdad," *New York Times*, 19 May 2002. Ajami's prediction that Baghdadis would greet U.S. troops with joy was quoted by Vice President Cheney in a speech at the Veterans of Foreign Wars 103rd convention, 26 August 2002.

18. See Elizabeth Drew, "The Neocons in Power," *The New York Review of Books* 50, No. 10 (12 June 2003).

19. Stephen Fidler and Guy Dinmore, "Debating How to Put Iraq Back Together Again," *Financial Times*, 22 March 2003, p. 9.

20. See Kanan Makiya's War Diary, New Republic Online, 18 April 2003.

21. Jonathan Steele in Baghdad, "Delegates Agree New Talks on Government," *The Guardian*, 29 April 2003.

22. Unedited Transcript, "The Day After: Planning for a Post-Saddam Iraq," Conference, American Enterprise Institute, Washington D.C., 3 October 2002.

23. See Paul Wolfowitz, Deputy Secretary of Defence, General Peter Pace, USMC, Vice Chairman Joint Chiefs of Staff, Alan Larson, Assistant Secretary of State for Economics, Business and Agricultural Affairs, testimony before the Senate Foreign Relations Committee, 2:35, pm, Thursday May 22, 2003.

24. See Susan B. Glasser, Basra, "Sheik's Appointment by British Triggers Protests and Accusations," *Washington Post*, 11 April 2003.

25. Quoted in Robyn Dixon, "A Dust-Up in Basra's Leadership Vacuum," *Los Angles Times*, 18 April 2003.

26. See Donald Macintyre in Amarah, "British Hope Colonial Past Can Inspire Law And Order," *The Independent*, 24 April 2003; and Glen Owen in al-Amarah, "British Law Is Template for New Legal System," *The Times*, 24 April 2003.

27. See Marion Farouk-Sluglett and Peter Sluglett, *Iraq Since 1958: From Revolution to Dictatorship* (London: I. B. Tauris, 2001).

28. See Peter Slevin, 'Iraqi Town Becomes Test for Reconstruction," *Washington Post*, 23 April 2003.

29. For a further expansion of this argument, see "Iraq after Saddam: The Quagmire of Political Reconstruction," *IISS Strategic Comment* 8, no. 4 (May 2002).

BIBLIOGRAPHY

Archive Sources

India Office Library, British Library, London (IOL).
Files of the Military Department:
  Mesopotamian Campaign and Commission of Enquiry
  L/MIL/5
Military Department Library:
  L/MIL/17
Files of the Political and Secret Departments:
  L/P&S/10
  L/P&S/15
  L/P&S/18
Official Publications Library, British Library, London.
Public Records Office, Kew, London (PRO).
Colonial Office:
  Iraq Administrative Reports
  CO 696
  Original Correspondence Iraq
  CO 730
Air Ministry:
  Overseas Commands
  AIR 23
Foreign Office:
  Political
  FO 371
National Archive of India, New Delhi: India.
Baghdad High Commission Files (BHCF)
Newcastle Library:
  Private Papers of Gertrude Bell.
The Sudan Archive Durham University Library
  Private Papers of:
  F. C. C. Balfour.
  Sir G. F. Clayton.
  Sir R. E. Windgate.
  Sir H. Young.

The Middle East Center Library, St Antony's College, Oxford University:
   Private Papers of:
   H. E. Bowan.
   H. R. P. Dickson.
   C. J. Edmonds.
   Sir J. B. Glubb.
   H. St. John B. Philby.
   A. L. F. Smith.
   Sir H. Young.

Book, Theses, Articles, and Unpublished Papers

Abrahamian, Ervand. "Oriental Despotism: the Case of Qajar Iran." *International Jour-
   nal of Middle Eastern Studies* no. 5. 1974.
Adas, Michael. *Machines as the Measure of Men: Science, Technology, and Ideologies of
   Western Dominance.* Ithaca, N.Y.: Cornell University Press, 1989.
Ahmad, Aijaz. *In Theory: Classes, Nations, Literatures.* London: Verso, 1992.
Ajami, Fouad. "Iraq and the Thief of Bagdad," *New York Times*, 19 May 2002.
Al Hasso, Nazar Tawfik. "Administrative Politics in the Middle East: The Case of
   Monarchical Iraq, 1920–1958," Ph.D. diss., University of Texas at Austin, 1976.
Al Khafaji, Isam. "A Few Days After: State and Society in a post-Saddam Iraq," in *Iraq
   at the Crossroads: State and Society in the Shadow of Regime Change*, ed. Toby Dodge
   and Steven Simon. London and Oxford: International Institute for Strategic Stud-
   ies and Oxford University Press, 2003.
———. "The Myth of Iraqi Exceptionalism." *Middle East Policy*, no. 4 (October
   2000).
Al Sayyid, Afaf Lutfi. *Egypt and Cromer: A Study in Anglo-Egyptian Relations.* London:
   John Murray, 1968.
Althusser, Louis. "Contradiction and Over-Determinations: Notes for an Investigation."
   In *For Marx*, by Louis Althusser, translated by Ben Brewster. London: Verso, 1990.
———. *Essays on Ideology.* London: Verso, 1984.
———. *Montesquieu, Rousseau, Marx.* London: New Left Books, 1977.
Amadouny, Vartan. "Infrastructural Development Under the British Mandate." In *Vil-
   lage, Steppe, and State: The Social Origins of Modern Jordan*, ed. Eugene L. Rogan and
   Tariq Tell. London: British Academic Press, 1994.
Ambrose, Stephen E., and Douglas G. Brinklet. *The Rise to Globalism: American For-
   eign Policy Since 1938.* Harmondsworth: Penguin Books, 1997.
American Enterprise Institute. "The Day After: Planning for a Post-Saddam Iraq."
   Unedited conference transcript. Washington D.C. 3 October 2002.
Anderson, Perry. *Lineages of the Absolutist State.* London: Verso, 1987.

The Arab Bulletin: Bulletin of the Arab Bureau in Cairo, 1916–1919. Introduction by Dr. Robin Bidwell. Slough: Archive Editions, 1986.

Arrighi, Giovanni. "The Three Hegemonies of Historical Capitalism. " In *Gramsci, Historical Materialism and International Relations*, ed. Steven Gill. Cambridge: Cambridge University Press, 1993.

Asad, Talal. "Two European Images of Non-European Rule." *Economy and Society* 2, no. 3 (1973).

Baloch, I. *The Problems of "Greater Baluchistan": A Study of Baluch Nationalism.* Stuttgart: Steiner Verlag Wiesbaden GMBH, 1987.

Baram, Amatzia. "Building Towards Crisis: Saddam Husayn's Strategy for Survival." Policy Paper no. 47. The Washington Institute for Near East policy, 1998.

———. "Neo-Tribalism in Iraq: Saddam Hussein's Tribal Policies, 1991–96." *International Journal of Middle Eastern Studies* no. 29 (1997).

Baram, Philip J. *The Department of State in the Middle East, 1919–1945.* State College, Penn.: University of Pennsylvania Press, 1978.

Barraclough, Geoffrey. *An Introduction to Contemporary History.* Harmondsworth: Penguin, 1990.

Barret, Michele. "Ideology, Politics, Hegemony: From Gramsci to Laclau and Mouffe." In *Mapping Ideology*, ed. Slavoj Zizek. London: Verso, 1994.

Barton, Frederick D., and Bathsheba Crocker. "Winning the Peace in Iraq." *The Washington Quarterly* 26, no 2 (spring 2003).

Batatu, Hanna. *The Old Social Classes and the Revolutionary Movements of Iraq: A Study of Iraq's Old Landed and Commercial Classes and of Its Communists, Ba'athists, and Free Officers.* Princeton, N.J.: Princeton University Press, 1989.

Bearse, George D. *British Attitudes to India, 1784–1858.* Wesport, Conn.: Greenwood Press, 1961.

Beck, Peter J. " 'A Tedious and Perilous Controversy': Britain and the Settlement of the Mosul Dispute, 1918–1926." *Middle East Studies* 17 (April 1981).

Beer, G. L. "The Future of Mesopotamia." In *African Questions at the Paris Peace Conference, with papers on Egypt, Mesopotamia and the Colonial Settlement*, by G. L. Beer. Edited with introduction, annexes, and additional notes by Louis Herbert Gray. London: Dawsons of Pall Mall, 1968.

Beer, G. L., and F. M. Graves. "The Territorial Settlement in Africa." In *The Settlement with Germany.* Vol. 2 of *A History of the Peace Conference of Paris, ed.* H. W. V. Temperley. London: Oxford University Press, issued under the auspices of the Royal Institute of International Affairs, 1969.

Bell, Gertrude. *The Arab of Mesopotamia.* Basrah: Superintendent Government Press, 1917.

———. *From Her Personal Papers, 1914–1926.* Vol. 2. Ed. Elizabeth Burgoyne. London: Ernest Benn, 1961.

————. *The Letters of Gertrude Bell.* Vol. 2. Selected and edited by Lady Bell. Harmondsworth: Penguin, 1939.

————. Preface to *The Desert and the Sown.* 1907. Reprint, Boston: Beacon Press, 1985.

Bhabha, Homi. "Signs Taken for Wonders: Questions of Ambivalence and Authority Under a Tree Outside Delhi: May 1817." *Critical Inquiry* 12, no. 1 (1985).

Bhaskar, Roy. "Marxist Philosophers from Marx to Althusser. " In *Philosophy and the Idea of Freedom,* by Roy Bhaskar. Oxford: Basil Blackwell, 1991.

————. *Reclaiming Reality: A Critical Introduction to Contemporary Philosophy.* London: Verso, 1993.

Bhattacharya, Neeladri. "Colonial State and Agrarian Society." In *Situating Indian History: For Sarvepalli Gopal,* ed. S. Bhattacharya and R. Thapar. Delhi: Oxford University Press, 1986.

————. "Pastoralists in a Colonial World." In *Studies in Social Ecology and Environmental History, Nature, Culture, Imperialism: Essays on the Environmental History of South Asia,* ed. David Arnold and Ramachandra Guha. Delhi: Oxford University Press, 1995.

Blunt, Lady Anne. *Bedouin Tribes of the Euphrates.* 2 vols. London: Frank Cass, 1968.

Bocco, Riccardo, and Tariq Tell. "Pax Britannica in the Steppe: British Policy and the Transjordanian Bedouin, 1923–39. " In *Village, Steppe, and State: The Social Origins of Modern Jordan,* ed. Eugene L. Rogan and Tariq Tell. London: British Academic Press, 1994.

Bowles, John. *The Imperial Achievement: The Rise and Transformation of the British Empire.* Harmondsworth: Penguin, 1977.

Brahimi, Lakhdar. "Report of the Panel on United Nations Peace Operations." UN document A/55/305 S/2000/809.

Brewer, Anthony. *Marxist Theories of Imperialism: A Critical Survey.* London: Routledge, 1990.

Brown, Judith M. *The Oxford History of the British Empire.* Vol. 4, *The Twentieth Century.* Oxford: Oxford University Press, 1999.

Bruce, Colonel C. E. "The Sandeman Policy as Applied to Tribal Problems of Today." *The Journal of Royal Central Asian Society* 19 (1932).

Bull, Hedley. *The Anarchical Society: A Study in World Politics.* London: MacMillan, 1995.

————. "The Revolt against the West." In *The Expansion of International Society.* Eds. Hedley Bull and Adam Watson, Oxford: Clarendon Press, 1989.

Burke, Edmund. "Reflections on the Revolution in France." In *The Portable Edmund Burke,* ed. Isacc Kramnick. New York: Penguin, 1999.

Busch, Briton Cooper. *Britain, India, and the Arabs, 1914–1921.* Berkeley: University of California Press, 1971.

————. *Mudros to Lausanne: Britain's Frontier in West Asia, 1918–1923.* Albany: State University of New York Press, 1976.

Bush, George W. "The President's State of the Union Address." Washington, D.C., 29 January 2002.

———. "President at 2002 Graduation Exercise of the United States Military Academy." West Point, New York, 1 June 2002.

———. "The President's 2003 State of the Union Address. Washington, D.C., January 2003.

———. "President Discusses the Future of Iraq at the American Enterprise Institute." Washington, D.C., 26 February 2003.

Cain, P. J., and A. G. Hopkins. *British Imperialism: Crisis and Deconstruction, 1914–1990*. London: Longman, 1993.

———. *British Imperialism: Innovation and Expansion, 1688–1914*. London: Longman, 1993.

Callinicos, Alex. *Theories and Narratives: Reflections on the Philosophy of History*. Cambridge: Polity Press, 1995.

Cannadine, David. *The Decline and Fall of the British Aristocracy*. London: Macmillan, 1996.

Carr, E. H. *International Relations Between the Two World Wars, 1919–1939*. New York: Harper Torch Books, 1947.

———. *Nationalism and After*. London: Macmillan, 1945.

———. *The Twenty Years' Crisis, 1919–1939*. Basingstoke: Macmillan, 1978.

Cetinsaya, Gokhan. "Ottoman Administration of Iraq, 1890–1908." Ph.D. diss., University of Manchester, 1994.

Cheney, Richard. "A Speech at the Veterans of Foreign Wars 103rd Convention," 26 August 2002.

Cirakman, Asli. "The Prejudice of Montesquieu: Intellectual Roots of Modern Eurocentrism." Paper presented at the Middle East Studies Association, 32nd Annual Meeting, Chicago, Illinois, 3–6 December, 1998.

Clarence-Smith, William Gervase. "The Organization of 'Consent' in British West Africa, 1820s to 1960s." In *Contesting Colonial Hegemony, State and Society in Africa and India*, ed. Dagmar Engles and Shula Marxs. London: British Academic Press, 1994.

Clifford, James. " On Orientalism." In *The Predicament of Culture: Twentieth-Century Ethnography, Literature, and Art*, by James Clifford. Cambridge, Mass.: Harvard University Press, 1988.

Cocker, Mark. *Rivers of Blood, Rivers of Gold: Europe's Conflict with Tribal Peoples*. London: Pimlico, 1999.

Cohn, Bernard S. *An Anthropologist Among the Historians and Other Essays*. Delhi: Oxford University Press, 1987.

———. *Colonialism and Its Forms of Knowledge: The British in India*. Princeton, N.J.: Princeton University Press, 1996.

———. "Representing Authority in Victorian India." In *The Invention of Tradition*, ed. Eric Hobsbawn and Terence Ranger. Cambridge: Canto, Cambridge University Press, 1993.

Colonial Office. *Iraq: Report on Iraq Administration, October 1920–March 1921.* London: His Majesty's Stationery Office, 1922.

———. *Iraq: Report on Iraq Administration, April 1922–March 1923.* London: His Majesty's Stationery Office, 1924.

———. *Report by His Britannic Majesty's Government on the Administration of Iraq for the Period April 1923–December 1924.* London: His Majesty's Stationery Office, 1925.

———. *Report by His Britannic Majesty's Government to the Council of the League of Nations on the Administration of Iraq for the Year 1925.* London: His Majesty's Stationery Office, 1926.

———. *Report by His Britannic Majesty's Government to the Council of the League of Nations on the Administration of Iraq for the Year 1926.* London: His Majesty's Stationery Office, 1927.

———. *Report by His Britannic Majesty's Government to the Council of the League of Nations on the Administration of Iraq for the Year 1927.* London: His Majesty's Stationery Office, 1928.

———. *Report by His Britannic Majesty's Government to the Council of the League of Nations on the Administration of Iraq for the Year 1928.* London: His Majesty's Stationery Office, 1929.

———. *Report by His Britannic Majesty's Government in the United Kingdom of Great Britain and Northern Ireland to the Council of the League of Nations on the Administration of Iraq for the Year 1929.* London: His Majesty's Stationery Office, 1930.

———. *Report by His Britannic Majesty's Government in the United Kingdom of Great Britain and Northern Ireland to the Council of the League of Nations on the Administration of Iraq for the Year 1930.* London: His Majesty's Stationery Office, 1931.

———. *Report by His Britannic Majesty's Government in the United Kingdom of Great Britain and Northern Ireland to the Council of the League of Nations on the Administration of Iraq for the Year 1931.* London: His Majesty's Stationery Office, 1932.

———. *Special Report by His Majesty's Government in the United Kingdom of Great Britain and Northern Ireland to the Council of the League of Nations on the Progress of Iraq during the period 1920–1931.* London: His Majesty's Stationery Office, 1931.

Cox, Jafana L. "A Splendid Training Ground: The Importance to the Royal Air Force of its Role in Iraq, 1919–1932." *The Journal of Imperial and Commonwealth History*, 13, no. 2 (January 1985).

Cox, Sir Percy, "Historical Summaries." In Gertrude Bell, *The Letters of Gertrude Bell*, vol. 2, selected and edited by Lady Bell. Harmondsworth: Penguin, 1939.

Cox, Robert. *Production, Power, and World Order: Social Forces in the Making of History.* New York: Columbia University Press, 1987.

———. "Social Forces, States, and World Orders: Beyond International Relations Theory." In *NeoRealism and its Critics*, ed. Robert O. Keohane. New York: Columbia University Press, 1986.

Cranston, Maurice. *The Romantic Movement.* Oxford: Blackwell, 1994.

Cromer, Earl of. *Modern Egypt.* 2 vols. London: Macmillan, 1908.

———. *Political and Literary Essays, 1908–1913.* London: Macmillan, 1913.

Dann, Uriel, ed. *The Great Powers in the Middle East, 1919–1939.* New York: Dayan Center for Middle Eastern and African Studies, Holmes & Meier, 1988.

Darwin, John. "Imperialism in Decline? Tendencies in British Imperial Policy Between the Wars." *The Historical Journal* 23, no. 3 (1980).

———. *Britain, Egypt, and the Middle East: Imperial Policy in the Aftermath of War, 1918–1922.* London: Macmillan, 1981.

———. "Decolonisation and the End of Empire." In *Historiography*, Vol. 5 of *The Oxford History of the British Empire*, ed. Robin W. Winks. Oxford: Oxford University Press, 1999.

Dawson, Graham. "The Blond Bedouin: Lawrence of Arabia, Imperial Adventure and the Imagining of English-British Masculinity. " In *Manful Assertions: Masculinities in Britain Since 1800*, ed. Michael Roper and John Tosh. London: Routledge, 1991.

Degroot, Gerard J. *Blighty: British Society in the Era of the Great War.* London: Longman, 1996.

DeNovo, John A. "On the Sidelines: The United States and the Middle East Between the Wars, 1919–1939. " In *The Great Powers in the Middle East, 1919–1939*, ed. Uriel Dann. New York: Dayan Center for Middle Eastern and African Studies, Holmes & Meier, 1988.

Deringil, Selim. *The Well Protected Domains: Ideology and Legitimation in the Ottoman Empire, 1876–1909.* London: I. B. Tauris, 1998.

Dewey, Clive. *Anglo-Indian Attitudes: The Mind of the Indian Civil Service.* London: Hambledon Press, 1993.

Dews, Peter. *Logics of Disintegration: Post-Structuralist Thought and the Claims of Critical Theory.* London: Verso, 1987.

Dirks, Nicholas B. "Introduction: Colonialism and Culture." In *Colonialism and Culture*, ed. Nicholas B. Dirks. Ann Arbor: University of Michigan Press, 1995.

Dirks Nicholas B. "From Little King to Landlord: Colonial Discourse and Colonial Rule." Nicholas B. Dirks (ed.), *Colonialism and Culture.* Ann Arbor: University of Michigan Press, 1995.

Dodge, Toby. *An Arabian Prince: English Gentlemen and the Tribes East of the River Jordan. Abdullah and the Creation and Consolidation of the Transjordanian State.* London: Center of Near and Middle Eastern Studies Occasional Paper 13, School of Oriental and African Studies, 1993.

———. "Cake Walk, Coup, or Urban Warfare: The Battle for Iraq." In *Iraq at the Crossroads: State and Society in the Shadow of Regime Change.* Ed. Tody Dodge and Steven Simon. London and Oxford: International Institute for Strategic Studies and Oxford University Press, 2003.

Dodge, Toby, and Steven Simon. Introduction to *Iraq at the Crossroads: State and Society in the Shadow of Regime Change.* London and Oxford: International Institute for Strategic Studies and Oxford University Press, 2003.

Dowson, Sir Ernest. *Government of el Iraq: An Inquiry Into Land Tenure and Related Questions with Proposals for the Initiation of Reform.* Letchworth, England: printed for the Iraqi Government by the Garden City Press, 1931.

Drew, Elizabeth. "The Neocons in Power." *New York Review of Books* 50, no. 10 (12 June 2003).

Dreyfus, Hubert L., and Paul Rabinow. *Michel Foucault: Beyond Structuralism and Hermeneutics.* Chicago: University of Chicago Press, 1983.

Durkheim, Émile. *On Morality and Society: Selected Writings.* Ed. Robert N. Bellah. Chicago: University of Chicago Press, 1973.

Eagleton, Terry. *Ideology: An Introduction.* London: Verso, 1994.

Edney, Matthew H. *Mapping Empire: The Geographical Construction of British India, 1765–1843.* Chicago: University of Chicago Press, 1997.

Embree, Anislie T. "Landholding in India and British Institutions." In *Land Control and Social Structure in Indian History,* ed. Eric Frykenberg. Madison: University of Wisconsin Press, 1969.

Engles, Dagmar, and Shula Marxs, eds. *Contesting Colonial Hegemony: State and Society in Africa and India.* London: British Academic Press, 1994.

Fairclough, Norman. *Discourse and Social Change.* Cambridge: Polity Press, 1992.

Farouk-Sluglett, Marion. "The Formation of the Iraqi State: Politics and Political Alliances Under the Mandate, 1920–1932." Paper presented at the British Society for Middle Eastern Studies Conference, Manchester, July 1994.

Farouk-Sluglett, Marion, and Peter Sluglett. "The Historiography of Modern Iraq." *American History Review* 96, no.5 (December 1991): 1408–21.

———. *Iraq Since 1958: From Revolution to Dictatorship.* London: I. B. Tauris, 1990.

Feierman, Steven. *Peasant Intellectuals: Anthropology and History in Tanzania.* Madison: University of Wisconsin Press, 1990.

Fields, Karen E. *Revival and Rebellion in Colonial Central Africa.* Princeton, N.J.: Princeton University Press, 1985.

Femia, Joseph. "Hegemony and Consciousness in the thought of Antonio Gramsci." *Political Studies* 23, no. 1 (March 1975).

Fernea, Robert A., and Wm. Roger Louis, eds. *The Iraqi Revolution of 1958: The Old Social Classes Revisited.* London: I. B. Tauris, 1991.

The Financial Times.

Fischbach, Michael Richard. "State, Society, And Land in 'Ajlun (Northern Transjordan), 1850–1950." 2 Vols. Ph.D. diss., Georgetown University, 1992.

Foreign Office. *Report by His Britannic Majesty's Government in the United Kingdom of Great Britain and Northern Ireland to the Council of the League of Nations on the Administration of Iraq for the Period January to October 1932.* London: His Majesty's Stationery Office, 1933.

Foucault, Michel. *The Archaeology of Knowledge and the Discourse on Language.* New York: Barnes and Nobles Books, 1993.

———. *Discipline and Punish. The Birth of the Prison.* Transl. Alan Sheridan. Harmondsworth: Penguin, 1991.

———. *The History of Sexuality.* Vol. 1 of *The Will to Knowledge.* Trans. Robert Hurley. Harmondsworth: Penguin, 1990.

———. *The Order of Things; An Archaeology of the Human Sciences.* London: Routledge, 1997.

———. "Truth and Power." In *Power/Knowledge: Selected Interviews and Other Writings 1972–1977,* ed. Colin Gordon. New York: Pantheon Books, 1980.

———. "Two Lectures at the College De France 1976: Lecture One, 7 January." In *Power/Knowledge: Selected Interviews and Other Writings 1972–1977,* ed. Colin Gordon. Pantheon Books, New York: 1980.

Fromkin, David. *A Peace to End All Peace: Creating the Modern Middle East, 1914–1922.* Harmondsworth: Penguin Books, 1991.

Frum, David. *The Right Man: The Surprise Presidency of George W. Bush.* New York: Random House, 2003.

Fussell, Paul. *The Great War and Modern Memory.* London: Oxford University Press, 1975.

Gallagher, John. "The Decline, Revival, and Fall of the British Empire." In *The Decline, Revival and Fall of the British Empire, The Ford Lectures, and Other Essays,* by John Gallagher, ed. Anil Seal. Cambridge: Cambridge University Press, 1982.

Gann, Rose. "Blind Alleys: The Limits of Textbook Ideology." *Politics* (May 1995).

Gerber, Haim. *The Social Origins of the Modern Middle East.* Boulder, Colo.: Lynne Rienner Publishers, 1987.

Germain, Randall D., and Michael Kenny. "Engaging Gramsci: International Relations Theory and the New Gramscians." *Review of International Studies* no. 24 (1998).

Giddens, Antony. *The Nation-State and Violence.* Vol. 2 of *A Contemporary Critique of Historical Materialism.* Cambridge: Polity Press, 1985.

Gill, Steven, ed. *Gramsci, Historical Materialism, and International Relations.* Cambridge: Cambridge University Press, 1993.

Gilmour, David. *Curzon.* London: Papermac, 1994.

Girouard, Mark. *The Return of Camelot: Chivalry and the English Gentleman*. New Haven, Conn.: Yale University Press, 1981.

Glubb, John. *Arabian Adventures: Ten Years of Joyful Service*. London: Cassell, 1978.

———. *The Changing Scenes of Life: An Autobiography*. London: Quartet Books, 1983.

———. *The Story of the Arab Legion*. London: Hodder and Stoughton, 1948.

Gong, Gerrit W. *The Standard of Civilization in International Society*. Oxford: Clarendon Press, 1984.

Gramsci, Antonio. *Selections from the Prison Notebooks*. Ed. and trans. Quintin Hoare and Geoffrey Nowell Smith. London: Lawrence and Wishart, 1971.

———. *The Gramsci Reader: Selected Writings 1916–1935*. Ed. David Forgacs. London: Lawrence and Wishart, 1988.

Graves, Philip. *The Life and Times of Sir Percy Cox*. London: Hutchinson, 1941.

Greenleaf, W. H. *The Ideological Heritage*. Vol. 2 of *The British Political Tradition*. London: Methuen, 1983.

The Guardian.

Guha, Ranajit. *A Rule of Property for Bengal: An Essay on the Idea of the Permanent Settlement*. Paris: Mouton, 1963.

———, ed. *Subaltern Studies I: Writings on South Asian History*. Delhi: Oxford University Press, 1982.

Haas, Richard N. "The 2002 Arthur Ross Lecture: Remarks to Foreign Policy Association." New York, 22 April 2002.

Habermas, Jurgen. *The Philosophical Discourse of Modernity: Twelve Lectures*. Trans. Fredrick Lawrence. Cambridge: Polity Press, 1987.

Haj, Samira. *The Making of Iraq, 1900–1963: Capital, Power, and Ideology*. New York: State University of New York Press, 1997.

Hall, H. Duncan. "The British Commonwealth and the Founding of the League Mandate System." In *Studies in International History: Essays Presented to W. Norton Medlicott, Stevenson Professor of International History in the University of London*, ed. K. Bourne and D. C. Watt. London: Longman, 1967.

———. *Mandates, Dependencies, and Trusteeship*. New York: Klaus Reprint Company, 1972.

Hall, Stuart, Bob Lumley, and Gregor McLennan. "Politics and Ideology: Gramsci." In *On Ideology*, ed. Center for Contemporary Cultural Studies. London: Hutchinson and Company, 1977.

Halliday, Fred. *Rethinking International Relations*. Basingstoke: Macmillan, 1994.

Headrick, Daniel R. *The Tentacles of Progress: Technology Transfer in the Age of Imperialism, 1850–1940*. New York: Oxford University Press, 1988.

———. *The Tools of Empire: Technology and European Imperialism in the Nineteenth Century*. New York: Oxford University Press, 1981.

Heder, Steve. "Cambodia, 1990–98: The Regime Didn't Change." In *Regime Change, It's Been Done Before*. Ed. Roger Gough. London: policyexchange, 2003.

Heller, Mark. "Politics and the Military in Iraq and Jordan, 1920–1958: The British Influence." *Armed Forces and Society* 4, no. 1 (November 1977).

Hirsh, Michael, "Bush and the World." *Foreign Affairs* (Sepember/October 2002).

Hoare, Sir Samuel. *A Flying Visit to the Middle East.* Cambridge: Cambridge University Press, 1925.

Hostettler, Nick. "Asiatic Mode of Production." Unpublished paper. Department of Political Studies, School of Oriental and African Studies. April 1993.

Hourani, Albert. Foreword to *The Role of the Military in Politics: A Case Study of Iraq to 1941,* by Mohammad A. Tarbush. London: Routledge Kegan Paul, 1985.

Hoverd, Margaret Jane. "Kurdish Ethno-nationalism in a Changing International Order: 'Power' and the Mosul Question." Master's thesis, School of Oriental and African Studies, 1997.

Howard, Michael. "The Military Factor in the European Expansion. " In *The Expansion of International Society,* ed.. Hedley Bull and Adam Watson. Oxford: Clarendon Press, 1989.

Hughes, Matthew. *Allenby and British Strategy in the Middle East, 1917–1919.* London: Frank Cass, 1999.

Hurd, Douglas. Foreword to *Regime Change, It's Been Done Before.* London: Policyexchange, 2003.

Ikenberry, G. John. "America's Imperial Ambition." *Foreign Affairs* (September/October 2002).

The Independent.

International Commission on Intervention and State Sovereignty. *The Responsibility to Protect.* IDRC, 2001.

International Institute for Strategic Studies. "Iraq After Saddam: The Quagmire of Political Reconstuction." *IISS Strategic Comment* 8, no. 4 (May 2002).

Ireland, Philip Willard. *Iraq: A Study in Political Development.* London: Jonathan Cape, 1937.

Islamoglu-Inan, Huri. "Introduction: Oriental Despotism in World-System Perspective." In *The Ottoman Empire in the World-Economy,* ed. Huri Islamoglu-Inan. Cambridge: Cambridge University Press, 1987.

———. *State and Peasant in the Ottoman Empire: Agrarian Power Relations and Regional Economic Development in Ottoman Anatolia During the Sixteenth Century.* London: E. J. Brill, 1994.

Issawi, Charles. *The Fertile Crescent, 1800–1914: A Documentary Economic History.* Oxford: Oxford University Press, 1988.

———, ed. *The Economic History of the Middle East, 1800–1914: A Book of Readings.* Chicago: University of Chicago Press, 1975.

Jabar, Faleh A. "Sheikhs and Ideologues: Deconstruction and Reconstruction of Tribes Under Patrimonial Totalitarianism in Iraq, 1968–1998." In *Tribes and Power:*

Nationalism and Ethnicity in the Middle East, ed. Faleh A. Jabar and Hosham Dawod. London: Saqi, 2003.

Jackson, Robert H. *Quasi-States: Sovereignty, International Relations and the Third World*. Cambridge: Cambridge University Press, 1993.

———. "The Weight of Ideas in Decolonization: Normative Change in International Relations." In *Ideas and Foreign Policy*, ed. Judith Goldstein and Robert Keohane. Ithaca, N.Y.: Cornell University Press, 1993.

Jeffery, Keith. *The British Army and the Crisis of Empire, 1918–1922*. Manchester: Manchester University Press, 1984.

Jentleson, Bruce W. *Coercive Prevention: Normative, Political, and Policy Dilemmas*. US Institute of Peace Peaceworks series, 2000.

Jwaideh, Albertine. "Aspects of Land Tenure and Social Change in Lower Iraq During Late Ottoman Times." In *Land Tenure and Social Transformation in the Middle East*, ed. Tarif Khalidi. Beirut: American University of Beirut, 1984.

———. "Midhat Pasha and the Land System of Lower Iraq." *St Antony's Papers*, vol. 16. Oxford, 1963.

———. "The *Sanniya* Lands of Sultan Abdul Hamid II in Iraq." In *Arabic and Islamic Studies in Honor of Hamilton A. R. Gibb*, ed. George Makdisi. Cambridge, Mass.: Harvard University Press, 1965.

———. "Tribalism and Modern Society: Iraq, a Case Study." In *Introduction to Islamic Civilization*, ed. R. M. Savory. Cambridge: Cambridge University Press, 1976.

Jwaideh, Wadie. :The Kurdish Nationalist Movement: Its Origins and Development." Ph.D. diss., Syracuse University, 1960.

Kabbani, Rana. *Imperial Fictions: Europe's Myths of Orient*. London: MacMillian, 1986.

Kant. Immanuel. "What Is Enlightenment?" In *Kant Selections*, ed. Lewis White Beck. New York: Macmillan, 1988.

Kasaba, Resat. "A Time and a Place for the Non-State: Social Change in the Ottoman Empire During the 'Long Nineteenth Century.' " In *State Power and Social Forces: Domination and Transformation in the Third World*, ed. Joel S. Migdal, Atul Kohli, and Vivienne Shue. Cambridge: Cambridge University Press, 1994.

Kaviraj, Sudipta. "On the Construction of Colonial Power: Structure Discourse, Hegemony." In *Contesting Colonial Hegemony: State and Society in Africa and India*, ed. Dagmar Engles and Shula Marxs. London: British Academic Press, 1994.

Kedourie, Elie. *The Chatham House Version and Other Middle Eastern Studies*. Hanover, N.H.: University Press of New England, 1984.

Keene, Edward. "The Colonising Ethic and Modern International Society: A Reconstruction of the Grotian Tradition in International Theory." Ph.D. diss., London School of Economics, 1998.

Kennedy, David. "The Move to Institutions." *The Cardozo Law Review* 8, no. 5 (April 1987).

Kennedy, Paul. *The Realities Behind Diplomacy: Background Influences on British External Policy, 1865–1980*. London: Fontana Press, 1985.

———. *The Rise and Fall of the Great Powers: Economic Change and Military Conflict from 1500 to 2000.* London: Fontana Press, 1989.

Keohane, Robert O. *After Hegemony: Cooperation and Discord in the World Political Economy.* Princeton, N.J.: Princeton University Press, 1984.

Kiernan, V. G. *The Lords of Human Kind: European Attitudes to the Outside World in the Imperial Age.* Harmondsworth: Penguin, 1972.

Kirkbride, Sir Alec. "Was Britain's Abdication Folly? II: Reflection on the Kedouries Version." *Round Table* (July 1970).

Kratochwil, Friedrich V. "Politics, Norms, and Peaceful Change." *The Review of International Studies* 24 (December 1998). Special edition: "The Eighty Years Crisis, 1919–1999," ed. Tim Dunne, Michael Cox, and Ken Booth.

Kumar, Dharma, ed., with Meghnad Desai. *The Cambridge Economic History of India.* Vol. 2, *Ca. 1757–1970.* Cambridge: Cambridge University Press, 1983.

Latham, Robert. "History, Theory, and International Order: Some Lessons from the Nineteenth Century." *Review of International Studies* no. 23 (1997).

Layne, Linda L. *Home and Homeland: The Dialogics of Tribal and National Identities in Jordan.* Princeton, N.J.: Princeton University Press, 1994.

Leman, Nicholas. "The Next World Order: The Bush Administration May Have a Brand New Doctrine of Power." *The New Yorker,* 1 March 2002.

———. "After Iraq: The Plan to Remake the Middle East. *The New Yorker,* 17 February 2003.

Lenin, Vladimir I. *Imperialism: The Highest Stage of Capitalism. A Popular Outline.* New York: International Publishers, 1993.

Lepenies, Wolf. *Ideas in Context: Between Literature and Science. The Rise of Sociology.* Cambridge: Cambridge University Press, 1992.

Litwak, Robert S. "The New Calculus of Preemption." *Survival* 44, no. 4 (winter 2002–2003).

Lockie, Liora. "Iraqi Politics 1931–1941." Ph.D. diss., University of London, 1988.

Lloyd George, David (Lord Lloyd of Dolobran). Foreword to *Iraq from Mandate to Independence,* by Ernest Main. London: George Allen and Unwin, 1935.

Longrigg, Stephen Hemsley. *Four Centuries of Modern Iraq.* Oxford: Oxford University Press, 1925.

———. *Iraq, 1900 to 1950: A Political, Social, and Economic History.* Oxford: Issued under the auspices of the Royal Institute of International Affairs by Oxford University Press, 1953.

The Los Angeles Times.

Louis, Wm. Roger. "The Era of the Mandates System and the Non-European World." In *The Expansion of International Society,* ed. Hedley Bull and Adam Watson. Oxford: Clarendon Press, 1989.

———. *In the Name of God Go! Leo Amery and the British Empire in the Age of Churchill.* New York: W. W. Norton, 1992.

————, ed. *Imperialism: The Robinson and Gallagher Controversy*. New York: New Viewpoints, 1976.

Lovejoy, Arthur O. "The Meaning of Romanticism for the History of Idea." *Journal of the History of Ideas* 2 (June 1941).

Lucas, John. *Modern English Poetry From Hardy to Hughes: A Critical Survey*. London: B. T. Batsford, 1986.

Lugard, F. G. (High Commissioner Northern Nigeria). *Instructions to Political and Other Officers on Subjects Chiefly Political and Administrative*. London: 1906; revised 1906.

Lugard, F. G. (Lord). *The Dual Mandate in British Tropical Africa*. London: Frank Cass, 1965.

Lyell, Thomas. *The Ins and Outs of Mesopotamia*. Cambridge: Allborough Publishing, 1991.

McCarthy, Thomas. Introduction to *The Philosophical Discourse of Modernity, Twelve Lectures*, by Jurgen Habermas, trans. Fredrick Lawrence. Cambridge: Polity Press, 1987.

McDowall, David. *A Modern History of the Kurds*. London: I. B. Tauris, 1996.

MacPherson, C. B. *Burke*. Oxford: Oxford University Press, 1980.

Makiya, Kanan "Kanan Makiya's War Diary." New Republic Online, 18 April 2003.

Mangan, J. A. *The Games Ethic and Imperialism: Aspects of the Diffusion of an Ideal*. Harmondsworth: Viking Penguin, 1986.

Main, Ernest. *Iraq From Mandate to Independence*. London: George Allen and Unwin, 1935.

Makdisi, Saree. *Romantic Imperialism: Universal Empire and the Culture of Modernity*. Cambridge: Cambridge University Press, 1998.

Mamdani, Mahmood. *Citizen and Subject: Contemporary Africa and the Legacy of Late Colonialism*. Princeton, N.J.: Princeton University Press, 1996.

Mann, Michael. "The Autonomous Power of the State: Its Origins, Mechanisms, and Results." In *States, War, and Capitalism: Studies in Political Sociology*, by Michael Mann. Oxford: Blackwell, 1988.

————. *A History of Power from the Beginning to A.D. 1760*, vol. 1 of *The Sources of Social Power*. Cambridge: Cambridge University Press, 1986.

Mannheim, Karl. *Conservatism: A Contribution to the Sociology of Knowledge*. Ed. trans. David Kettler and Volker Meja. London: Routledge Kegan Paul, 1986.

Marx, Karl. "The British Rule in India." In *Surveys From Exile: Political Writings*, vol. 2, by Karl Marx, ed. David Fernbach. Harmondsworth: Penguin, 1973.

————. *Capital: A Critique of Political Economy*. Vol. 1, trans. Ben Fowkes. Harmondsworth: Penguin, 1990.

————. "The Eighteenth Brumaire of Louis Bonaparte." In *Surveys From Exile: Political Writings*, vol. 2, by Karl Marx, ed. David Fernbach. Harmondsworth: Penguin, 1973.

Mastanduno, Michael. "Models, Markets, and Power: Political Economy and the Asia Pacific, 1989–1999." *Review of International Studies* 16, no. 4 (October 2000).

Mayer, Arno J. *Politics and the Diplomacy of Peacemaking: Containment and Counter-revolution at Versailles, 1918–1919.* London: Weidenfeld and Nicolson, 1968.

Meadwell, Hudson. "Secession, States, and International Society." *Review of International Studies* no. 25 (1999): 371–87.

Mejcher, Helmut. *Imperial Quest for Oil: Iraq, 1910–1928.* London: Ithaca Press, published for the Middle East Center St. Antony's College, Oxford University, 1976.

———. "Iraq's External Relations 1921–26." *Middle Eastern Studies,* no. 13, October 1977.

Mendilow, Jonathan. *The Romantic Tradition in British Political Thought.* Kent, Croom Helm, 1986.

Migdal, Joel S. *Strong Societies and Weak States: State-Society Relations and State Capabilities in the Third World.* Princeton, N.J.: Princeton University Press, 1988.

Mitchell, Timothy. *Colonizing Egypt.* Berkeley: University of California Press, 1991.

———. "The Limits of the State: Beyond Statist Approaches and Their Critics." *American Political Science Review* 85, no. 1 (March 1991).

———. *Rule By Experts,* Berkeley: University of California Press, 2002.

Monroe, Elizabeth. *Britain's Moment in the Middle East, 1914–1917.* London: Chatto and Windus, 1981.

Montesquieu, Charles de Secondat, Baron de. *The Spirit of Laws.* Trans. Anne M. Cohler, Basia Carolyn Miller, and Harold Samuel Stone. Cambridge: Cambridge University Press, 1989.

Morris, James. *Farewell the Trumpets: An Imperial Retreat.* Harmondsworth: Penguin, 1978.

Mouffe, Chantal. "Hegemony and Ideology in Gramsci." In *Gramsci and Marxist Theory,* ed. Chantal Mouffe. London: Routledge Kegan Paul, 1979.

Muhsin, Khalid Abid. "The Political Career of Muhammad Ja'far Abu al-Timman (1808–1937): A Study in Modern Iraqi History." Ph.D. diss., School of Oriental and African Studies, 1983.

Musgrave, P. J. "Social Power and Social Change in the United Provinces, 1860–1920." In *Economy and Society. Essays in Indian Economic and Social History,* ed. K. N. Chaudhuri and Clive J. Dewey. Delhi: Oxford University Press, 1979.

Musselwhite, David. "The Trial of Warren Hastings." In *Literature, Politics, and Theory: Papers from the Essex Conference on the Sociology of Literature, 1976–1984,* ed. Francis Barker, P. Hulme, M. Iversen, and D. Loxley. London: Methuen, 1986.

The National Security Strategy of the United States of America. Sepember 2002. http://www.whitehouse.gov/nsc/nss.html.

The New York Times.

Northedge, F. S. *The League of Nations: Its Life and Times, 1920–1946.* Leicester: Leicester University Press, 1986.

Olson, Robert. "The Battle for Kurdistan: The Churchill-Cox Correspondence Regarding the Creation of the State of Iraq, 1921–1923." *The International Journal of Turkish Studies* 5, no. 1 (1993).

———. "The Second Time Around: British Policy Towards the Kurds (1921–1922)." *Die Welt des Islams* 37 (1987).

Omissi, David E. *Air Power and Colonial Control: The Royal Air Force, 1919–1939.* Manchester: Manchester University Press, 1990.

Ormsby-Gore, W. G. A. (MP, late Member of the Permanent Mandates Commission). "The Mandatory System." In *The Settlement with Germany,* vol. 6 of *A History of the Peace Conference of Paris,* ed. H. W. V. Temperley. London: Oxford University Press, issued under the auspices of the Royal Institute of International Affairs, 1969.

Osterhammel, Jurgen. *Colonialism: A Theoretical Overview.* Trans. Shelly L. Frisch. Princeton, N.J.: Markus Wiener Publishers, 1997.

Owen, Roger. "Class and Class Politics in Iraq Before 1958: The 'Colonial and Post-Colonial State.' " In *The Iraqi Revolution of 1958: The Old Social Classes Revisited,* ed. Robert A. Fernea and Wm. Roger Louis. London: I. B. Tauris, 1991.

Packer, Geolrge. "Kanan Makiya, Dreaming of Democracy." *New York Times Magazine,* 2 March 2003.

Parry, Benita. "Problems in Current Theories of Colonial Discourse." *The Oxford Literary Review* 9, nos. 1–2 (1987).

Perham, Margery. Introduction to the fifth edition of *The Dual Mandate in British Tropical Africa,* by Lord Lugard. London: Frank Cass, 1965.

Phillips, Anne. *The Enigma of Colonialism: British Policy in West Africa.* London: James Curry, 1989.

Pieterse, Jan P. Nederveen. *Empire and Emancipation: Power and Liberation on a World Scale.* London: Pluto Press, 1990.

Plamenatz, John. *The English Utilitarians.* Oxford: Basil Blackwell, 1958.

Poggi, Gianfranco. *Images of Society: Essays on the Sociological Theories of Tocqueville, Marx, and Durkheim.* Stanford, Calif.: Stanford University Press, 1972.

Polanyi, Karl. *The Great Transformation: The Political and Economic Origins of Our Time.* Boston: Beacon Press, 1957.

Porter, Dennis. "Orientalism and Its Problems. " In *Colonial Discourse and Post-Colonial Theory: A Reader,* ed. Patrick Williams and Laura Chrisman. Hempstead: Harvester Wheatsheaf, Hemel, 1993.

Public Broadcasting Service. "Front Line Special: The War Behind Closed Doors." http://www.pbs.org/wgbh/pages/frontline/shows/iraq/themes.

Rabinow, Paul. Introduction. In *The Foucault Reader. An Introduction to Foucault's Thought,* ed. Paul Rabinow. Harmondsworth: Penguin, 1991.

RAND, *America's Record on Nation Building.* Forthcoming, 2003.

Ranger, Terence. "The Invention of Tradition in Colonial Africa." In *The Invention of Tradition,* ed. Eric Hobsbawn and Terence Ranger. Cambridge: Cambridge University Press, 1993.

Rhodes, Edward. "The Imperial Logic of Bush's Liberal Agenda." *Survival* 45, no. 1 (spring 2003).

Robinson, Ronald. "Non-European Foundations of European Imperialism: Sketch for a Theory of Collaboration." In *Studies in the Theory of Imperialism*, ed. E. R. J. Owen and R. B. Sutcliffe. London: Longman, 1972.

Robinson, Roland, and John Gallagher with Alice Denny. *Africa and the Victorians: The Official Mind of Imperialism*. 2d ed. Hampshire: Macmillan Education, 1992.

Rogan, Eugene L. *Frontiers of the State in the Late Ottoman Empire: Transjordan, 1850–1921*. Cambridge: Cambridge University Press, 1999.

Rogan, Eugene L., and Tariq Tell, eds. *Village, Steppe, and State: The Social Origins of Modern Jordan*. London: British Academic Press, 1994.

Rosenberg, Justin. *The Empire of Civil Society: A Critique of the Realist Theory of International Relations*. London: Verso, 1994.

Royal, Trevor. *Glubb Pasha: The Life and Times of Sir John Bagot Glubb, Commander of the Arab Legion*. London: Abacus Books, 1993.

Ruggie, John G. *Constructing the World Polity: Essays on International Institutionalization*. London: Routledge, 1998.

———. "International Regimes, Transactions, and Change: Embedded Liberalism in the Post-War Economic Order." In *International Regimes*, ed. Stephen Krasner. Ithaca, N.Y.: Cornell University Press, 1982.

Rupert, Mark. "(Re-) Engaging Gramsci: A Response to Germain and Kenny." *Review of International Studies* no. 24 (1998).

Said, Edward. *Orientalism: Western Conceptions of the Orient*. Harmondsworth: Penguin, 1991.

Saiedi, Nader. *The Birth of Social Theory: Social Thought in the Enlightenment and Romanticism*. Lanham, Md.: University Press of America, 1993.

Salih, Khaled. *Nation-Building and the Military: Iraq, 1941–1958*. Gotenborg Studies in Politics no. 41. Gotenborg University, 1996.

Sasson, Sir Philip (Under-Secretary of State for Air), Anniversary Lecture, "Air Power in the Middle East." *Journal of the Royal Asian Society* 20 (1933).

Sayer, Derek. *The Violence of Abstraction: The Analytic Foundations of Historical Materialism*. Oxford: Basil Blackwell, 1987.

Scott, David. "Colonial Governmentality." *Social Text* no. 43 (fall 1995).

Scott, James C. *Seeing Like a State: How Certain Schemes to Improve the Human Condition Have Failed*. New Haven, Conn.: Yale University Press, 1998.

Schumpeter, Joseph. *Imperialism and Social Classes*. New York: Meridian Books, 1958.

Shannon, Richard. *The Crisis of Imperialism, 1865–1915*. London: Paladin, 1974.

Sherman, A. J. *Mandate Days: British Lives in Palestine, 1918–1948*. London: Thames and Hudson, 1997.

Showstack Sassoon, Anne. "Passive Revolution and the Politics of Reform." In *Approaches to Gramsci*, ed. Anne Showstack Sassoon. London: Writers and Readers, 1982.

Sluglett, Peter. *Britain in Iraq, 1914–1932*. London: Ithaca Press, published for the Middle East Center, St Antony's College, Oxford University, 1976.

———. "Formal and Informal Empire in the Middle East." In *The Oxford History of the British Empire*, vol. 5, *Historiography*, ed. Robin W. Winks. Oxford: Oxford University Press, 1999.

———. "Profit and Loss from the British Mandate: British Influence and Administration in Iraq, 1914–1932." Ph.D. diss., St Antony's College, University of Oxford, 1972.

Smith, Bruce James. "Edmund Burke: Political Order and the Past. " In *Politics and Remembrance: Republican Themes in Machiavelli, Burke, and Tocquville*, by Bruce James Smith. Princeton, N.J.: Princeton University Press, 1985.

Spruyt, Hendrik. "The End of Empire and the Extension of the Westphalian System: The Normative Basis of the Modern State Order." In *Continuity and Change in the Westphalian Order*, ed. James A. Caporaso. Oxford: Blackwell, 2000.

Stedman Jones, Gareth. "The History of U.S. Imperialism." In *Ideology in Social Science: Readings in Critical Social Theory*, ed. Robin Blackburn. London: Fontana/Collins, 1979.

Stevenson, John. *History of Britain: British Society, 1914–1945*. Harmondsworth: Penguin, 1984.

Stivers, William. *Supremacy and Oil: Iraq, Turkey, and the Anglo-American World Order, 1918–1930*. Ithaca, N.Y.: Cornell University Press, 1982.

Stokes, Eric. *The English Utilitarians and India*. Oxford: Oxford University Press, 1959.

———. *The Political Ideas of English Imperialism*. Inaugural Lecture given in the University College of Rhodesia and Nyasaland. Oxford University Press, London: 1960.

Stoler, Ann Laura. *Race and the Education of Desire: Foucault's* History of Sexuality *and the Colonial Order of Things*. Durham and London: Duke University Press, 1995.

Storrs, Ronald. *Orientations*. Definitive edition. London: Nicholson and Watson, 1949.

Stoyanovsky, J. *The Mandate for Palestine: A Contribution to the Theory and Practice of International Mandates*. London: Longman, 1928.

Sullivan, Shanon. "State and Society in Iraq During the British Mandate, 1920–1932." Master's thesis, School of African and Asian Studies, London, 1992

Tabachinick, Stephen E., ed. *The T. E. Lawrence Puzzle*. Athens, University of Georgia Press, 1984.

Tarbush, Mohammad. *The Role of the Military in Politics: A Case Study of Iraq to 1941*. London: Routledge Kegan Paul, 1985.

Taylor, A. J. P. *English History, 1914–1945*. Oxford: Oxford University Press, 1990.

Taylor, Charles. *Philosophy and the Human Sciences: Philosophical Papers 2*. Cambridge: Cambridge University Press, 1995.

———. *Sources of the Self: The Making of the Modern Identity*. Cambridge: Cambridge University Press, 1994.

Temperley, H. W. V., ed. *The Settlement with Germany*. Vol. 2 of *A History of the Peace Conference of Paris*. London: Oxford University Press, issued under the auspices of the Royal Institute of International Affairs, 1969.

The Times.

Thomas, Bertram. *Alarms and Excursions in Arabia*. London: George Allen & Unwin, 1931.

Thomas, William. *The Philosophic Radicals: Nine Studies in Theory and Practise, 1817–1841*. Oxford: Clarendon Press, 1979.

Thompson, John B. *Studies in the Theory of Ideology*. Cambridge: Polity Press, 1990.

Thornton, A. P. *The Imperial Idea and its Enemies: A Study in British Power*. London: Macmillan, 1959.

Thornton, Thomas Henry, C.S.I., D.C.L. *Colonel Sir Robert Sandeman: His Life and Work on Our Indian Frontier. A Memoir, with Selections from His Correspondence and Official Writings*. London: John Murray, 1895.

Tidrick, Kathryn. *Heart Beguiling Araby: The English Romance with Arabia*. London: I. B. Tauris, 1981.

Tocqueville, Alexis de. *Democracy in America*. Vol. 2. New York: Vantage Books, 1990.

Toulmin, Stephen. *Cosmopolis: The Hidden Agenda of Modernity*. Chicago: University of Chicago Press, 1992.

Townsend, Charles. "Civilization and Frightfulness in Air Control in the Middle East Between the Wars." In *Warfare Diplomacy and Politics: Essays in Honor of A. J. P. Taylor*, ed. Chris Wrigley. London: Hamish Hamilton, 1986.

Towle, Philip Antony. *Pilots and Rebels: The Uses of Aircraft in Unconventional Warfare, 1918–1988*. London: Brassey's, 1989.

Toynbee, Arnold. "Was Britain's Abdication a Folly?" *The Round Table* (April 1970).

Tripp, Charles. *A History of Iraq*. Cambridge: Cambridge University Press, 2000.

———. "What Lurks in the Shadows?" *The Times Higher*, 18 October 2002.

———. "After Saddam." *Survival* 44, no. 4 (winter 2002–2003).

Turner, Bryan S. *Marx and the End of Orientalism*. London: George Allen and Unwin, 1978.

———. *Weber and Islam: A Critical Study*. London: Routledge Kegan Paul, 1974.

Van Alstyne, Richard W. "Woodrow Wilson and the Idea of the Nation State." *International Affairs* 37, no. 3.

Wagner, Peter. *A Sociology of Modernity: Liberty and Discipline*. London: Routledge, 1998.

Waldron, Jeremy, ed. *Nonsense Upon Stilts: Bentham, Burke, and Marx on the Rights of Man*. London: Methuen, 1987.

Warriner, Doreen. *Land and Poverty in the Middle East*. London: Royal Institute of International Affairs and Oxford University Press, 1948.

The Washington Post.

Weliwita-Gunaratne, C. "The Role of Gertrude Bell in the Formation of Modern Iraq, 1918–1921." Master's thesis, School of Oriental and African Studies, London, 1983.

Wendt, Alexander. "Anarchy Is What States Make of It: The Social Construction of Power Politics." *International Organization* 46, no. 2 (spring 1992).

———. *Social Theory of International Politics.* Cambridge: Cambridge University Press, 1999.

Westrate, Bruce. *The Arab Bureau: British Policy in the Middle East, 1916–1920.* State College, Penn.: Pennsylvania State University Press, 1992.

White, Freda. *Mandates.* London: Jonathan Cape, published under the auspices of the League of Nations Union, 1926.

Wiener, Martin J. *English Culture and the Decline of the Industrial Spirit, 1850–1980.* Harmondsworth: Penguin, 1992.

Williams David. "Aid and Sovereignty: Quasi-States and the International Financial Institutions." *Review of Internatinal Studies* 26, no. 4 (October 2000).

Williams, Raymond. "The Organic Society and Human Perfection." In *Edmund Burke: Appraisals and Applications,* ed. Daniel Ritche. New Brunswick, N.J.: Transaction Publishers, 1990.

Williams, Wilbur Laurent. *The State Of Iraq: A Mandate Attains Independence.* Foreign Policy Reports, Foreign Policy Association, vol. 8, no. 16 (12 October 1932).

Wilson, A. T. *Loyalties, Mesopotamia.* Vol. 1, *1914–1917: A Personal and Historical Record.* London: Oxford University Press, 1930.

———. *Loyalties, Mesopotamia.* Vol. 2, *1917–1920: A Personal and Historical Record.* London: Oxford University Press, 1931.

Wilson, Mary. *King Abdullah: Britain and the Making of Jordan.* Cambridge: Cambridge University Press, 1987.

Wilson, Woodrow. "Address Delivered to the Senate, January 22nd, 1917." In *Readings in World Politics,* vol. 2. Chicago: American Foundation for Political Education, 1957.

———. "A Speech Before a Joint Session of Congress, January 8th, 1918." In *Readings in World Politics,* vol. 2. Chicago: American Foundation for Political Education, 1957.

Winks, Robin W. "On Decolonisation and Informal Empire." *American History Review* 81, no. 3 (1976): 540–56.

Winstone, H. V. F. *Gertrude Bell.* London: Constable, 1993.

Wolfowitz, Paul. Deputy Secretary of Defence's testimony before the Senate Foreign Relations Committee. 22 May 2003.

Woodruff, Philip. *The Men Who Ruled India.* Vol. 2, *The Guardians.* London: Jonathan Cape, 1954.

Woodward, Bob. *Bush at War.* New York: Simon and Schuster, 2002.

Yapp, M. E. *The Near East Since the First World War: A History to 1995*. 2d edition. London: Longman, 1996.

Young, Crawford. *The African Colonial State in Comparative Perspective*. New Haven, Conn.: Yale University Press, 1994.

Young, Major Sir Hubert. *The Independent Arab*. London: John Murray, 1933.

Young, Robert. *White Mythologies: Writing History and the West*. London: Routledge, 1990.

Young, Tom. " 'A Project to be Realized': Liberalism and Contemporary Africa." *Millennium: Journal of International Studies* 24, no. 3 (1995).

Youngs, Tim. *Travellers in Africa: British Travelogues, 1850–1900*. Manchester: Manchester University Press, 1994.

Zinni, Anthony. Speech at the Middle East Institute. Washington D.C. 10 October 2002.

Zizek, Slavoj. "Introduction: The Spectre of Ideology. " In *Mapping Ideology*, ed. Slavoj Zizek. London: Verso, 1994.

Zubaida, Sami. "Review Article: Exhibitions of Power." *Economy and Society* 19, no. 3 (August 1990).

ACKNOWLEDGMENTS

At the end of May 2003, in the aftermath of the U.S. invasion, I found myself walking through the central government district of Baghdad. I had just left the old Republican Palace on the banks of the Tigris and was walking towards the center of the city to catch a ride. It was from the grand quarters of the Republican Palace that Saddam Hussein had ruled over Iraq. I had just spent the afternoon at the palace interviewing staff from the newly formed Coalition Provisional Authority; the hub of U.S. attempts to rebuild the Iraqi state after the invasion. In the late afternoon sunshine I struggled to understand how these American administrators were intending to reform the institutions of state they had so recently seized from the Baathist ruling elite.

As I walked passed the burnt-out hulks of government ministries, I came across small groups of American soldiers manning checkpoints in the security compound surrounding the palace. They had fought their way up from Kuwait in the expectation that they would be welcomed into Baghdad as liberators. They now found themselves the focus of increasing societal resentment, losing comrades every day to an enemy they were supposed to have defeated several weeks earlier.

The themes that dominated my impressions of that afternoon, the interviews in the opulent marble halls of the palace and the conversations with disorientated young GIs many miles from home, are those that have come to form the hub of my own research agenda as an academic: how society is understood, how people set about trying to create states, and how the states they build interact with society. I have sought answers to these questions by focusing on the birth and evolution of the postcolonial state in the international system, using Iraq as a prime example. All these questions appeared, on that afternoon, to be personified in the bewilderment, fear, and alienation of a group of young men, trying to impose order on a society they had little or no understanding of.

This book is an attempt to understand why the first attempt at regime change and state building in Iraq failed. It uses the tools of social theory and political sociology to interrogate the colonial archive, seeking to understand the perceptions and hence the agency of those British officials who spent eighteen years trying to build a stable state in Iraq. Ultimately, it was their failures that brought war and foreign intervention back to Iraq in the first few years of the new millennium. If the United States can possibly avoid the misperceptions and mistakes of the state builders who went before them, the Iraqi people just might have a chance at getting the better life they so richly deserve.

Researching, writing, and then publishing should ultimately, by its very nature, be a collective endeavor. In finishing this book I have incurred a great many debts to people who have taken the time to engage in extended discussions with me. This book was conceived, researched, and largely written while I was studying and teaching at the School of Oriental and African Studies, University of London. It was finished while I was an associate fellow of the Royal Institute of International Affairs and brought to publication while I was a research fellow at the Centre for the Study of Globalisation and Regionalisation, the University of Warwick. I would like to thank the Politics Department at SOAS and Rosy Hollis of the Middle East Programme at RIIA. Richard Higgott, the Head of CSGR at Warwick, has provided me with wise academic counsel throughout.

Several groups of people have been influential in shaping the ideas and research that went into this book. First, I would like to thank Kathryn Dean, Sudipta Kaviraj, John Sidel, and Tom Young for taking the time to discuss comparative politics and social theory with me. I gained a great deal from taking part in the Foucault and Colonialism discussion group and workshop at SOAS and would like to thank Shruti Kapila and David Arnold for organizing them. I would also like to thank Fred Halliday, Yosi Kostiner, Roger Owen, Tariq Tell, Mai Yamani, and Sami Zubaida for enlightening me on many and varied aspects of politics in the Middle East.

Charles Tripp. my Ph.D. supervisor and mentor, has continued to provide me with the wise and patient counsel that has guided me through research and writing.

Whilst looking at the Baghdad High Commission archives in New Delhi, Ian Brown was kind enough to extend to me the paternal hand of SOAS many miles away from home.

In helping me with my continuing struggle to work on and understand Iraq, I would like to thank Khaireddin Haseeb, Faleh Jabar, Raad

Al Kadiri, Zuhair Al Kadiri, Isam Al Khafaji, Tim Niblock, and especially Peter Sluglett.

Most advice and inspiration has been given to me by, and the greatest influence upon my thinking has come from, fellow researchers that I have been lucky enough to work along side over the previous decade. At SOAS these have included Ali Ansari, Grace Carswell, Bill Dorman, Nick Hostettler, and David Williams, and in India I would like to thank Ian Barrow and Kriti Kapila.

I would like to thank Karin Barry for proofreading the original text. It was Michael Dwyer who took that text from my office in Warwick and convinced me not only that it should be published but also that it should be published now and it was Peter Dimock at Columbia University Press whose wise and sympathetic editing made the text more readable.

I would like to thank the Economic and Social Research Council and the School of Oriental and African Studies for funding the research for this book. I greatly benefited from presenting drafts of different chapters at the British and French Mandates in Comparative Perspective conference, organized by IFEAD (Damascus), the University of Utah, and Mémoires méditerranéens/IREMAM, Aix-en-Provence, Workshop on Late Colonialism in the Middle East, the Middle East Center, the Henry M. Jackson School of International Studies, the University of Washington, The Middle East Mandates in Comparative Perspective workshop, the University of Utah, *Past and Present* fiftieth-anniversary conference, Institute of Historical Research, University of London, the Middle East Study Group, Birkbeck College, and the Centre of Middle Eastern and Islamic Studies, University of Durham. I would like to thank these institutions and the participants in the meetings for their comments.

Such extended periods of travel, research, and writing places unfair burdens on one's family. I would very much like to thank my mother, Pat Dodge, and brother and sister, Jane Dodge and Matthew Dodge, and the Day family for their unceasing faith and support over the years.

My greatest thanks and the largest debt of gratitude is due to Clare. It is she who chased me back into graduate study, made sure I stayed there, and provided endless support and enthusiasm and it is to her I would like to dedicate this book.